The Nature of The Soul

Works in this series include:

The Nature of The Soul

Creative Thinking

The Soul and Its Instrument

The Disciple and Economy

Leadership Training

Ashramic Projections

Introduction to The Path of Initiation,
Vols. I & II

Healing

Applied Wisdom

Printed editions of the above works are available through Wisdom Impressions.

II

The Nature of The Soul

By Lucille Cedercrans

Wisdom Impressions Publishers, LLC
Roseville, MN

The Nature of The Soul
by Lucille Cedercrans

Third edition, 2011

Wisdom Impressions is a group of practitioners of The Wisdom. Our purpose is to help create the appearance, support the teaching, and facilitate the distribution of The Wisdom.

Wisdom Impressions Publishers, LLC
P.O. Box 130003
Roseville, MN 55113

Copyright © 2011 by Wisdom Impressions Publishers, LLC
ISBN **978-1-883493-38-7 $19.95**

The Great Invocation

From the point of Light within the Mind of God
Let light stream forth into the minds of men.
Let Light descend on Earth.

From the point of Love within the Heart of God
Let love stream forth into the hearts of men.
May Christ return to Earth.

From the centre where the Will of God is known
Let purpose guide the little wills of men—
The purpose which the Masters know and serve.

From the centre which we call the race of men
Let the Plan of Love and Light work out
And may it seal the door where evil dwells.

Let Light and Love and Power restore the Plan on Earth.

"The above Invocation or Prayer does not belong to any person or group but to all Humanity. The beauty and the strength of this Invocation lies in its simplicity, and in its expression of certain central truths which all men, innately and normally, accept—the truth of the existence of a basic Intelligence to Whom we vaguely give the name of God; the truth that behind all outer seeming, the motivating power of the universe is Love; the truth that a great Individuality came to earth, called by Christians, the Christ, and embodied that love so that we could understand; the truth that both love and intelligence are effects of what is called the Will of God; and finally the self-evident truth that only through *humanity* itself can the Divine Plan work out."

Alice A. Bailey

V

Editors' Foreword

The *Nature of The Soul* is part of a series of courses on self-initiated spiritual growth and development. These courses are designed to facilitate step-by-step unfoldment from individuality to group awareness and conscious service to the One Life. This conscious service is called the path of discipleship, and those who walk this path are called Disciples.

The courses prepare the student for the inner work of the Disciple. This inner work is accomplished through meditation which is the creative activity of the Soul or consciousness. Thus, each of the texts in this series is a course in the art and science of meditation.

The first in this series, *The Path of Initiation, I & II,*[1] introduce the beginning student to the basic concepts and practices of the Wisdom teachings.

The next in the series, *Creative Thinking,* is a course in the cleansing or purification of the persona, in aspiration to the Spiritual Soul. If actively practiced, it will prepare the persona (mind, emotions, and body), to become a vehicle of the higher self or Overshadowing Soul.

The next in the series, *The Soul and Its Instrument,* is a course in integrating the persona in cooperation with the Spiritual Soul. If actively practiced, it will prepare the integrated persona to become a vehicle of service to humanity and the One Life.

The final course in the series, *The Nature of the Soul,* is designed to facilitate step-by-step unfoldment from individuality to group awareness and conscious service to

---

[1] Originally titled: *"Introduction to The Path of Initiation."*

VI

the One Life. It is not an intellectual treatise, but a course in self-initiated spiritual growth and development. Three overlapping layers include: Meditation exercises for the Soul-mind-brain alignment, exploration of the Seven Rays, and Creativity from the level of the Soul in the establishment of the Plan on earth.

The first incarnation of *The Nature of The Soul* was in 1953, as a series of ten loose-leaf lessons. In the late 1950's *The Nature of The Soul* (or N.S.) was revised and expanded into the present 40 lesson course.

This third bound edition of *The Nature of The Soul* is a faithful reproduction of the original loose-leaf editions. The only changes are minor corrections of grammar, punctuation, and design. Every effort was made to retain the subjective quality and outer flavor of the earlier editions.

The text was carefully scrutinized by the staff of Wisdom Impressions. Whenever a correction would have changed the meaning or quality, the original text was retained.

We have added a Table of Contents, Directory of Techniques, Study Guide, and Index. While not part of the original text, practitioners of the course have found them helpful.

Sincerely,

The Editors

May, 2011

Table of Contents

Directory of Techniques

The inner disciplines listed below are an essential part of *The Nature of The Soul* course. Like all such disciplines, they are designed to produce specific effects in the consciousness, bodies and environment of the student. When these disciplines are practiced in the proper order and manner, they facilitate unfoldment from individuality to group awareness. However, they can be abused.

Combining these disciplines with drugs, or other techniques, or using them for selfish purposes, is dangerous. If you have any questions about the use or effects of these disciplines, we recommend that you obtain instruction from a trained Teacher of The Wisdom.

XII

XVI

INTRODUCTORY

Foundational Concepts for Contemplation:

Inner Government of Planet;
Three Divine Laws
(Evolution, Reincarnation, Karma);
The Path of Initiation
(Birth, Baptism, Transfiguration,
Crucifixion, Ascension)

1

INTRODUCTORY

The human family stands today upon the threshold of a new experience, that of Soul consciousness. Every man, woman, and child incarnate upon the planet is being brought closer to this happening by the force of evolution itself. Just as man is differentiated from the animal, in that he is a self-conscious human being, so shall he make yet another advance in awareness to become a Soul-conscious son of God. No longer must he walk in the shadow of spiritual ignorance, for the Light of his Soul is moving upon his horizon.

This movement of the Soul toward expression within and through its lower counterpart can be seen within the mass consciousness of the whole human family. In no area of that mass is it stilled, but moves constantly to produce an awakening of man to Its presence. Men and women everywhere are becoming restless, dissatisfied and overburdened with the world of material values they have created for themselves. They seek new values which will bring lasting peace to their world, little knowing as yet the nature of that peace.

In recognition of, and cooperation with this activity of the Soul, a New Thought-Form Presentation of The Wisdom has been created and placed in availability for those who seek it. It can be contacted as an abstraction via the activity of meditation, and must then be translated into a concrete form by the one who meditates.

This series of instructions is an interpretation of that new thought–form, and has been written in an effort to aid man in the search for his Soul.

For those who seek authority behind the written word, the truth of this text must be proven via its application. A formulated concept is of value only if it can be worked out as a living truth within the life and affairs of Humanity. Therefore, do not look to the source of this teaching for its authenticity, but to the application of it within your own life and affairs.

This series of instructions has been built up from a foundation of certain basic concepts which can be briefly outlined as follows:

A. INNER GOVERNMENT

1. That there is one Cosmic Center governing all life within the manifest Cosmos. This we define as the One God, Whose nature is both Immanent and Transcendent.

2. That the sum total of life in and upon our planet constitutes a Planetary Being, Who, under the impulse of that Creative Cosmic Center of which He is an outpouring, directs the life and affairs of the Planet according to a Divine Purpose. This Divine Purpose He shares with those other Planetary Beings who make up our solar system. This Great Life is defined as the Planetary Logos.

3. That the Logos works out His purpose via three major Planetary Centers:

   a. Shamballa - The head center where the Will of our Logos is known. Here a group of Lives formulate the Will of God into the Divine Plan for the whole of the Planetary Life and affairs as it works out through the various kingdoms in nature.

Introductory

b. Hierarchy - The heart center where the Love, or Pure Reason of our Logos is known. Here a group of Lives headed by The Christ, step down the Will of God and the larger Plan itself into a relationship with Humanity. Via the energy of Love, the Logoic Purpose is worked out for humanity as the Evolutionary Process, or Divine Plan of the Soul. This inner governing body we refer to as the Hierarchy of Masters, each Master being an individualized focal point within the consciousness of The Christ.

c. Humanity - The throat center where the Will and Love of God are worked out into manifestation via the energy of intelligent activity. The intelligent direction of the Will, and the intelligent application of Love within the life and affairs of Humanity, will bring to successful fruition the greater Purpose and Plan of the Planetary Logos Himself.

4. That there is a world group of disciples who consciously function within the body of Humanity in cooperation with the Hierarchy. They do not at any time receive orders from the Hierarchy, but do cooperate in such a way as to assure the manifestation of the Divine Plan within the body of Humanity.

These men and women are not confined to any organization, race, creed, color, or station in life. They are quietly working within all parts of the world, within every department of human living, for the spiritual health and welfare of humanity. They invoke the unseen aid of the Hierarchy through their own efforts to serve the Plan, and are called "accepted disciples."

5. That there is another group of men and women, who are working under the inspiration and guidance of the disciples in the world, and who are consciously aspiring to the state of discipleship via their own self initiated service activities. They are called "probationer disciples."

6. That there is a vast group of seekers in the world, some of whom are as yet unaware of the above information, who stand ready to receive the teaching that will place them in the group of probationers. These are sometimes inspired consciously or unconsciously to aid in the working out of the Divine Plan for Humanity. They are a supportive group and will always be found on the side of good or right. These people are called "aspirants."

7. That there is an inner governing agency within every individual which can, through right aspiration, be invoked to intervene in his life and affairs. This we call Overshadowing Spiritual Soul.

B. <u>DIVINE LAW AND ORDER</u>

That emanating from the Central Cosmic Center there are certain impulses which become the Divine Laws that maintain order in the manifest Cosmos. Three of these, along with others not enumerated at this time, work out in our planetary scheme in the following manner:

1. The Law of Evolution

   This is the Divine Law governing the Consciousness aspect of all life. It is related to the Purpose of God and means, simply, that any created state of consciousness is in a process of growth, regardless of its outer appearance and condition. Thus, man evolves to become the Soul conscious Son of God, while He in turn evolves to become an individualized focal point within the consciousness of The Christ.

2. The Law of Reincarnation or Rebirth

This could be called the grading system of the evolutionary process within the human family. The Soul incarnates not once in human form, but many times until It masters the form nature, and controls Its vehicles as the Instrumentality of the Divine Plan.

3. The Law of Karma

Here is the great Law of Balance, that which makes evolution possible. It controls the displacement of energies within the manifest Cosmos, directing a return of each flow of energy, from any given point, back to its Source in similar type, strength, and quality. Thus, whatever a man thinks, feels, or does shall return again to him as the balance of energy displaced within his own individual system. Via this law a man meets with those opportunities for growth which he himself has created, and thus evolves in the school of experience from instinct to intellect, from intellect to intuition, and from intuition to inspiration. Thus does knowledge itself become Wisdom, and the Soul master of Its own fate or karma. Upon such mastery, the incarnating consciousness is freed from the Wheel of Rebirth into a higher frequency range of activity.

The Nature of The Soul

C. THE PATH OF INITIATION

That after the personality has reached a certain place in the evolutionary process, his growth becomes a conscious, self-initiated activity. In cooperation with the Plan of Evolution the incarnating entity initiates those experiences which will expand the awareness of the personal self to include the awareness of the Spiritual Soul. This expansion covers five states of consciousness, sometimes referred to as the five initiations. They are enumerated and explained as follows:

1. The Birth of The Christ

   Here the personality has awakened to the essential truth of his Being. He recognizes that truth as his spiritual identity in nature, and is, therefore, enabled to relate as the Christ-Child to his Father Who is in Heaven. He is born again in Christ consciousness, and endeavors to live, stand, and walk in the Light of the Christ, sharing that Light with all of his associates. It is at this point that brotherhood, for him, becomes a fact in nature.

2. The Baptism

   In this initiation the individual willingly undergoes a purification process. Through self-initiated disciplinary training, which usually covers a period of several incarnations, he subjects his emotional nature to the Divine Law and energy of Love. Thus he purifies his lower desire nature, transmuting it into aspiration to God via a fixed ideal which he identifies as The Christ.

3. The Transfiguration or Illumination

   This is the first major initiation in which the

whole consciousness becomes illumined, so to speak, with the Light of Logoic Purpose. He undergoes a great awakening and begins, with Wisdom, to glimpse the cause back of all that he sees. He is cognizant of the reality underlying all form manifestation and begins to think in terms of, and to work with energy.

Such a one directs his life and affairs from the level of the Soul, functioning in the world as an accepted disciple of The Christ.

4. The Crucifixion

This is the initiation in which the individual crucifies that part of his being which stands between himself and the full embodiment of his Spiritual ideal. He sacrifices his personality ambition and desire to the One Life indwelling all forms. He gives himself completely, works for, and is subservient to that Life. After release from personal desire and ambition, he comes back to work in the world, but with one difference: his motive is love of Humanity, and all that he does is in service to his brothers.

5. The Ascension

This initiation is so advanced that very little can be said about it. It is freedom from, and mastery of, the three planes of human endeavor: the physical, astral-emotional and mental. The individual is released from the Wheel of Rebirth, and if he does incarnate again, it is only in times of crisis, for the guidance of Humanity.

Man today is undergoing a difficult transition of which he knows little. As a race, he is completing the first initiation and approaching the second, fluctuating between the emotional aspect of his nature and the mental. He is learning to react to life intelligently rather than with just his emotions. As he becomes more and more polarized in the mental aspect, he comes closer to the revelation of his own Soul.

Still, man does have the freedom of choice, and should he decide to continue along his selfish path of separativeness, he will undergo another period of dark ages in which the Spiritual Soul will be unrealized, and the completion of the first initiation awaiting yet another opportunity.

This course of instruction is written in an effort to show how the individual aspirant and disciple in the world can help Humanity make the right choice.

There are certain suggestions which can be offered as to the manner in which the lessons are studied. First, let us consider group consciousness, for this will eventuate as man comes into a realization of himself as a Soul, and tends to subordinate his personality to the Soul.

Groups of individualities come into incarnation because of a long period of association which results in karmic relationships, and a certain aspect of the Divine Plan to work out together.

Those of you who are attracted to this teaching would do well to consider these relationships. All of those about you are Souls who are, in a peculiar manner, related to you and the working out of the Plan. As you progress in realization, others will be drawn to you, and if you progress rightly, you and the others will experience a group consciousness whose motive is Service, and whose goal is the manifestation of the Divine Plan, as you have grasped it for Humanity.

A few words of warning may be inserted here regarding

groups. Since you are functioning at this time as personalities, a certain amount of friction may occur, and unless carefully handled, the group will not survive as such. Let Divine Love guide you in this enterprise. Recognize each one as a Soul, and therefore as your brother. Let loving kindness dictate your attitude in all of your relationships, and give to each the freedom to express himself as he sees fit. Set yourselves up not as judges, or as one above the other, but as brothers on equal footing, each striving to perfect himself in order to serve the many.

The Nature of The Soul

LESSON 1

Beginning Stages of Soul Definition:

The Holy Trinity or Triangle of Manifestation;
The Triune Nature of the Human Soul
(Spiritual, Human, Animal);
The Question of Motive and the Four
Guidelines of Approach to these Teachings

LESSON 1

In the approach to an understanding of the Soul, consideration is first given the basic concept underlying all manifestation. Any appearance in form is but the working out, or breathing forth (to use an occult term) of the three Principles of Deity. These three Principles which have been referred to as the Holy Trinity, and symbolized in geometric form as the Triangle of manifestation, are the three Persons in One: God the Father, God the Mother or Holy Ghost, and God the Son.

The occult student divorces them from personality, and considers these three basic Principles as that which can be seen as the underlying cause of every appearance in form. He defines them in several terms in an effort to understand the inner meaning of the outer world.

They are considered first from the perspective of polarity. The Father Aspect is seen as the Positive Pole, the Mother Aspect as the Negative Pole, and the Son Aspect as that which is created by the interplay of energy between the two. Thus the three principles are enumerated as:

1. Positive Pole — Spirit
2. Magnetic Field — Consciousness
3. Negative Pole — Matter

Spirit and Matter are seen as the two polarities of one energy, and consciousness as the magnetic field created by the resulting interplay of frequency between the two poles.

The Nature of The Soul

The next step in the occult approach to an understanding of Truth, or reality is:

1. Positive Pole   — Divine Will
2. Magnetic Field   — Divine Love
3. Negative Pole   — Divine Intelligence

When Positive Will is impressed upon Negative Intelligence, the expression of Love is born. The continuing interplay between Will and Intelligence produces an evolution of that Love, according to a Divine Purpose which is inherent in the Will, via a Divine activity which is inherent in the Intelligence. Thus we see the manifest world about us, and begin to glimpse (but a ray as yet) the Light of its inner meaning. That Light is somewhat increased when we put all of our definitions together into a synthesis:

Father Aspect	Son Aspect	Mother Aspect
Positive Pole	Magnetic Field	Negative Pole
Spirit	Consciousness	Matter
Divine Will	Divine Love	Divine Intelligence
Purpose	Evolution	Activity
Monad	Soul	Man

Soul is a term used to define the consciousness aspect, the second Person in the Holy Trinity. The evolution of that consciousness into the expression of Perfect Love results in The Christ, full-grown Son of God.

We differentiate the Soul, then, as the infant or child Son, and the Christ as the adult Son. We recognize The Christ as both an over-shadowing and an indwelling Principle. The over-shadowing consciousness of Christ is that which is not imprisoned or limited to the form nature. Thus "I and the Father are One." The indwelling Christ is that Divine Pattern present within the Soul which ensures and guides its growth into adulthood.

The combination or synthesis of Purpose, Evolution, and Activity which will finally manifest as The Christ in outer expression, we refer to as the Divine Plan.

Here then is the basic formula upon which the whole of occult study is produced and from which it proceeds. Establish the key formula clearly in your mind, learning to reduce any appearance in form back to its essential reality via the basic symbol of its cause. Later you will come to understand cause and effect according to the manifesting relationship of the effect to its cause. This may seem somewhat abstract and meaningless now; however, if you will apply the key given in the above information, its meaning will gradually clarify.

For example, the three basic principles can be further translated into:

| 1. Power | 2. Light | 3. Form |
| 1. Cause | 2. Meaning | 3. Effect |

The Soul is a created consciousness, and yet it can be traced back to the essential triangle of cause, meaning that God is consciously aware of Himself and His creation. Thus "man is created in the Image and Likeness of God." He is within the Image, growing into that Likeness, hence the creative process, insofar as appearance is concerned, is not yet complete.

We see the Soul of our Planetary Logos as one vast body of consciousness manifesting in myriad forms. Those general forms which we recognize are differentiated into five kingdoms in nature, namely: the mineral, vegetable, animal, human, and Spiritual. Each kingdom in nature is one identified Being, or Soul, contained within the Logoic awareness.

The Nature of The Soul

The Soul, or Life, of the human kingdom is composed of the sum total of consciously identified human beings contained within its ring-pass-not. We see the Soul of humanity then as one Soul manifesting within its many vehicles.

Because of the differentiation of the form, and the apparent difference in the evolution of the Soul itself, it is difficult for the beginner to grasp this concept of Oneness. Each Soul is but an individualized expression of the Over Soul, and all are consciously, or unconsciously, working toward one purpose and goal. The One Life builds many forms, each one created for the purpose of evolution and expression. Each form conveys a degree of developed and developing consciousness, plus Soul expression.

The appearance of the many can be explained in the following manner: An individualized Soul is likened unto an atom in the body of the One Soul, which has acquired conscious awareness of itself. It is not in the beginning conscious of that Life in which it lives, moves, and has its being, but because of its inherent characteristics, it is swept into incarnation to develop its awareness, thus aiding the evolution of the One Life. All of this time the central directing Will and the Intelligence are aware of the new birth, aiding it in its long period of growth, until it, too, becomes conscious of that Life of which it is but an individualized expression, color, or tone.

The purpose of evolution, insofar as man's mind has been able to comprehend, is at-one-ment, complete with individuality.

The Soul of a human being, that is, the sum total of his consciousness, is defined in three major classifications, as follows:

Lesson 1

1. The Spiritual Soul on its own plane. This is that aspect of the individualized entity which is not as yet incarnate in form. Its life and affairs are maintained above the frequency range of the brain consciousness, until such time as the persona has evolved to permit Its incarnation. The Divine Purpose of the individualized expression, that is, Its relationship to the One Life, is maintained here in what is often referred to as the "superconscious," and directed downward as the motivating impulse for spiritual growth. The essence of the experience gained during each lifetime is absorbed into the Spiritual Soul as Wisdom—that Wisdom which will be necessary to the working out of its Purpose when at last it descends into incarnation. The Spiritual Soul relates man to God.

2. The human Soul in the three planes of human endeavor. This is that aspect of the individualized entity which has incarnated and identified with form. It thinks of itself as "I," functions within and through the brain as the persona, and evolves via its experience with form into an identification with its Spiritual counterpart. At the height of its growth it merges with the Spiritual Soul, incarnates again into a human vehicle, and masters the form nature. At this point the persona has been absorbed by the Spiritual Soul, and the life in form is a Conscious Soul Incarnate. Thus the Fifth Kingdom (Heaven) is brought to earth. The human Soul relates man to humanity.

3. The animal Soul. This is that aspect of the individualized entity which lies below the threshold of awareness, still identified completely with the form nature. It produces the instinctual reactions of man which result in the lower animal nature expressed through the emotional and physical

The Nature of The Soul

vehicles. This aspect has to be absorbed into, and transmuted by the human, and finally the Spiritual Soul. The animal Soul relates man to the animal Kingdom.

It might be added here that there is something of the Soular life of the mineral and vegetable kingdoms expressing within man, as well as the above, and thus all kingdoms in nature meet and manifest within humanity. This is a point to be kept in mind for it later leads to an understanding of the part humanity plays in the evolution of Logoic consciousness.

I would like to take this opportunity to explain something to the earnest student in regard to his understanding of the teaching. All teachers of The Wisdom realize the difficulty presented, particularly to the beginner, in grasping the concept of Truth which is projected. He is confronted with a bewildering array of new, and to him, meaningless terms with answers to the reason for his being, which he has never really expected to find. If he is not very careful at this stage, he is liable to become so confused as to what is Truth, that he may delay his own growth unnecessarily long.

First, examine very carefully your motives. For what and why are you seeking? What will you do with this teaching once you have grasped it? Do you have the betterment of mankind in mind, or do you seek for self-glorification?

Remember, the Conscious Soul is a part of the Whole. His desire is the evolution of that Life in which he lives, moves, and has his being. Any activity in which the Spiritual Soul is engaged is in service to his brothers.

If there is anyone who seeks attainment for the glorification of the separated self, it would be better if he dropped out — if he waited until such time as his motives became rightly oriented. He will, as he learns through painful experiences the emptiness of the illusion about him, the inevitability of change, the dissatisfaction when a long-sought goal is finally reached, the inability to find fulfillment. All of these painful experiences finally cause man to seek fulfillment in service. His motives become pure, and he is at last ready to begin his long climb up the mount of initiation.

This path of initiation is strewn with many obstacles, constituting the baser nature of man himself. He must be willing to see himself as he is, to find and overcome those negative qualities within his own instrument which have been acquired in the world of illusion, and are revealed in the Light of the Soul. It takes great courage to meet, see, and overcome that which constitutes the separated self. It takes courage to sacrifice that part of oneself which separates him from the Soul, and that courage is born of right motive.

The student who does not consider these things, who is not honest with himself, but continues to seek from the selfish purposes of the little will, only brings great suffering upon himself. The keynote of the accepted disciple is harm-less-ness. See to it that you cultivate this quality if you would escape the pitfalls which encompass so many.

There are certain rules of procedure which will aid the student who is honest with himself, and who sincerely aspires to learn for the sake of others. They are listed and explained as follows:

1. Achieve and maintain flexibility of consciousness. This is more commonly known as an open mind, and it is an attitude of the greatest importance to the aspirant.

    It is impossible to know all there is to know

about any one subject. All truth is relative to a man and his present stage of consciousness. Whenever he thinks he has arrived at full and exact knowledge about any one subject, he has become crystalized in his thinking, thereby closing the door upon Wisdom. Get the feel of a vast field of knowledge, which man has not even touched, lying back of all things considered factual.

2. Accept as Truth only that which you comprehend with both the heart and mind. There is within the basic structure of the inner, subjective man (the combined head and heart) a built-in intuitive response mechanism which has been placed there by the Soul. This is not the built-in emotional response mechanism, but rather a higher correspondence of that, which is responsible for the inner guidance known and experienced by many. It does not speak to you in either voice or formulated thought, but produces a response of instantaneous inner knowing which supersedes thought.

   Do not then be blind in your acceptance, accepting as fact a statement which comes from so-called authority. You can and will develop the intuitive response to Truth which will guide you along the path of Light.

3. Do not look at that which you cannot accept as a falsity. Remember, that for another it might be the greatest of Truth. Simply allow that which you do not comprehend and cannot accept to pass. Do not make an issue of it. Wait, and later you will see it in the Light of your own Soul, recognizing its place in the scheme of things.

4. Become receptive to the transference of concepts.

Lesson 1

This is difficult at first, yet extremely important. Remember, a word or a grouping of words is not the concept it is attempting to convey. It is a door through which the aspirant may pass into greater understanding.

All Truth loses something of itself as it takes on the outer wrappings of description. Nonetheless, it can be contacted as abstract concept if the mind is not imprisoned within, or caught up in, the glamour of its outer form. Very often a student is literally bewitched by the vehicles in which Truth makes its appearance, and as a result he learns and repeats volumes of words which hold little, if any, meaning to him.

Attempt to intuit the world of meaning—to sense the depth and fullness of that meaning—and to grasp in realization some understanding of it. This will stimulate into greater activity the intuitive faculty, and you will gradually become receptive to the transference of concepts.

LESSON 2

The Trinity in Relationship to Humanity:

The Trinity Further Defined
(First, Second, Third Logos);
Three Statements of Identity
("I Will To Be," "I Am," "I Create");
The Soul's Use of The Persona
in Building a Vehicle of Manifestation

LESSON 2

Consciousness, that being which is capable of awareness in any stage, we call Soul, and define it as animal, human, or Spiritual, according to Its degree of developed awareness. The nature of consciousness, whether it be that of an animal, man, or a Spiritual Soul incarnate, is essentially divine, since its only parent is God.

This concept is essential; inherent divinity must be grasped, not only as an abstraction, but as a fact in nature, by every student who would become initiate in the Wisdom. Thus, right and wrong, good and evil, any appearance of the pairs of opposites must be understood and resolved into harmony within the mind of the serious student. This is wisdom, and its practical application in the world of affairs is the self-appointed task of every disciple of The Christ.

We attain to such wisdom via a study of, and meditation upon, "The Nature of the Soul" as It manifests Itself in form. Thus, we turn our attention again to the basic triangle of manifestation in order to arrive at the essential impulses, characteristics and attributes of the Soul.

1. Father Aspect   Positive Pole   Divine Will

2. Son Aspect   Magnetic Field   Consciousness or Soul, Divine Love

3. Mother Aspect   Negative Pole   Divine Intelligence

The Nature of The Soul

These three principles of Deity are also referred to as:

1. The First Logos
2. The Second Logos
3. The Third Logos

The First Logos, or the First Aspect of Deity, is the Positive Pole, because His Nature is Positive to all else. Here is the first impulse which initiated creation and the last impulse which brings it to its final conclusion during any one cycle.

The Third Logos, or the Third Aspect of Deity, is the Negative Pole because His Nature is in direct opposition to that of the First Logos. He is negative to (can be impressed by) the motivating Will Impulse.

The Second Logos, or Second Aspect of Deity, partakes of both Divine Will and Divine Intelligence, since He is the created result of both. His nature is composed of the Positive and Negative Aspect, plus Divine Love or Pure Reason, which is His peculiar quality.

The Second Logos, or Son Aspect, is the sum total of all that is in expression at any given time. Here then, in His higher aspect, is our God, and in His lowest aspect, ourselves, consciousness, Soul, Son of God in manifestation.

It is the Divine Nature of that Son or Soul that we are approaching in our minds in an effort to arrive at Wisdom through understanding. We do this through analogy. What are the inherent aspects within the Soul which are analogous to the Son in His highest state? How do these aspects work out in the consciousness of the persona?

First, as the Divine Will Impulse, the motivating Impulse back of all manifestation. This Divine Will

Lesson 2

Impulse moves constantly within the Soul, producing via its impact upon intelligence the characteristic of intelligent will within a man. Such will is essentially Divine since it is the sounding Logoic Word meaning "I Will to Be".

The constant sound or vibration of Will upon Intelligence within consciousness results in a progression of experience which evolves the consciousness to hear, to respond, and to grow in awareness of its essential meaning. Thus we find man demonstrating the Will to live, to progress, to prosper.

Secondly, as the Impulse of Divine Love emanating from the Heart of God (Christ) to impact upon the heart of man (Soul). What is Divine Love or Pure Reason but perfect consciousness? Thus, man is conscious of Being. His sound goes forth as the "I Am" and it is essentially Divine, since it is the word of the Son or Christ, the Second Person in the Holy Trinity. Thus is produced within man the characteristic of identification, i.e., the expression or assertion of that degree of Son, Soul, or Love which is realized.

Thirdly, as the Impulse of Divine Intelligence constantly impacting upon the consciousness to produce manifestation or intelligent activity. Here sounding within the Son, or Soul, is the inherent word of the Mother, the Third Person in the Holy Trinity: "I create." Thus, forms are built through which the consciousness experiences and evolves the Positive and Negative polarities of His Being. His activity is essentially Divine because it is an inherent characteristic bestowed upon Him by the Intelligence of God. He must create—he must act in accordance with His inherent will, and His degree of identification with Christ.

The synthesis of the above three manifest the attributes of the Soul, which will be explained and clarified in a later lesson.

The Nature of The Soul

What is a man, then, when observed from the perspective of reality? He is the synthesis of the three-fold word of God sounding in time and space . . .

1. I Will to Be

2. I am

3. I create

. . . or Christ as it is translated by Christianity, or Buddha as it is translated by Buddhism, etc.

From the moment of the birth of an individual Soul, a self conscious unit within the greater consciousness of the Second Logos, the process of human evolution begins. The new birth of awareness is swept into activity by the Divine Impulses of the Will, Intelligence, and Love which are inherent within it. These, working under the Divine Laws of Evolution, Reincarnation, and Karma, build the first cycle of vehicles for the incarnating Soul, with little attention being given the building process by the consciousness itself. In the beginning, the process automatically proceeds according to Divine Law, and the inherent Plan.

Later, however, when the Spiritual Soul has evolved a certain degree of Wisdom (awakened, via its experience with form, to its essential Reality and its Divine Nature), it takes a more specific part in the building process.

It observes the growth of the persona (that aspect of its consciousness which is imprisoned within and identified with the form) and determines what further experiences under Divine Law are needed. Then, consciously manipulating Divine Will and Intelligence, the Spiritual Soul creates the vehicles of incarnation.

Lesson 2

This is an important concept to bear in mind. The Soul does not seek out a vehicle already created and then incarnate into it, but rather He builds the persona vehicles via a meditation process.

An aside note may be inserted here for later meditation and reflection:

"The Spiritual Soul is in deep meditation throughout the whole of Its incarnating cycle."

In cooperation with the individual Souls of the personality parents concerned (determined by evolutionary development and karma) the Spiritual Soul proceeds with the process of creation from His own plane of affairs. Procreation is, then, but the effect of a cause initiated on Spiritual Soul levels.

Such information may be somewhat startling to the beginner on the occult path, therefore, it is suggested for all those to whom these concepts are new, proceed slowly and without intensity of mind. Do not attempt to either accept or reject the information at this time, nor even to understand it in its entirety. The above concepts carry implications which, when later comprehended, will flood the mind with Light.

Much depends upon your approach. Too great a stimulation may bring that for which your consciousness is not yet ready. On the other hand, too great a struggle to grasp the inner meaning of esoteric concepts may result in an unconscious repulsion of that meaning.

Consider the text then, with the ease born of detachment, i.e., *"It may or may not be true. I shall observe and in so doing permit clarification of my mind."*

The Spiritual Soul, when it is building its vehicle of incarnation, forms it according to the needed experience,

The Nature of The Soul

colors it with the necessary qualities to draw, under the law of attraction, the needed lessons, and so grows rich in Wisdom. Each succeeding form or vehicle is capable of greater Spiritual expression, until finally the Spiritual Soul builds a vehicle of such high vibratory frequency, that it can carry the sum total of His developed Spiritual consciousness, and so manifest perfection in form. This final incarnation frees Him from the wheel of re-birth.

LESSON 3

Rebuilding the Instrument of the Persona:

Character Building
(The Persona's response to the Soul
impulse to start on the Path of Return);
Invocation and Evocation
(The basic tools of relationship
between the Soul and Persona);
The Disciplines of the Average Human Being
and the Aspirant in Relation to Character
Building, Meditation and Alignment,
Basic Instruction on Meditation

LESSON 3

We have stated thus far that the Divine Impulses of Will, Love, and Intelligence impacting upon the incarnate consciousness produce three inherent characteristics within the evolving persona. These characteristics themselves are evolved within and with the persona until they are expressed as a synthesis of Soul-planned activity. Thus is the evolution of the man concluded in the human sense, and the conscious Soul incarnated into form.

It is during this stage of personality growth that the process of character building is emphasized as the path of return for the Son of God. The conscious "I" begins to glimpse and to build an ideal of his Divine Prototype, the Spiritual Soul, and endeavors to rebuild his instrument, to expand his consciousness, and to fashion his life and affairs according to that ideal. In the beginning his vision will be distorted and incomplete due to the lack of clarity in his mind. It will also be clouded with many glamours in accordance with the emotional content of his feeling nature, but in most cases it will suffice to stimulate him into a new effort of conscious growth.

Little realizing the importance of the evolutionary step he is taking, this one approaches the path of initiation, whereon he will initiate his own Spiritual development with whatever aid he may invoke through the invocative strength of his own efforts.

I should like to seemingly digress for a few moments for the purpose of bringing your attention to bear upon the idea of invocative strength.

The Nature of The Soul

Many of you who are attracted to this series of instruction are already somewhat acquainted with the concept of invocation and evocation. However, we shall define the terms used, for the sake of clarity, and proceed with our subject from that definition.

Invocation is the calling down into active play of that Deity which overshadows an individual or a group of individuals. That which is invoked may appear in one of many forms, such as an idea, an experience, or in the case of a needy humanity, even as the incarnation of an initiate consciousness. Thus, Divine Intervention is brought into being via the magnetic pull of the invocative center, which is acting as a positive pole of magnetic attraction within the three worlds of human endeavor.

Evocation is a calling forth into expression of that Divine Potential which is latent within the manifest form. Thus, the indwelling Christ, that Divine Spark or Seed within the consciousness of the mass, can be attracted into expression via the magnetic pull brought to bear upon it by a conscious Son of God living within the body of humanity.

Invocative strength is developed within the aspirant via his self-initiated efforts toward Spiritual growth, and his expression of that growth. "God help me," will meet with success in accordance with the proven sincerity of its speaker. If such an appeal is made via action, then will the aid be forthcoming from whatever level the aspirant has been able to reach.

Character building is the first and, it might be added, the most important process used in the development of invocative strength. The evolving persona is attempting to become Soul infused. He attracts that Soul infusion (Divine Intervention) via his effort to embody his ideal of the Soul. Each successful expression of a Soul quality establishes him more definitely as a positive pole of Spiritual magnetic attraction within his environment.

Such Spiritual magnetism works in two directions. It attracts that which is above it in frequency down into manifestation, and that which is occluded or imprisoned within the form nature upward and outward into manifestation. Thus, the Overshadowing Christ is brought down into incarnation and the Indwelling Christ is brought up to be merged with Its Divine Prototype.

At a later date an actual technique can be given those of you who qualify, for the purpose of utilizing this information to the betterment of humanity and the working out of the Plan. In the meantime, attempt to understand its inner meaning and to relate yourselves to it.

As the aspirant actually takes his place upon the path of initiation, the character building process is entered into as a science which utilizes certain techniques based upon a knowledge of the characteristics of a Soul-infused persona. The vision then becomes more clear, more definite, and more possible of embodiment. It is no longer distorted and clouded, a vague dream of self-glorification, but a vision of radiant beauty which is based upon the real truth of the Soul of humanity. What the aspirant himself can and will attain to, all of humanity can and will reach, and hence his vision no longer includes just himself, but becomes the Divine Plan which includes every man, woman, and child upon the planet.

The characteristics of the Soul-infused persona are the manifestation of Divine Will, Divine Love, and Divine Intelligence within and through the form nature.

Thus, we see that the disciplines exercised by the aspirant during this period of growth are somewhat different from those of the average person who is attempting to build character.

The average man patterns his disciplines after the moral and ethical standards of the society and civilization in which he lives. This, however, is not enough for the aspirant. He maintains the ethical and moral code of his society, plus that code which is based upon the Spiritual standards of his Soul. He does not kill a physical body simply because such is the law of his brothers; he goes even further. He is harmless in thought, word, and deed, because that is the Divine Law which his Soul recognizes and obeys. His disciplines then, are the positive acts of embodiment of a Spiritual ideal, which he himself has constructed in his response to the Overshadowing Spiritual Soul.

Before we go into a comprehensive study of the characteristics of the Soul-infused persona, I should like to insert basic instruction upon the subject of meditation. This will give the student a technique with which he may realize and embody the information given in the following lessons.

Meditation is a technical process whereby Soul contact is realized and Soul infusion achieved. It is safely carried out as a daily practice only after the persona has dedicated his vehicles to the Soul. If there are any of you, then, who have not and do not make such dedication, do not proceed any further with this instruction, for it could be disastrous to you. At this point you are entering the upward way which leads the errant son into the province of his Father. You will be invoking into your vehicles the higher frequency of Spiritual energies, which can be safely wielded only for the betterment of humanity. Deliberate misuse of a Spiritual energy or power brings quick retribution (karma) to the user; hence the protection of the masses is insured by Divine Law.

Lesson 3

The first step in any well ordered meditation is that of alignment. Alignment is the establishment of a path-of-least-resistance for the flow of energy between any two given points. In this case, the alignment is to be between the persona, focused in the physical brain, and the Spiritual Soul in Its own sphere.

The persona is composed of three aspects: the physical or dense body, the emotional-feeling nature, and the mind. The objective of the first stage of alignment is to render the physical body and the emotional nature quiescent and under complete mental control. This is brought about in a two-fold manner, as follows:

1. The two lower aspects of the instrument must be relaxed. Wherever there is tension, there the mind is held a prisoner. An emotion, particularly of a negative nature, will produce a physical tension, which holds the attention of the mind fastened to the body and the problem, without freedom to seek, recognize or create a solution. Any attempt to strain or lift the mind from its prison will only serve to strengthen its hold; therefore, the process must be that of relaxed alignment which results in a freeing of the mind. This is accomplished in the following manner:

    a. Become physically relaxed and comfortable. Make the body as comfortable as possible in a sitting position. Beginning with the feet, relax each muscle, tendon, and, finally, cell, of the entire body. Speak to the separate parts, telling them to relax. Know that the nervous system carries the message to them and that they will obey.

    b. Become emotionally calm and serene. Speak to the emotions, telling them to relax, to become at peace. Let each emotion become quiescent until there is a noticeable serenity pervading the feeling nature.

2. Establish a point of focus. When the physical body and the emotional nature are at peace, the personality consciousness will naturally focus in the mind. The mind, which is no longer held a prisoner to the lower aspects, naturally focuses its attention in the world of mind. It does not leave the body, but it can become attentive to the Soul. It is poised and alert. This is facilitated in the following manner:

   a. Establish a deep, easy rhythmic breath, that which seems natural and comfortable.

   b. Taking seven deep breaths, the student lets his conscious attention come to a point of focus within the forehead. Do not create a point of tension here. Simply settle easily in the forehead and realize that you are an integrated personality focused in your mental nature.

The next step is to align yourself (the focused consciousness) with the Soul via the mind. In the past, beginners have made the mistake of trying too hard. Let us eliminate that mistake now. Do not try to place the locality of the Soul. It is everywhere equally present, and to place it, before understanding, only limits your thinking. Instead, align yourself with the Soul by turning your attention to the concept of a Soul. Spend a few moments in silent contemplation of being aligned with your Higher Self via the medium of mental substance.

You are now ready to enter into communication with the Soul, to contact it via a seed-thought. The mind is given a thought which quickens its vibratory frequency in such a manner as to span the distance in awareness between the persona focused in the mental nature and the Overshadowing Soul.

Let your first seed-thought be that of "dedication."

"I, the personality, dedicate my consciousness and my bodies to the Soul."

This serves to identify and bridge the two states of awareness in time and space.

The seed-thought is then dropped. The words are no longer spoken. This is the most difficult stage of the entire meditation for beginners and for many of their seniors. The tendency of the mind to repetition swings the student into the habit of affirmation, and this is the polar opposite of the condition required for Soul contact. Just so long as the mind is speaking, it is closed to communion with the Soul. It must become quiet, attentive, alert.

The seed-thought is dropped as words. The energy of the thought remains as a line of contact (a bridge in mental substance) and needs no repetition.

The mind is still, attentive, receptive. When the moment of absolute silence has come, the Soul makes itself known.

I should here like to insert a few words of warning. Cast out all preconceived ideas you may have formulated as to what Soul contact is. You have probably heard stories of various phenomena experienced during meditation. Some of the common ones are: light, communication in the form of words, pictures, etc. This is all well and good and may be true of the persons concerned, but it is not a criterion.

The Nature of The Soul

Each individual experiences his contact in an individual manner. Some never see light, never see pictures, never hear or sense words. All of these phenomena are forms dictated by the personality, not the Soul. The purest form of Soul communication is instantaneous knowing. Anything else is a means, not the goal.

Accept that which results from your meditation as the best method suited to your development, and do not covet another's way. This is most important.

3. The meditation form is concluded via what we define as the descent, in the following manner:

   a. Turn the attention to the mental nature, and know it to be impulsed by the Divine Will Impulse;

   b. Turn the attention to the emotional nature and know it to be cleansed and purified by the energy of Divine Love;

   c. Turn the attention to the physical brain and nervous system and know them to be galvanized into right action.

   Spend a few moments radiating Divine Love to humanity.

LESSON 4

The Divine Plan and Divine Energy:

The Divine Plan;
Divine Energy in Relation to
Purpose, Power, and Will;
Negativity and Its Relationship to
Understanding the Underlying
Plan and Purpose;
The Law of Cause and Effect

LESSON 4

The characteristics of the Soul-infused persona are basically three types of energy which are available to the individual, or the group, for expression in the three worlds of human endeavor. These energies in their free state are the potentials of the Divine Plan, and in expression they are the manifestation of that Plan in the life and affairs of humanity.

The perfect manifestation of the Plan is obviously the result of an appropriation of a Divine potential of energy, and its direction into appearance in accordance with its Divine Intent. To appropriate energy for any other reason is an act of the errant son⊥ and carries a retaliation, so to speak, from the Plan⊥ itself.

This is an important concept to grasp. The Divine Plan is always in⊥ manifestation, regardless of outer appearance. That manifestation may be a becoming, or a perfection, but it is always there, moving within the appearance to restore order out of chaos; working out through the appearance into the Light of Day. War, for example, is the Divine Plan, as a becoming, for it must eventually teach man the error of his violence, while world unity and peace would be the Divine Plan in a phase of perfect expression.

Divine Energy, then, operates according to its own laws, which are invoked the moment it is moved from a potential into an actual expression. Each energy is impressed with a Divine Intent, which, when violated, results in a manifestation of a negative effect in the life and affairs of its violator. The succession of negative effects in the life and affairs of an individual will eventually awaken within him a need to learn the right use of energy. This phase of the evolutionary process we call the path of experience, for it proceeds via the trial and error⊥ methods, with little conscious effort made toward Spiritual development.

The Soul-infused persona is attempting to appropriate energy and to direct it into manifestation according to its Divine Intent. This activity we define as service to the Plan, and those who are engaged in the activity we define as disciples.

There are many stages of discipleship⊥ from that of the probationer⊥ up to, and beyond, that of the accepted disciple⊥ working from within one or another of the Hierarchial ashrams. The path of initiation is actually the path of⊥ discipleship which leads finally to the Overshadowing Christ.

Please bear the above concepts in mind as we proceed with a study of the characteristics which constitute, for the beginner, the ideal of the Soul. As you envision that ideal with greater clarity, such concepts will hold real meaning for you.

As the energy of Divine Will impacts upon the consciousness of a beginner on the path, we see it manifesting within his mind as the Will to Good. This is the first major step he takes in his re-orientation to the Soul. His little will, which has heretofore been concerned with the affairs of the separated persona, is aligned with the Will of God, as he begins to think in terms of the betterment of humanity. Thus, the good of the many becomes the motivating impulse⊥ underlying all of his activity. He is moved by that impulse to express goodwill⊥ toward his friends, relatives, and associates, so brotherhood becomes, for him, a fact in nature.

As this one envisions the ideal, that ideal begins to

Lesson 4

include the right use of Will energy. He begins to think in terms of the three component parts of this First Aspect of Deity:

1. Purpose
2. Power
3. Will

His will is derived, then, from the Purpose and Power of God. He begins to glimpse a Divine Purpose (Intent) working out through every situation he sees manifesting about him. He knows that the Power of God to manifest the good, the true, and the beautiful is inherent within that underlying purpose, so he seizes upon it, as his own. He makes himself receptive to Divine Intent ("not my will, Father, but Thine") and via an acceptance of it, invokes the Power of God⊥ into manifestation.

In this way, the beginner on the path becomes the probationer disciple, and begins to contribute his energies to the forces of Light upon the planet. He serves the Divine Purpose which underlies all manifestation.

This results in an attitude which is quite different from that of the average reformer in the world. Rather than attempting to stamp out so-called evil via inhibition, the probationer calls forth the Divine Purpose from within the form to manifest the good, the true, and the beautiful.

A negative situation is not seen, then, as something which must be stopped. It is seen as a result of misuse of available energy, as ignorance of Divine Intent, and, as such, it is recognized as a vehicle of manifestation for the Divine Plan.

The probationer grounds the Plan (aids its manifestation) by recognizing its existence within the form, and calling it forth into appearance in the Light of Day.

The Nature of The Soul

The disciple, then, looks upon disease, hunger, war, etc., as necessary vehicles through which the Will of God⊥ is making itself known. How else is a man or the world of men to know the Greater Purpose?

The ills of the bodies become secondary⊥ factors, important only in their disclosure of the ills of the consciousness. The body cannot, must not, be healed to cover a sick and Spiritually ignorant consciousness. In such cases, the disease goes inward to later erupt with greater violence and pain. Such an eruption may be delayed for an entire incarnation, only to bring the soul back into a crippled and pain-ridden vehicle for which there is no known cure.

How, then, can we be of service in a world which is characteristically painful? How can health, peace, and goodwill be made manifest in the life and affairs of humanity in the face of such odds?

The answer is not so difficult, nor so hidden, as it would appear. It remains only for the aspirants in the world to become disciples, to arrive at those attitudes which, in their sum-total, constitute discipleship.

We like to think of our God as a kind and benevolent Father, yet we do not recognize the Wisdom of His ways.

If a man be sick, if a world be at war, let us then recognize a Divine Purpose underlying the condition. Let us accept the sickness, and the war, as being a vehicle through which the consciousness involved is presented with an opportunity for Spiritual growth. Let us serve by becoming receptive to God's Will, to Divine Purpose, in any event, and by calling it forth from within the event to grow and bloom as a flower of Truth. The beauty and fragrance of the flower will then dispel the sickness and the wrong relationship manifesting between brothers.

Lesson 4

At this point, I should like to present you with a service technique which can be utilized by an aspirant to discipleship to great advantage.

When you are presented with a condition of negativity, whether in your own life or the life of a brother, carry out the following technique:

A. Establish your own alignment with:

   1. your Soul,
   2. The Christ,
   3. The Father.

B. Recognizing that the manifesting condition is a result of the working out of Divine Law and Order, become receptive to the Divine Purpose which is inherent in this particular situation.

C. Upon recognition of Purpose, whether in detail or in generality, call it forth, from within whatever limitation is its prison, as a manifesting reality. See it take root within the consciousness aspect, grow there, and bloom as Truth.

D. Then, and only then, see the radiance of Truth dispelling the darkness cast by the shadow of ignorance. See that radiant Light emerge from the consciousness and shine forth through the form nature, transmuting, as it does, the outer form into a true reflection of inner reality.

E. Speak the words:

   "May the Divine Plan manifest Divine adjustment⊥within this condition in Divine Law and Order."

Sound the OM, and turn your attention elsewhere.

The Nature of The Soul

Divine Will manifests also as perseverance, which is a needed asset in the life of any disciple. The beginner must learn to work without always noting immediate results in the world of form, and this is often difficult. He is so enthusiastic; he has sensed the vision, and grasped a bit of the Divine Plan for humanity. Very often he feels a sense of urgency, a need for haste. In his attempts to manifest the Plan as he has seen it, he meets with seeming failure, not once, but many times. Often he does not realize that there is no real failure, but that out of that which appears as such, success is one step closer.

In his first attempts to serve, he makes many mistakes, and in viewing these, he feels a certain self-disgust, an inadequacy to meet the need of the times. He forgets that all through this period of learning he is being watched, and trained, and aided wherever possible. He will pass out of this period of probationership as a skilled worker, one of the trusted and dependable disciples upon whom the Hierarchy builds its hope for humanity.

There is another factor to be considered here, and that is the law of cause and effect. Cause originates in the inner world of thought, and effect is the manifestation of that thought in form. We find that every situation is an effect of a state of consciousness, and that to successfully change the situation, we must work with the consciousness aspect which is its cause. Therefore, the disciple works from above, downward. He extends his awareness into the world of mind, and of the emotions, as well as the world of form. He has sensed something of the Divine Plan. He then works to establish a state of consciousness within the mental sphere, a condition within the astral-emotional sphere, and intelligent activity in the physical.

Very often there will be a period of apparent chaos

manifesting in the world of form as a result of his efforts, and the beginner often becomes discouraged. The wise disciple realizes that often change will manifest in just this manner as karma is precipitated and adjusted. He continues his work, maintaining strength in the calm assurance of his Soul that all is well. He perseveres until his goal is realized.

During the coming week use the following seed-thought in your meditation exercise:

"I am receptive to the Purpose, Power and Will of God, as it is stepped down to me from my Soul. I serve that Purpose, Accept Its Power, and do the Will of God."

The Nature of The Soul

LESSON 5

The Seven Rays and the Right Use of Will:

Introduction to the Seven Rays;
Ray Make-up of Human Kingdom,
Planetary, and Solar Logoi;
Synthesis;
Glamour of Self-Importance;
Will Energy as it Impacts
the Instrument of the Persona;
Right Uses of First Ray Energy

LESSON 5

In our consideration of the characteristics of Divine Will, we must bear in mind that it is basically an energy expression of Divinity. God expresses in this Solar system via seven ray energies, which are in themselves seven subsidiary frequencies of the Cosmic Ray of Divine Love-Wisdom.

In order to more clearly understand this subject of energy expression, it is necessary to consider again the two polarities of the basic Trinity.

Positive	Negative
Spirit	Matter

In Lesson One it is stated "Spirit and Matter we see as the two polarities of one energy."

Spirit is matter vibrating at its highest frequency; matter is Spirit vibrating at its lowest frequency. These two polarities, plus the consciousness aspect or magnetic field created by the interplay of frequency between them, we define as the basic cause of all manifestation.

The three aspects, in a cosmic sense, manifest as three frequencies of energy which are defined as the Cosmic rays of:

1. Divine Will & Power
2. Divine Love-Wisdom
3. Divine Intelligence

These in turn are differentiated into four minor

frequencies which are defined as the Cosmic rays of attribute.

4. Harmony
5. Cosmic Definition or equation
6. Ideation
7. Divine Law and Order

A Solar system embodies one of the major rays (Divine Love-Wisdom, in our case) and differentiates it again into seven subsidiary frequencies which are the seven sub-rays of the embodied Cosmic ray.

Our Solar Logos is then in a process of embodying the Second Aspect, Divine Love, or the consciousness of a Cosmic Heavenly Man.

Cosmic Love is the lesson which He is learning, Cosmic Consciousness the goal toward which He is evolving, and the perfect expression of Wisdom or Pure Reason within His life and affairs, the goal He has set for Himself.

A Planetary Logos embodies one of the seven Solar rays (in our case, Divine Intelligence) and again differentiates it into seven subsidiary frequencies which become the seven planetary rays.

Our Planetary Logos makes His approach to Cosmic Love or Cosmic Consciousness via the embodiment of Divine Intelligence. He attempts to arrive at and express Cosmic Love through Intelligent Activity and its seven subsidiary frequencies. He is still attempting to embody Cosmic Consciousness, remember, as is the Solar Life of which He is a part, but indirectly, via the expression of a Divine characteristic inherent in the consciousness aspect of the Solar Logos. That characteristic is not the basic third or matter aspect, but rather the Divine Intelligence the Son inherits from the Mother.

All Life within the Planetary body is conditioned by:

1. Cosmic Love via its third Solar subsidiary, Divine Intelligence,
2. And several of the seven Planetary subsidiaries.

The Major Planetary Rays are defined for further clarity as:

1. The Will to Know Love in it highest aspect,
2. The Love of Wisdom,
3. The Intelligent application of Mind in Love,

and the minor four as:

4. The balancing of the pairs of opposites to produce harmony out of discord,
5. Application of Intelligence in Concrete knowledge and science,
6. Devotion to an Ideal,
7. Order through ceremony and sacrifice.

The seven rays, whether Cosmic, Solar or Planetary, always maintain their basic nature since original Impression of Divine Intent is maintained. They are only stepped down in frequency by the Cosmic, Solar, or Planetary consciousness appropriating them.

To carry this correspondence even further, we find the Soul of humanity in a process of embodying the third Solar ray of Divine Intelligence, while an individual Soul may be found on any one of the Planetary seven.

The rays of the persona are in turn subsidiary to the Soul ray.

The Nature of The Soul

Synthesis is the lifting in frequency of any subsidiary seven into its original expression.

EXAMPLE

1. In the Solar Life, synthesis is the lifting of the Solar Seven into Cosmic Love.

2. In the Planetary Life, synthesis is the lifting of the Planetary Seven into a Solar expression of Intelligent Love.

3. In the individual human sense, synthesis is the lifting of the personality rays into an expression of the Soul ray.

We see every appearance in form as but a combination of certain ray energies, knowing that the so-called solid form is but the slowest rate of frequency of the energies involved. This appearance is the appearance of the matter aspect, the negative pole of manifestation, while Spirit is but the highest rate of frequency of the same energies involved. Between these two is the magnetic field, the Soul or consciousness aspect, which is found occupying every range of frequency between Spirit and matter.

It is realized that the above information is highly technical and will be difficult for some; however, it is not only necessary to you as foundational occult knowledge, but it holds illumination for those whose intuitions are awakening in a Spiritual sense. Learn it, as you would learn any other text, and then reflect upon its inner meaning. Do not be concerned if that meaning, and Spiritual significance, is not readily apparent, for it will reveal itself in due time.

The above technical information can serve in one sense now, however. It can dispel the glamour of importance

Lesson 5

which many occult students tend to build around themselves. Once it is understood that our Solar Logos, that Life in which our Planetary Logos lives and moves and has His being, is evolving toward Cosmic Consciousness, the individual will not make the mistake of thinking he has attained to the same state. He will take his proper place, eliminating the swelled sense of ego, and work toward the achievement of his own evolutionary goal.

This is important and possibly one of the hardest experiences of the occult path. If it reduces man in his own eyes, it expands God at the same time, and gives the individual a truer sense of proportion.

When the human being begins to glimpse the vision of his Soul, and to be impressed by the Wisdom of his Soul, his first reaction is egotistical. He thinks of himself as different from the rest of humanity, and little realizing the error of his way, becomes more dangerously separative than when he was a persona without thought of Soul. The antidote is absorption of a few occult facts, plus the realization that what is happening to him is as natural as any process of growth. He is not different, nor unique, above or below his brothers. He is simply entering into an experience which every man, woman, and child upon the planet either has already, is now, or will, in due course of time, share with him.

If you have been using the seed-thought given in the last lesson as a regular meditation exercise, you have invoked into your instrument from Soul levels a greater impact of Will energy than heretofore.

Let us now observe the natural effects of such an impact upon each of the three aspects of the persona.

The moment such energy impacts upon the mental body, it stirs the consciousness therein toward some kind of drive. The individual has availed himself of more motive power, so to speak, which activates the motives already present. Thus, spiritual ambition, which is the drive for Spiritual attainment as a separated persona, stirs its head and the aspirant begins to think in terms of a position of power, of wide influence. Instead of serving those whom he is dedicated to serve, or responding to their needs naturally, he is conscious only of himself and his need to satisfy his ego. He wants to be somebody in a Spiritual sense.

At the same time, the real mental impulse to be of service to the Divine Plan, to discipline the persona, to evolve as a member of the human family, is activated too, and the pairs of opposites make an appearance within the mind nature to be resolved into harmony.

The conflict between the two motives will produce confusion, discord, ups and downs in the thought-life, until they are resolved via rededication and a sane attitude toward them.

The aspirant and probationer disciple realizes first that motive is an evolving part of his consciousness. If he had attained purity of motive, he would not be where he is now.

He accepts, then, the fact that via the process of evolution he has embodied the pairs of opposites, and that he has now entered that stage of growth and development wherein he will resolve them within himself, gradually transmuting the one into an expansion of the other.

While he does not feed the wrong motives of which he becomes consciously aware, he does not indulge in guilt because of them. They are there. They are indicative of his place in the evolutionary scheme, and of the work ahead. He develops a sense of humor, laughs at himself and his faults, and forges ahead to promulgate the good, the true and the beautiful.

Lesson 5

This is right use of Will energy on mental levels and it results in Divine Strength. The man is tempered to endure the path of initiation and its revelation of his baser nature.

As the Will energy passes from the mental into the emotional nature, it produces the same type of conflict there; desire versus aspiration. It activates the so-called good and bad, very often producing emotional disturbance. The aspirant simply wills to Love. He floods his emotional nature with Love via the direction of his thought, and calms the troubled waters. He assumes the same attitude toward the emotional situation as he does toward the mental, bringing the reality of his Soul into being within this aspect of his nature. Thus, he becomes a harmonizing agent in the world of affairs.

On the physical plane, he simply puts into action his reoriented thoughts and feelings. He realizes that his Will is the stepped-down energy of God impressed with a Divine Intent. The wielding of Divine Intent produces order within his life and affairs.

During the period of his probationership as a disciple, the individual uses Will energy in the following manner:

1. To seek out and know the Divine Plan as it is held in focus by the Christ. This he does via meditation, study and observation.

2. To render his instrument fit for service to the Divine Plan. This he does via Soul-imposed disciplinary training, which involves the invocation of Divine Will Impulse into his own inner nature.

3. To embody to the best of his ability that degree of Soul quality which he can touch with his heart and mind. This he does via aspiration.

The Nature of The Soul

4. To initiate a defined service activity on mental, emotional, and physical levels, which bears no hope of tangible return or obvious results. In other words, let him find a service which is performed from behind the scenes, to no one else's knowledge.

During the coming week continue with the same seed-thought, noting the effects of the impact of Will energy in your life and affairs. Determine, via an observation of your daily activity, the ways in which you can put such energy into right use. As an assignment, bring a brief written statement of such discoveries to your next class.

LESSON 6

The Question of Identity and the Second Ray:

Second Ray as Magnetic Field,
as Image of God, as Consciousness;
Our Identity as Soul;
The Nature of Divine Love-Wisdom
as Reason, Perfect Understanding,
Right Relationship;
Second Ray in Relation to
the Astral Body manifesting
as Desire and Aspiration;
Embodying Second Ray in Terms
of Harmlessness and
Relating to Others as Soul;
Detachment

LESSON 6

We have defined the consciousness aspect as the magnetic field created by the interplay of frequency between Positive Spirit and Negative Matter. Here is the created Son, the Love-Wisdom aspect of the Divine Expression.

There is a great mystery underlying these terms used as synonymous to describe the second Logos.

What is the magnetic field? It is the essential area of activity resulting from a flow of force alternating between the two poles. Force in this instance is constituted of the various frequencies that the One energy takes as it plays between Its positive and negative polarity.

The essential area of activity is consciousness, or Soul. This is the conscious thinking, feeling, creating entity. This is the God of our manifest Cosmos beyond which the highest developed minds in our Solar system cannot go. About Him it has been said: "And having pervaded the universe with a fragment of myself, I remain."

Our Christian Bible states, "God created man in the Image and Likeness of Himself."

The essential area of activity, the magnetic field of consciousness, is the Image of God. It is the first (counting from above) manifestation of God that man's mind can attain to, and this only in theory thus far. And yet, man is not only created in the Image, but he is a part of It.

The beginner often has difficulty with this concept of

The Nature of The Soul

himself as Consciousness, for what is it? It is, insofar as he is concerned, an intangible something he cannot see, hear, taste, smell, or touch. Consciousness to him is formless, and yet out of it emerges all of the forms that are. He cannot confine it, limit it, or pin it down to a specific; therefore, comprehension of himself as a consciousness seems impossible.

To further confuse the issue, a teacher cannot limit it to a specific, but can only explain what it is not. It is not the body, the emotions, nor the mind; it is that which creates and uses them. The teacher can only say, "You are a consciousness. You were before the form of your body, you are now within that form, and you will be long after it is gone."

Here is the old problem of identity, which characterizes the occultist, beginner and adept.

The beginner can help himself to begin to know, by following a very simple meditation exercise as follows:

1. Turn attention to the physical body and realize that you are not your body.

2. Turn attention to the emotional nature and realize that you are not your emotions.

3. Turn attention to the mind and realize that you are not your thoughts.

4. Focus the attention in the ajna and meditate for three minutes on the following seed-thought:

   "Having pervaded this body, emotions and mind with a fragment of myself, I remain."

The next step in the knowing process is to try to under-

Lesson 6

stand why the occultist defines consciousness as Divine Love-Wisdom. Here is another mystery almost more overpowering than that of consciousness itself. Divine Love is a concept which defies Logic and Reason, yet these two are born within it.

Some schools have gone so far as to say "God is Love." We say God is Love, God is consciousness, for they are one and the same. We go further and say that man is a developing, growing, consciousness, therefore he is a developing, growing Love.

From above downward, we may put it yet another way.

1. Divine Love is the consciousness of God's Being.

2. Divine Love is the consciousness of Christ, the adult son.

3. Divine Love is the growing consciousness of the human Soul, the child son.

Divine Love is not the Law. It is the manipulator of the Law. It is Pure Reason, that which Is.

Regardless of ray makeup, predominant characteristics or environing circumstances, every man's essential nature is Love. This alone, when all else fails, will reach him and this is the concept that every occultist is endeavoring to embody, regardless of the path or method he may be taking at the moment.

This simple, yet so difficult concept, is the golden key to initiation. The key which opens every door in the awareness to every field of knowledge until finally the world of meaning itself is entered, and known in its totality. If you would learn, would become wise, then give your attention to Love, for Love created all knowledge. It lies within and behind everything that is.

The Nature of The Soul

Thus far, we have talked in abstractions, yet it remains to bring the concept down to the here and now, to relate it as one of the Divine characteristics of the Soul-infused persona.

In the Soul-infused persona, Divine Love-Wisdom manifests as quality, the quality of his relationships, that which determines the activity resulting from any two or more being related.

Where the quality of a relationship is characterized by Divine Love, there is perfect understanding, and where there is perfect understanding, there is perfect application of knowledge. Wisdom is the ability to put concrete knowledge into intelligent activity, the knowing how to apply that which you know to the highest good of all concerned.

Divine Love-Wisdom, in this stage of development, we understand as describing a Divine Relationship in which there is Divine understanding resulting in Divine Activity.

The man is in right relationship with His God, The Plan, his brothers, and himself. Thus his activity is in service to The Plan.

This manifests and predominates first in the astral-emotional nature, the vehicle through which the feeling aspect of consciousness is developed. This energy body is a great transmitter of force which can be, and often is, of a destructive nature. When the Love aspect is highly developed, however, the astral body is an instrument of healing, transmutation, and the Power factor in the work of manifestation. In this stage it constitutes the desire body of the Soul, and through the Power of Right Desire or Aspiration, it attracts all that is needed for the Divine work.

Lesson 6

Divine Love manifests first in the consciousness of the beginner on the path, as right aspiration. He has become, over a long period of time on the path of experience, discontented with the kind of life he is living. He longs for something else to give Purpose to his life, and not knowing what that something else might be, is driven from place to place, from religion to religion, from philosophy to philosophy in search of Truth.

At last he recognizes that that Truth is greater than he, or anyone else as a personality, for he realizes that the persona of itself is without a Purpose. He sees the Truth, then, as his own Higher Self, his Christ-Self in Reality, and to that he aspires.

He endeavors to see the vision of himself as he really is, and in so doing, he becomes aware of the Ideal. He glimpses a vision of the ideal, at first distorted by the clouds in his own mental-emotional aura, later, clear and beautiful.

After having seen the vision (if only in part), he then sets out to embody it, to become that in manifestation. He undergoes a period of self-imposed discipline in which he fashions his thought-life, his emotions, and his physical actions to portray the ideal he has found.

In this manner, the instrument is literally rebuilt. The inner thought-life gradually undergoes a transformation which eliminates negativity and the nonessentials, to build in those thought-patterns which characterize the Soul-infused persona. The emotional life assumes an attitude of serenity and radiatory Love, while the physical body, from the cellular structure to the whole vehicle itself, is galvanized into right action.

During this rebuilding process, the aspirant endeavors to practice harmlessness. He lifts the vibratory frequency of his bodies via a strict disciplinary training,

69

The Nature of The Soul

which has to do largely with his attitude toward others, and so becomes harmless in thought, word, and deed. Only then is he ready for initiation.

In reorienting his affairs to the life of the Soul, the aspirant finds Divine Love-Wisdom manifesting next as a recognition of others as Souls. This is the first step toward the attainment of the common goal of man; the manifestation of brotherhood. He recognizes, first, those of his immediate group, as his brothers in Christ, and gradually all of the connotations of this relationship seep into his consciousness. He experiences the greatest of all gifts, the richness and fullness of the Love of God in man.

One of the most important steps taken toward this goal is the attitude of detachment. As an effect of Divine Love, it is actually an attachment to the Soul of all life which results in a detachment from the form.

As stated previously, disciples who are thrown together in the life of the personality, to work out some aspect of the Plan, often meet with great difficulty. There are differences in personality reactions, differences in opinion, in type and method of work, and in ray makeup. This causes friction where the attention is focused in the world of form.

The aspirant learns first that his brother is a Soul, and therefore they are both a part of the One Life. He then learns to attach importance only to the Oneness of the Soul, and to attach no importance to the differences of the persona. This is at first difficult, since the aspirant has been concerned with the affairs of the persona over a period of many lifetimes. It necessitates a placing of values upon the constant realities, rather than changing conditions, an attainment of right perspective.

This is most easily facilitated when the aspirant can lift

his focal point of attention above the area where old thought-forms can influence him. His task is to stand steady in the Light of that Truth which he is attempting to embody. He begins to actually take up his residence in the head, that place where he practices his daily meditations.

Here it is possible for him to abstain from criticism in thought, word, and deed. He goes even further and recognizes neither vice nor virtue in the persona. Thus, his focal point of attention is shifted beyond the mask to the reality, and Truth communicates itself to him. He is neither attracted nor repelled by the persona, but is at-one with the Soul, thus right relationship on the plane of the personality is the natural manifestation, and the disciple finds that he is free to work in harmony with any and everyone.

During the coming week, please utilize the following seed-thought in your daily meditation exercise:

"I stand receptive to that Love which is my Soul, and Truth is made known to me."

The Nature of The Soul

LESSON 7

Second Ray as It Impacts the Instrument:

Second Ray in the Mental Body as Reason or Compre-
hension and Its Relationship to Intelligence;
The Precipitation of Love via Hierarchy,
the Soul, and Its Instrument;
Love in the Astral Body and the Pairs of Opposites;
The Need to Manifest Love in Physical-Dense

LESSON 7

Divine Love-Wisdom, which is the basic energy and the basic Law of our Solar system, is actually the very essence of consciousness itself, and is usually found predominating somewhere in the disciple's equipment. Even those disciples who work along first or Third Ray lines of force do so in an approach to the final embodiment of Love.

The major concept in regard to the Second Ray, and one which is very little understood until after a certain initiation, is its relationship to the reasoning process. The intellect which we attribute as a faculty of a man's intelligent mind, is in actuality a faculty of consciousness itself, which wields the will and the intelligent substance available to it, to produce order out of chaos. According to the degree of developed awareness (consciousness of Love) will be determined the ability of a man to think. This developed awareness of Love is actually a presence which underlies and moves within the mind.

The individual mind itself, or a man's mental body, is created out of Will and intelligent substance, by a focal point of self-identification within the consciousness of the Planetary Logos. The focal point of individuality grows in its awareness of self as Love, through experience, gradually building a mental body capable of comprehending that Greater Life of which it is only a part.

Love, then, produces comprehension. It is the energy which relates many experiences in such a way as to produce a pattern, an evolution, and, finally, intelligent, productive thought.

The Nature of The Soul

After a man consciously enters the path of initiation, he becomes more apparently intelligent, because he is becoming more aware of Love. That so-called intelligence grows until it becomes Wisdom and hence we define Love-Wisdom in its highest aspect as Pure Reason. Such reason is all comprehensive, or all knowing, because it is instantaneous. It supersedes the reasoning process of the average man, which sees and can only relate, then, to the form aspect, because it goes beyond the form, to the triadal reality or cause of form to relate all factors into one harmonious whole. Nothing is left out, but everything is included through the Power of Love to perceive and to relate. Thus, we say Perfect Love produces perfect understanding.

If the probationer would learn more, if he would perceive the Plan, and relate himself to it, let him so fix his attention on Love, not as an emotion, but as reason and as consciousness, so as to literally invoke it into his own mind. In this way, he will attract all of the various parts of the Plan into his mind where they can be perceived, and related into that assemblance of thought which produces the "vision," speaking in occult terms.

Love finds its source, insofar as humanity is concerned, in the Planetary Heart Center, known as the Spiritual Hierarchy.

It seeks its point of entry into the individual man via his Soul, to pass unnoticed, and unappropriated (in most cases), through the mind into the feeling nature (the astral-emotional body), where it is reflected into the brain consciousness as emotion.

The alignment, then, with Love, or the Heart of God, for most men is as follows:

Lesson 7

1. The Spiritual Hierarchy

2. The individual Soul

3. The mental body

4. The astral-emotional body (feeling aspect of consciousness)

5. The brain consciousness

Seldom is this energy utilized by the man in the region of pure (higher) mind, where thought is created, but it passes unimpeded through this area to impact upon the feeling aspect of consciousness, where it is interpreted as an emotion. It is then reflected into the lower mind, in which the brain consciousness functions, to be evaluated as a series of thoughts, which are in reality little more than emotions given form in mental substance. Thus, an average man interprets experience according to its impact upon the Love energy within his own emotional nature.

Little wonder, then, that humanity's reactions to its own livingness are oft-times so irrational, so unreasonable. Little wonder that its affairs do not reflect Light. The Light of Reason has been shadowed by the clouds of Spiritual ignorance, which dwell in that area between higher Mind where pure thought is possible, and the brain, the area where a man's emotions veil Truth.

Do not forget that the brain is not the creator of thought, but rather the instrument, and in many cases, the victim of thought. If such thought-forms as impact upon a man's brain are largely emotional in content or so-called reason, then so will his reactions to life be emotional. If he lives in his solar plexus center, his outer life will portray the fogs which are characteristic of this place where (in occult terms) water is transmuted into steam. The man who lives here cannot see clearly, for his vision is distorted by fog.

There is much for the aspirant to understand in the above. If it seems difficult, that is because the information is intended to arouse the Spiritual intuition. Dwell upon it, then, and come to know why the emotions are likened unto fog.

The serious student who studies and meditates upon this lesson will see the obvious path which lies before him.

First he must lift himself up into his head where he will take up residence and live consciously. Just how conscious is the average individual? Just how often do you know why you do what you do? Is not the so-called normal human being largely caught up in a maze of activity seldom produced or even aided by his own conscious thought? Do you know what a thought is, free of emotion? The feeling aspect of consciousness is capable of functioning in the mind too, as abstract intuition, rather than emotion. This is a concept well worth thinking on.

Poised in the head, and endeavoring to live in the mind, the probationer will then realize his alignment with the Heart of God.

The alignment is a vertical one. He will think upward, be receptive to Love as it reaches him from the Hierarchy via his Soul and mind. Then as it passes into the mind (as the energy of Soul consciousness), he will appropriate it for the Purpose of knowing Truth. If he is confused as to what Truth, he will seek out the truth of any situation with which he is concerned, but from a focus in his head via the energy of Love.

Endeavor to think in terms of Love in the mind many

times a day. Consciously and deliberately avail yourselves of it on mental levels by reasoning with it. Let all approaches to understanding, all thinking processes, be with Love.

The next step is to manifest a positive expression of it in the emotional nature. Sweep this aspect of yourself with Love many, many times a day.

In the student's approach to an understanding of this particular energy, he examines it from the perspective which sees the pairs of opposites as they are made manifest by the Second Ray. Thus, he comes to understand in illumining flashes of perception his own inner psyche, and this, of course, renders loving understanding of another's problems possible.

Grasp this concept clearly, that regardless of the individual's own ray make-up, his particular life problem will somehow be involved with the energy of Love. No matter whether recondite or apparent, clear reevaluation of the psyche will reveal this to be so.

Consider the polar opposite of Love, as it is manifested within the human nature. What is that polar opposite? It often comes as a shock to the Second Ray probationer to realize that the opposite of Love is hate. Negative Second Ray manifests as hate in its various tones and colors. The normal Love aspect of the individual is either turned inward toward himself, which automatically excludes others from its expression, or in extreme cases, it is choked off completely and the individual hates even himself.

Since Love is the energy which perceives and relates, we find that its negative manifestations negate and distort the reasoning faculty of the consciousness so that right use of even the lower mind is impossible. Such a one experiences extreme difficulty in learning. He is not lacking in basic intelligence, but his consciousness is unable to properly relate data in mental substance in such a way as to produce knowledge. He is without the necessary quality of Love to use his mind properly.

When a child is unloved, when his natural expression of Love is negated by the environment, his normal reasoning faculty is hampered, and for him the educational process becomes a serious problem. If the adults who are primarily concerned with the growth and development of such a child could but realize this lack, either within himself or his environment, a solution of his problems could be readily found.

The practical application of technique, whether in the case of the child, an adult brother, or the probationer himself, is simple. Since Love is the energy of consciousness itself, every person is endowed with it, either as a potential or as an actual expression. That which we interpret as good is basically an expression or an effect of Love. Hence, there is good within all men, and there is the ability to learn Truth regardless of outer appearances.

That good, or Love, is attracted outward into expression from within every person the disciple contacts. This is one of his major service activities and it qualifies all of his relationships.

Recognition of the basic good, call it the Inner Christ, or what you will, of every man, woman, and child the individual contacts, and a conscious effort to draw that good forth into manifestation, is the duty of one who claims or aspires to discipleship.

This can only be accomplished through a positive recognition, and a silent proclamation of that good or Love. No amount of criticism, of interference into another's life and affairs will evoke Love from him. Love evokes Love.

Lesson 7

Thus, the way of the disciple is clearly enunciated.

During the coming week continue to use the same seed-thought in your daily meditation. As an assignment, please bring a written explanation of the effects your meditations on Love are producing within your consciousness and its life and affairs.

The Nature of The Soul

LESSON 8

Third Ray as It Impacts the Instrument:

Intelligent Activity and the Nature of Substance
(Inertia, Activity, Creativity);
The Impacts of Third Ray on the Instrument as
Mental Polarization and Conscious Form Building;
The Role of Transmutation

LESSON 8

The third Divine characteristic of the soul-infused persona is defined as Intelligent Activity. It is an energy expression inherited from the mother aspect, and has to do with the very nature of substance.

Substance is not only intelligent, but in its essence it is intelligence itself. It has two characteristics which are of major importance to the student during this phase of his development. Since it is the negative pole of all manifestation, in its free or first state it is completely negative, quiescent, impressionable. It is then inert. The moment it is impressed with a Divine Intent (the Will aspect), it becomes active. These two characteristics, that of inertia and of activity, make possible its form building nature.

Thus, we see intelligence, substance, or the mother aspect, as it is in itself. When it is acted upon by the Will, as in the first Trinity or Cause, its basic inertia controls its excitation to create only the forms carried in the Divine Intent of the Will, and thus an ordered Cosmos comes into Being.

The Son aspect of the first Trinity inherits not only the Will and Intelligence of His parents, but the characteristics of both. The abilities to direct the Will, and to act intelligently are His, and thus out of Himself, He, in turn, creates.

Man, a descendant of God in the long line of descendants, inherits in lesser degree these same characteristics which have to be developed and perfected in the course of his evolution.

The Nature of The Soul

He is constituted of (1) a Positive Pole, which is the Spirit, the Motivating Will aspect, (2) a Negative Pole which is Matter, the Intelligence aspect, and (3) a consciousness. Since his Spirit is derived from the Father, and his Substance from the Mother, they are not essentially his, though he partakes of them. He is essentially the consciousness or magnetic field which resides within the frequency ranges between the two poles. As such, he inherits within himself the characteristics of the Father: Purpose, Power and Will, and the characteristics of the Mother: Inertia, Activity, and Creativity. As a consciousness, he evolves to manipulate both Spirit and Matter, or Will and Intelligence. Thus, finally he can state, in full awareness: "I and the Father are One."

Intelligent Activity, then, from the perspective of the Spiritual Soul, is the ability of the consciousness to control the motion of substance, to fix and maintain it in a desired orbit. This leads to initiation and adeptship.

The training process which leads to such attainment is entered into consciously, when the ordinary forces of evolution have brought a man to that place where he sees intelligent activity as the working out of God's Plan on earth, and seeks to take a part in it. Then, the evolutionary process is speeded up, and he lives with greater rapidity, due to an ever–expanding consciousness, through each phase of the eternal moment. What would have taken many incarnations to achieve in consciousness, only takes one; hence, his so-called sudden transformation. Intelligent activity then speeds up the entire process of growth and development, so a man may sense a goal or ideal, expand his consciousness to embody that ideal, and realize its manifestation within his life and affairs in one, short lifetime.

Here is that Divine Activity of the Plan which, once realized and accepted, becomes analogous to the Law of

Lesson 8

Grace taught to the mass by Christianity.

The impact of Divine Intelligence upon a probationer disciple results in three major effects within his consciousness and instrument.

1. The first manifestation is that of apparent chaos. This is the result of an activation of old forms, plus a mental awakening. The individual has been undergoing a series of experiences which, in one sense, are not seen. They are felt in pleasure and pain, happiness and sorrow, loss and gain. Very often these experiences appear to be unrelated, and without meaning. Then one day the individual awakens to the facts of life. He realizes that everything he has undergone has been for a definite purpose. He sees a pattern and realizes the Soul as its motivating cause.

He begins to take a mental (note the difference between mental and emotional) interest in what is going on within and without himself, as well as others.

At the same time, he is recipient of a flow of Divine Energies pouring down from the Soul through the various aspects of the persona. As we have already discovered, this energy activates the desirable as well as the undesirable, causing a growth of all that lies within the total state of consciousness.

As it passes through the mental aspect, thoughts of self, as well as thoughts of service, expand and grow out into manifestation. The mental body is activated and the individual becomes aware of his own thought-life.

As the energies pass through the emotional nature, all desire remaining is fanned into a flame to rise in conflict with the newly awakened aspiration. Very often the student is amazed to discover within himself emotions he had not known he was capable of entertaining. He becomes aware of his own subconscious wish life.

As the energies pass through the physical instrument and out into the environment, the effects are many and varied, for here in concrete form the subjective thought-life and astral-emotional life are precipitated. There may be an appearance of many small illnesses, or even a serious illness, while on the other hand, there may appear healings which are miraculous to the onlooker.

In the beginning, the manifestations, whatever they are, seem to be in a state of upheaval, as one opposes the other. Hence, the first manifestation of intelligent activity in the life of an aspirant or probationer disciple is chaos. It does not make sense to the ordinary human mind.

This is the first danger upon the path for the beginner, the trial accompanying initiation. The young disciple must look past the appearance to the inner reality, realizing that via this outer chaos, Divine Order shall be reestablished in his life and affairs.

2. The second manifestation of Intelligent Activity which must take place within the life of the disciple now is that of mental polarization. He has to shift his focal point of attention from the astral-emotional nature into his mental body and this is no easy task.

An individual who is focused in the astral body is controlled by his emotions and influenced by the emotions of others. He is pulled this way and that by the forces of this aspect of his instrument, and of the emotional world in which he lives. Astral forces are the power factor of manifestation. He, then, is controlled by power on the rampage, so to speak, and cannot see with a clear inner vision because he is blinded by his own desires and feelings. He is lost in the midst of illusion, actually a part of that illusion since he is, after all, only an actor in a great drama, unaware of himself as an actor. He is suffering the triumphs and the tragedies of the role he plays, unaware of his true identity.

Let the student realize that if an emotion, any emotion, be it that of yourself or another, can deflect your action or your thought from any Truth which you have at some time grasped, there, in that area of the astral body, a part of your consciousness is polarized.

The whole effort during this stage of growth is to lift the consciousness bit by bit, out of the area where the emotion is in control, into that area of mind where Truth formulated into thought is the controlling factor in the life and affairs.

This is intelligent activity, and when the consciousness in the brain will cooperate with the Soul, the shift can be made with amazing rapidity and the least discomfort.

It would be of very great advantage to every student who is attracted to these lessons to realize that herein lies the cause of his difficulty on the path.

Why do so many men and women today seek out the psychiatrist, the analyst, and even the hypnotist, in a frantic effort to both understand himself, and to attain some little measure of control over his environment? Because the mass of humanity is undergoing that chaos which precedes mental polarization.

The most perfect therapy one can undergo during this difficult period is the spiritual therapy exercised by the Soul as It focuses the Light of Intelligence into Its instrument, and the consciousness imprisoned therein. That Light reveals, cleanses and purifies.

The Nature of The Soul

The aspirant and probationer disciple establishes a triangle between his Soul, his subconscious, and himself as the observer. He takes his place in the center between the brows, and allows the Soul to throw Its Light into the subconscious. Then he observes, without taking part in, the content revealed. Via such observations and perfect alignment, the Soul is permitted, then, to clarify the self to the self.

The emotions are permitted to reveal themselves to the observer, but he does not take part in them. He is not swayed or controlled by them. He realizes the Truth and transmutes emotion into its polar opposite.

Example

The disciple has established the triangular alignment between himself focused in the center between the brows, his Soul via his aspiration to it, and his subconscious via his recognition of its existence.

He then becomes the observer, permitting (not demanding, but permitting) the Soul to reveal what it will of the content within the subconscious.

He then becomes aware of an emotion. Let us say it is an intense resentment of some person known during childhood. The original resentment manifests now in his adult life toward anyone who is in a position of authority. This is revealed with sudden clarity.

He then transmutes the negative force by realizing and projecting love to:

    a. himself as a child
    b. the person originally involved
    c. the original situation
    d. and all persons who are in positions of authority anywhere in the world.

Lesson 8

Via this technique of Soul therapy, the consciousness makes its shift from the astral-emotional body into the mental body.

3. The third manifestation which the energy of intelligent activity takes in the life and affairs of the probationer disciple is that of conscious form building.

We shall go into this in more detail in the next lesson.

In the meantime, utilize the following seed-thought in your daily meditation.

"I stand receptive to that Divine Intelligence which produces the activity of the Plan. Right Action is revealed to me and I am made whole."

The Nature of The Soul

TRANSMUTATION TECHNIQUE

This technique can be utilized each evening before retiring, or as it is needed.

1. Make the usual three-fold lower alignment and focus the consciousness in the ajna center.

2. Integrate the consciousness in aspiration to the Soul.

3. Visualize a triangle of light between the:

   Soul

   yourself as the observer in the ajna

   subconscious

4. Repeat slowly and carefully:

   "The Light of the Soul is thrown downward into the instrument to reveal, cleanse, and purify that which is karmically ready to be brought to Light in Divine Law and Order. I stand clear, observing only."

5. Transmute whatever negativity is revealed into its polar opposite via the application of Love.

6. Meditate for three minutes on the concept: *"THE TRUTH SHALL MAKE ME FREE."*

Spend a few moments radiating the Light of Truth through the instrument and into the environment.

LESSON 9

Prerequisites to Conscious Form Building:

Love as Prime Energy
and Force in Building Forms;
Perfection of One's Own Instrument
as First Intelligent Activity;
Need for Mental Polarization,
Love in the Mind, the Energy
of a Subservient Will, and
Aspiration to Serve
when Undertaking White Magic;
Conscious Adaptation and
Control of the Instrument

LESSON 9

As the Soul infuses the persona with the energy of Love, which is, remember, the energy of consciousness itself, that Divine characteristic defined as Intelligent Activity begins to make its appearance. Not until the Love aspect is sufficiently developed, can the energy of Divine Intelligence be molded into those forms which are the expression of Intelligent Activity, from the perspective of the Spiritual Soul.

You will remember that we defined the Third Planetary ray as "The intelligent application of mind in Love." This means, literally, that the heart must be wedded to the head, that a man's mind must be so infused with Love that his activity is an intelligent application of it in all times and places. It is the consciousness of Love which wields Spirit and Matter (Will and Intelligence) in that exact equation which results in the perfected form.

Thus, we come to the art and science of form building, which is the *modus operandi* of the White Magician who works with increasing devotion to manifest the Divine Plan within the body of humanity. This one molds substance into those forms which will carry the consciousness of the Divine Plan out into appearance in the Light of Day.

The probationer disciple utilizes the form building technique to perfect his own instrument, and in so doing trains himself to enter into the field of White Magic as a disciple of The Christ. When his three-fold instrument, his environment, and every aspect of his life and affairs conforms to the subjective Truth he has grasped, then he can be trusted to work with those techniques which will serve the betterment of a needy humanity.

This is the great stumbling block for so many would-be disciples who cry out desperately for techniques with which to serve. They forget that their service must be rendered through their own instruments, and that while humanity is served through imperfect vehicles, nonetheless a certain degree of conformity must be attained before a disciple can be trusted with the secrets of White Magic.

What is meant by the term "perfected instrument"? Certainly the reference is to the good, the true, and the beautiful, but as it is conducted from within to without. The meaning does not refer to a superficial covering of good health, nice appearance, abundant supply, or anything of the kind. A man may be bedridden and still render a specific and valuable service in the world sense.

It is the consciousness aspect that determines the condition of the instrument. What is the subjective influence being radiated by the man in the brain through his vehicles? This is the question of major importance, not, what is the condition of his physical health? Or, what is his financial status?

There are certain prerequisites to learning the art and science of form building which I shall list here.

1. A certain degree of mental polarization. The man must be capable of establishing and maintaining for at least three minutes a concentrated mental focus which cannot be disturbed by emotional impact.

    Most students have acquired this ability via the common need to earn a living, others through meditation practice, and still others through educational effort.

2. The ability to wield Love from a mental level and so control the astral body. This is not so common and most students have yet to acquire it. The transmutation technique given in the previous lesson will aid the earnest student in his effort to build in this prerequisite.

3. A developed Will which is subservient to the Divine Will of the Plan itself. In other words, the developed personal will is willing to accept the Divine Plan in all instances.

4. An intense aspiration to use the mind for the betterment of humanity. The student seeks knowledge, but not for the sake of knowledge alone. He must be motivated from an inner need to make his contribution to a better world for the race of men.

The first concept the student disciple will learn as he approaches this science, is that the forms with which he is primarily concerned are the forms within his consciousness. What does he think in relation to all things, both individually and collectively? What does he feel? What inner patterns mold and hold his consciousness, and so condition his outer life and affairs?

He then compares that which is in manifestation with the ideal mold. To what patterns would he fit his consciousness if he were free to do so? What would he have himself think and feel? And, finally, what would he have himself do?

After such inner search, and comparisons, he then becomes receptive to the Plan his Soul would set in operation. What qualities, what characteristics, what forms would his Soul place within the consciousness? What lessons has the Soul been attempting to teach these many years?

After receiving the clear impression or vision of the ideal from his Soul, he accepts it and then sets out to build it in the eye of his mind. Carefully and with utmost conformity to the transmitted ideal, he builds the forms of thought he would have his mind take, the forms of feeling he would have his emotions follow, and the outer activity that would most perfectly conduct the new state of consciousness into appearance.

For the probationer, the outer act will always relate to the harmonizing, the balancing, and to the Divine Order of his present environment. He will meet those responsibilities in the physical world which are his dharma or duty, with the spiritual fulfillment which they demand.

This is conscious adaptation, and it is one of the manifestations of Intelligent Activity. The probationer learns to adapt himself to his environment, and finally to adapt his environment to the best that is within him. He and his outer life slowly adjust to the Soul, and so Divine Law and Order reasserts itself, first in his consciousness, and finally in the outer form. Right relationship is the result. A clue can be given the earnest student in the following words:

> "Alone I stand upon the scales, and reaching out I bring into all relationships that peculiar motion which results in balance."

At this point, it is wise to consider the world in which we live. It is in a constant state of flux. That which today appears constant and unchanging, is, tomorrow, a thing of the past. All form is temporary, ever passing, ever assuming new patterns and pictures, and these changing even in the act of forming.

Lesson 9

Consciousness grows through its ability to adapt to the changing conditions about it. Contrary to average thought, it is not resistance which produces growth, but rather adaptation, that capacity which allows consciousness to lend itself to a manifesting condition, and to come through whole and unharmed. This can be seen in war, in the case of bodily harm, such as the removal of a limb, and even in cases of insanity. The consciousness grows <u>because</u> of the experience, not in spite of it. Even though a man be unconscious of this innate ability to adapt, he constantly does so, and when the adaptation can be conscious, we see rapid growth.

The aspirant and probationer, once he begins to grasp this fact, realizes that while he as a personality may have been resisting conditions within his environment, his consciousness has been lending itself to them. Following this example, the man then stops fighting and begins to cooperate with his Soul. He enters into the condition, but he does so in a detached impersonal manner, first as the observer, and, later, as the actor. He enters as the actor only after becoming aware of Soul Purpose.

In other words, if his condition is one of ill health, of poverty, etc., he stops resisting and consciously adapts, asking what is the lesson to be learned here? Why has my Soul projected me into this situation? He withdraws the persona from the field of action for a time and re-enters it as the observer. He quietly enters into his environment, seeing in it only the good, the true, and the beautiful, seeking out the growth provided by the condition, and slowly but surely the environment responds to the flood of positive energy exerted upon it. With the new change, the consciousness again adapts.

As the student studies the art of form building, he learns to see all form as substantial intelligence in controlled motion, created to convey a purpose, and to result in a desired goal. The individual's own form is regarded as an instrument. Its purpose is eventually revealed and its goal is seen. The qualities which that form has been specially constructed to portray are realized, and the man sets out to embody them. He builds the forms (inner first) which will further the expression of the Soul.

Several points should here be remembered:

1. The form is Intelligent Activity made manifest.

2. All activity in manifestation must take form in one or more frequency ranges.

For example, speech is one form the activity of thought takes as thought is made manifest on the physical plane. Its purpose is communication or relationship. Its goal is unity or at-one-ment.

The probationer disciple observes all of his activities, noting the particular form each one tends to take, recognizing, for example, the form his thought takes in speech, in feeling, and in deed. He sees his own thought portrayed in form, notes the quality of the thought via the clarity and the desirability of the forms used to portray it.

This often brings him to the sudden realization that his intelligent activity has been carried out in a rather hit-or-miss sort of way. He then sets out to put a semblance of order into it.

1. He observes and guards his speech, and in so doing becomes more cognizant of his thought life, the unconscious as well as the conscious. He becomes aware of the type, strength, and quality of mental energy with which he is constantly working, as well as his right, or wrong, use of it. He

learns the Purpose of his mental body, recognizing it as an instrument of the Soul, and at the same time as a body of cause for lower manifestation. He sees it as an instrument and an intermediary between a higher state of consciousness and a lower one, and not as consciousness itself.

2. He observes and transmutes his emotions, and so becomes aware of his astral body, the power factor of manifestation. He watches how it would distort his thought, when its Purpose is to perfectly reflect and give body to the Divine Plan as formulated by his mind.

3. He disciplines his physical activity to conform to his mental picture of the Soul. He recognizes that activity which is a response to the form side of life, and that which is a response to the Soul. He sees his activities as being either vehicles for an expression of the higher or the lower consciousness, and he learns to initiate that activity which blends or merges the two states of consciousness into one. Thus, man becomes in awareness a living Soul.

Continue to use the same seed-thought in your daily meditation.

The Nature of The Soul

LESSON 10

The Soul as It Relates to the Holy Trinity:

Relationship to God the Father;
Relationship to the Hierarchy and Christ
(Clarification of Contact with a "Master");
Relationship to the Mother
or Holy Ghost Aspect

LESSON 10

As we view the ideal of the Soul which the student at this point is attempting to embody, we find that it is based upon the three major expressions of Divinity.

1. <u>It is endowed with, and motivated by, the Divine Will of Logoic Purpose</u>. This links humanity, both individually and collectively to the Planetary Logos, the Father of our Christian Bible. This means that a man's will is an extension of God's Will, that his purpose is contained within the larger Purpose, and that his power is the Power of Logoic Intent.

Once this is completely accepted and understood, the Father is known. That Divine Being, Who with His Will released the Divine Spark which became our individual identity or Soul, is recognized.

Thus are we enabled to consciously relate to The Father, to direct our aspiration to a knowable Source, rather than to a vague and indefinable God.

This concept may be somewhat difficult for the beginner of occult study to accept, for it cuts into and destroys the crystallization of thought and superstition which has evolved in most minds anent The Father. He is shrouded in a veil of mystery and confusion, hidden from human perception via superstition and misinterpretation, yet the mass is told to direct their aspiration, hopes and prayers to Him. This has resulted in an inability of the human mind to relate to his Divine Source, the Father of his being, hence the maladjustment of a humanity who cannot relate to its Parent.

The Nature of The Soul

In considering this concept, we first realize that our immediate Creator is much closer to us than we had heretofore considered. The Father of each Soul within this humanity is The Logos — the Central, directing, Life who ensouls, and indwells, the planet earth, and all life therein.

This concept may give rise to conflict regarding the One God—"That Cosmic Creative Center About Whom Naught May Be Said"—therefore, one must consider very carefully the whole question. Who and What is God?

We know that there is One Center, One Life, out of which all lesser lives stream forth. From this Center issued the Cosmos, the Heavenly Man, and the Great Avatars. Yet, about Him naught may be said by the human mind, other than that He is the Ultimate Source which shall receive us when we have evolved, or have been lifted up into a much higher state than that of our Logos.

Contained within this One Life are many Logoi, Cosmic, Solar, and Planetary, Who, being created in the Image and Likeness of their Father, in turn create of Themselves. We the human children are the Sons of God, but our Sonship is in our own Planetary Logos. We are in Him, He in us, and so it is.

If the student can accept this concept now, and grasp its essential meaning, a Divine adjustment can take place within his psyche which will have deep psychological effects within his personality. This is perhaps one of the most important Truths with which you will ever be impressed, therefore; think deeply upon it.

Your alignment with God is direct and real, for it is via your will straight through to the Will of the Logos Who created your Soul. Think upon this, my brother, and then go back to the prayer of the Master Jesus. When you silently say, "Our Father," do so with conscious knowledge of Who He is, relating to Him as His Divine Child. Do not be afraid to thus identify, and to pour forth your Love and Thanksgiving to Him.

Thus does your Will relate you to the Father. Thus do you take one of the first steps upon the path of initiation which leads to a complete realization of your Spiritual identity; and thus do you truly begin to embody the ideal of the Soul.

2. The ideal of the Soul is qualified by Divine Love-Wisdom. It is the consciousness of Divine Love in which Wisdom is inherent. Thus is Its quality derived from the heart (consciousness or Soul aspect) of our Planetary Logos. This links humanity both individually and collectively to The Christ and His Spiritual Hierarchy, Who Embody the Heart of our God. Man is related to the Masters of the Wisdom, those Divine Beings Who have fully realized and grown into Their Sonship via this Identity in Christ. These are the Elder Brothers of the human race, the guides and watchers of our civilization, the Teachers and Saviors of our Souls.

While we may not normally meet with These, for They live in a frequency range which is beyond our perception, we may relate to Them as younger brothers, fashioning our lives after the Truths which They have embodied. Those Truths are contained within the Teachings of such appearances as The Buddha and Jesus of Nazareth.

Let it be known that the Soul is in contact with the Hierarchy, for each Soul has been given into the keeping of one or another of the Masters until such time as he has attained to his own adulthood.

This, too, is an important concept to grasp and understand, yet there is danger here. At this point, the student must be extremely careful not to lose the truth of the concept by clouding it round with glamour.

First, he realizes that each Soul has its particular and specific relationship with one of the Elder Brothers— that each Soul is watched and guided on Soul levels through the various stages of its evolutionary development, and that the Elder Brother can aid only within certain limitations which are defined as follows:

A. His contact is with the Soul only, never the persona.

B. That contact is via abstract concepts and energy, never via thoughts or words, except in the case of a Divine Incarnation, such as the Master Jesus.

   In other words, a Master of the Wisdom may impart certain Truths to the Spiritual Soul, via the transference of concepts on higher mental levels. The man in the brain must merge his consciousness with that of the Soul to realize such communion, or receive an imparted Truth into his awareness via a contact with his Soul. The words or pictures used to translate the Truth will be his own, formulated within his own brain as it translates the inflowing abstraction into concrete form.

C. An imparted Truth must always take the form of an abstraction, be universal in its application, and relate only to teaching. In other words, a Master is not permitted to advise as regards a personality problem, or to direct a persona along any course of action. The individual's own will is left free in every instance.

D. The Master releases His Divine Energy, Truths, and Protection to the disciple according to the disciple's effort to serve the Plan. In other words, He responds to the disciple's invocative strength.

Each one of you may then realize that you have a specific relationship to the Hierarchy, that the Wisdom of your Soul is expanded by a Master, and hence your growth is aided by the loving guidance of an Elder Brother. Relate to Him, then, via your love and appreciation, your receptivity to Truth, and your application of Truth in service. When you have done, and are doing these three, then you may consciously invoke both the Wisdom and the energy of your Master into your planned service activity.

3. The ideal of the Soul is seen as being endowed with the ability to create, to control the motion of substance. This links him finally with the Mother Aspect, the Holy Ghost, or Divine Mind. As He makes a specific contact with this aspect, it will be through the Angel of the Presence, that energy body of Light which houses His overshadowing Christ self.

Here indeed is a concept which contains a great mystery. The Soul is in contact with the substance out of which all forms are made via his own Angel of the Presence, and is therefore enabled to control the motion of substance and so create the forms his service shall take.

The medium of the form building process, which is the Mother aspect insofar as this planet is concerned, is the Divine Mind. Here the Logoic Will first impresses substance, or intelligence, with His Purpose, and the archetypal forms appear. These archetypal forms are given further substantial body in the world mind (part of the Divine Mind) by those Souls who consciously serve the Plan.

The Nature of The Soul

The student at this point makes his contact with that energy which is substance via his receptivity to the Light of his own Angel of the Presence. He aspires to work with that Light, to build forms out of it for the betterment of mankind.

He becomes receptive to *"that Mind which was in Christ,"* endeavoring always to make right use of mental substance. This "Mind which was in Christ" he visualizes as the blue-white Light of Christ which permeates his mental body from above. As he is recipient of it, he reciprocates by directing his will to good, and his will to love to the Holy Ghost aspect, on Monadic levels via the Angel of the Presence.

The result is an increasing knowledge of the archetypal forms, and hence knowledge of the Divine Plan, plus an ever-increasing ability to mold intelligence into those forms which carry the Divine Plan into outer manifestation.

Via the three-fold realization carried in the above, the ideal is found to include a conscious relationship with:

The Planetary Father

The Planetary Christ or Elder Brother

The Planetary Mother

These are related to and are the Source of his Spirit or Will, his Soul or Consciousness, and his Intelligence.

One other point here in regard to the Intelligence aspect. It was out of the negative intelligence that the Soul created Its own vehicle of incarnation. That vehicle, the body, emotions, and mind, is a crystallization of the Mother aspect. Its substance was impulsed into activity by the Divine Will of the Soul, qualified by the

Lesson 10

Divine Love of the Soul, and molded into a form by the Intelligent Activity of the Soul.

It is constantly revitalized and re-energized by those vital energies which are carried by the Mother aspect.

The vehicle is fluidic, and subject always to the Divine Will.

The ideal of the Soul includes, then, complete control of the form nature.

Please utilize the following seed-thought in your daily meditation exercise.

> *"I am the Soul. I blend and merge the three Lights to become the Light Divine. I am that Light."*

As an assignment, please explain in your own words your vision (understanding) of the Ideal.

The Nature of The Soul

LESSON 11

The Trinity as It Relates to the Persona:

First Ray and Aspiration
(In Emotions as Desire, In Mind as Ambition);
Reorientation of Selfish and Separative Will
into State of Cooperation and Inclusiveness;
Second Ray and Meditation
(As Tool for Illumination and Service);
Third Ray and Application

LESSON 11

The three major planetary rays, which the probationer disciple is attempting to perfect within himself in the character building process, are three types of energy which reach and influence him according to his aspiration, meditation, and application. We shall now consider at some length this three-fold method of contacting, accepting, and embodying the divine energies of the Soul. This will give the student a further understanding of the law, and clear the way for an eventual contact in awareness with the Soul.

A. ASPIRATION

In order to more clearly understand this activity, it is wise to consider first its correspondence on a lower level, namely—desire.

Desire, which is a phenomenon of the emotional nature of a personality, is based upon the selfish will of the man in the brain. The term self-ish, as used in these lessons, has to do with anything which concerns the separated self. It is the attitude of exclusion which can at times be very subtle and difficult for the individual to see within himself.

The desire for personal attainment, even though such attainment be considered spiritual, is selfish, and characterizes almost all probationers upon the path. It separates the individual in awareness from his brother. His desire has created a barrier of thought and emotion which revolves around him in such a manner as to isolate him in awareness from others. Thus, he is rendered insensitive to anything which does not have a

The Nature of The Soul

direct impact upon him as a separated, all-important personality.

The individual recognizes and eliminates this personality tendency by realizing with both the heart and mind that he is a part of the whole, and that he is dependent upon each part, and the whole. This concept must mean more to him than just a theory which he is able to comprehend with his intellect. It must be known as Truth in the heart as well as the mind so that the student is merging within himself both the heart and the head approach. He then realizes that he is important (and important is an incorrect term) only insofar as his relationship to each part, and the whole, is correctly recognized and balanced.

In our consideration of desire, we learn that the selfish will which centers itself in the little "I", acts upon the emotional nature as a vibratory influence. A bombardment of electrical impulse passes from the little "I" seated in the brain, to the emotional polarization located in the region of the solar plexus, via the nervous system. This calls forth from the emotional nature a vibratory activity commonly called desire.

The emotional body of most persons, as seen by a clairvoyant, is in an almost constant turmoil. There are vortices of energy very similar to whirlpools in a stream or river, into which the energies of the individual are pulled. These vortices represent the many desires which tend to direct the life and affairs of the individual.

They are spasmodically stimulated by the little will impulse, but without a definite rhythm, being, therefore, somewhat unpredictable and erratic. In this case, we see an individual who is completely ruled by his emotions, who is without purpose and who is a so-called victim of circumstance at all times.

116

Lesson 11

There is a difference when desire is coupled with purpose. The individual then tends to become one-pointed, manifesting less turmoil within the astral-emotional body. There will only be one or two large vortices, and a more definite rhythm will have been established. This rhythm attracts and repels, and so we see periods of intense desire, with later gratification through the fulfillment of that desire.

The gratification of desire always leads, sooner or later, to disillusion, and so the individual is still dissatisfied. This naturally leads to a substitution of goal and a new period of intense desire, until the individual awakens to the fact that desire is a betrayer. He then turns from it, and enters into the activity of aspiration.

In summing up desire, it is an activity of the emotional nature impulsed by the selfish will of the persona. It is always separative, being confined to the satisfaction of the individual concerned, and therefore largely responsible for the lack of brotherhood in the world today.

Aspiration is the result of an electrical impulse projected from the Soul (focused in the region of the pineal gland) to the emotional aspect (located in the region of the heart) via the energy underlying all substance. Thus is the vibratory activity of the emotional nature quickened, and this aspect literally lifted up out of the lower levels of the astral sphere where desire characterizes it, to the higher levels of aspiration.

This body of energy, when seen by a clairvoyant, is relatively quiescent. It is likened unto a calm, still pool of clear water, which reflects only the vertical impact of the Divine Plan as formulated by the mind of the disciple.

There is, then, first the impulse from the Soul, which stimulates the aspiration into being. The aspirant begins by a sort of longing, a yearning toward Light.

The Nature of The Soul

Just as a flower reaches toward the light of the sun, so the aspirant reaches toward the light of the Soul. This he does with his whole being.

Just as a flower grows and blooms and radiates beauty, so does the aspirant grow and bloom and radiate divinity. This radiation of the aspirant is characterized by his giving, in the form of activity, of the energy he has received from the Soul. This continual reaching toward the Light, and in turn the giving or sharing of that Light, has been termed aspiration.

This in turn evokes a further response from the Soul and the aspirant is the recipient of greater Light. In this manner, through a cyclic ebb-and-flow of energies, a call from the personality with response from the Soul, we see man bloom as a Soul-infused personality.

The term itself, "aspirant," as applied to an individual, denotes a certain development, and is not carelessly used in connection with all students. The aspirant is one who is engaged in the invocation of the Divine Will Impulse. This is a most important concept and should be contemplated by all sincere students. In this manner, the First Aspect of Divinity is brought into active manifestation within the individual environment. As the aspirant becomes a probationer, and later an accepted disciple, he does not outgrow or leave behind the activity of aspiration. This is something that evolves with him as he treads the path of initiation.

When the aspirant is well into this phase of growth, his mental attitude can best be described by the following words:

"Not my will, O Soul, but Thine."

Deliberately, and often at great seeming cost to the personality, this call is sounded forth. The little will of the personality, which has ruled for a long time, is subordinated to the will of the Soul, and not without battle.

Those forms which are out of harmony with Soul Purpose undergo a disintegrating process. This disintegration includes any discordant form, whether it be a thought-form, an emotional form, physical form, or an activity form. Thus is the attention of the aspirant lifted up and the eye opened.

That aspirant who is also a probationer disciple establishes a constant alignment between his brain and the Divine Will Impulse of the Soul. This he does in the following manner:

1. He recognizes first the fact of the existence of the Soul.

2. He mentally and emotionally accepts the Will of the Soul.

3. He visualizes a line of light reaching out from his brain extending through his mind to his Soul. His aspiration is then directed to the Soul via this line.

4. He maintains the line of contact at all times, subordinating his activities and his personal will to the Divine Will of the Soul.

This alignment is not given for use as a meditation exercise. It is to be used as a mental activity which is simultaneous with the routine of daily living. Let the eyes remain open, the brain subjectively attentive, and the physical instrument outwardly busy as usual. Do not use the alignment given as a meditation form.

In summing up aspiration, we say it is an activity of the

higher emotional nature and the mind, which is impulsed by the Soul. It is always concerned with the Divine Plan, being therefore inclusive, eventually producing within the mind and heart of the aspirant the recognition, acceptance, and practice of brotherhood.

B. MEDITATION

Meditation, when rightly carried out, brings the aspirant into contact with the illumining aspect of the Soul. It makes possible the recognition and the eventual embodiment of the quality of the Soul.

The activity of aspiration puts the student in tune, so to speak, with the Soul, while meditation expands the consciousness of the personality to touch the periphery of, and to finally merge with the consciousness of the Soul.

I should like to take this opportunity to point out to those of you for whom meditation seems dull and unrewarding its importance, not only to your own individual development, but as a service activity as well.

First, as regards your individual development, meditation is the open door into initiation. It is the way into Light which is tread by all disciples of The Christ. It is via this activity that the inner Kingdom of God, the world of meaning, and the "Secret Place of the Most High" is entered and known. Every activity of the accepted disciple has been first contemplated and worked out in cooperation with the Divine Plan via meditation. There comes a time in the life of every individual when further spiritual progress is dependent upon this activity, for it is literally the footpath of the Gods.

Meditation, to be fruitful, must be entered into by the occultist who is also the mystic, for the whole being, the entire focus of consciousness, is centered in the mind in order to focus upon Truth. Do not, then, enter into meditation in a half-hearted attempt to comply with instruction. Let the whole being be flooded with love of the activity in order to accomplish the most by it.

As a service activity, which each one of you can initiate here and now, meditation is one of the most important. Via this activity the disciple is enabled to focus within himself not only the Divine Plan or Hierarchial intent, but the precipitating energy of the Divine Plan as well. He becomes an instrumentality through which the Christ focuses His effort to guide, instruct and uplift the mass consciousness.

Every disciple who offers himself in this way serves a much greater cause than he can possibly realize. For as he experiences the realization of a Truth, the strength of his realization broadcasts that Truth into the mass mind where other members of humanity may pick it up as their own thought. In this way those Divine ideas which spring forth from the Hierarchy to the disciple, from the Spiritual Soul to the man in the brain, are again transmitted into the mental body of humanity as a whole, where many members of humanity can both be influenced by them, and in turn, become an influence in the activity of the Divine Plan. Realize this importance, and consider the service which you render each time you contemplate in meditation a concept of Truth, each time you contact, focus within yourself, and transmit a Divine energy which underlies a concept of Truth.

C. APPLICATION

After careful study of A and B, the student realizes that the Will of the Soul is contacted by his persistent aspiration, and that the Love-Wisdom of the Soul is contacted by his ability to meditate. The Third Aspect, that of Intelligent Activity, is contacted by the applied effort of the student to live Truth. This application which is put forth by the sincere student, not only brings his life and affairs into intelligent activity, but it also makes it possible for him to manifest in activity the other two aspects of the Soul which he has contacted.

In the next lesson, we shall consider application as the disciple's ability to establish and control his vibratory activity. In the meantime, give this lesson careful attention, for it contains much that is of advantage to you. Continue to use the same seed-thought for meditation.

Let there be Light.

LESSON 12

Application and Embodiment of Truth:

Harmlessness;
Purification of Thoughts;
Control of Speech;
Proper Direction of Emotions;
Communicating the Quality
of Our Inner Being
via Physical Actions

LESSON 12

A disciple is defined as one who has entered into awareness of himself as a Soul, and who works in the world as
such.

This "work" of the disciple is actually the establishment of
a certain type and quality of vibratory impact upon his
environment, and his ability to control that impact at all
times. In this way, the disciple creates a particular auric
influence which becomes a part of his service equipment.

The inner subjective man creates his vibratory impact
as he goes about the task of daily living. Every thought,
feeling, word and deed which he sets into motion carries
a specific vibratory frequency. As that frequency impacts upon another individual or group of individuals, it
wields an influence either for so-called good or bad.

The student is taught first of all to aspire toward harm-
less-ness. He learns that only as his vibratory impact is
in harmony with the Divine Plan is he harm-less. He
then sets out to bring his four-fold vibratory activity
under conscious control in accordance with those concepts which he knows as Truth.

In order to arrive at a clear understanding of this phase
of the character building process, we shall study sepa-
rately each aspect of the four-fold vibratory activity of
the student.

A. THOUGHT

We know that all things which can be defined as "something" in the world of form maintain a life of their own,

manifest in time and space according to the law of Cycles, and have a definite effect upon all other lives. This we call the vibratory activity of Life. All things carry a vibratory frequency which determines their cyclic activity in and out of the world of affairs, their manifestations in time and space, and their effect upon all other lives.

This is as true of a thought as it is of a Solar Life. For this reason, we speak of thoughts as thought-forms. They are actually ensouled ideas, given concrete form.

While it is true that the human cannot originate an idea, and only a very few can originate a thought, still he does receive the original idea or thought within his own mind, where he gives it individual tone and color. It has then become his own, carrying the frequency which he imposed upon it as a part of his influence in the world.

The great minds ensoul an idea, give that abstract idea form as thought, and set it forth to accomplish a specific purpose.

The majority of the race have not as yet reached this stage of development. They are controlled almost entirely by the "great minds" as they (the mass) receive, accept, and embody the thoughts created for them by the few. From this embodiment emerges a culture and civilization. The results will be good, and untrammeled by distortion, if the "great minds" are capable of clarity, and if the mass is receptive. Motive plays an important part here. The unscrupulous and the unenlightened enslave the masses. The true world server makes for humanity a better place in which to live and grow. Thus, we see the world of thought as the body of cause for the manifesting conditions and circumstances of the human family.

The student looks at his own thought-life in this light.

He observes the result of his thought upon himself as well as upon others within his sphere of influence. Does the vibratory impact of his thought result in Love, Peace, and Harmony? Is it a vehicle for the manifestation of the Divine Plan? If not, there is much need here for self-imposed disciplinary training. Is he in the process of becoming, via the process of evolution, a liberator or an enslaver of the masses? Herein lies a part of the answer to his degree of harm-less-ness, and the key to the type and quality of mental energy he uses.

B. SPEECH

The words of the student also have a life of their own— are the cause of certain manifestations in time and space—and have an effect upon all other lives.

Sound affects the substance of which all forms are made. It sets into motion, or modifies, the already established motion of substance. The vibratory impact of sound can result in the movement of substance, which is either constructive or destructive.

When sound takes the form of a word, a decree has been made. That word or grouping of words will manifest in time and space. If students could observe the effects produced by the words sounded forth from almost any individual, they would be sorely shocked. The broken bodies, the sick emotions, the chaotic conditions which result from the words spoken by humanity are painful for the true clairvoyant to look upon. A word once spoken, cannot be recalled. A chain of effects has been set into motion and will result in physical–plane manifestation.

When one considers that a word is not only a manifestation of a thought, but that it is also the direction into physical–plane manifestation of a thought, one pauses before he speaks.

There is another point here which is of great importance to the student. Do his words convey his own thought-life, or that of another? Is he directing into manifestation a planned activity which was clearly formulated in his own or a senior's mind, or is he simply the mouth-piece (tool of manifestation) for any thought which impacts upon his mind from whatever source?

The probationer disciple speaks and because he has become recipient of a certain degree of Soul energy, his words manifest with greater strength and speed than do those of many of his brothers. They have a definite influence upon those within his environment. They often form and determine the conditions to manifest within his sphere of influence. Thus do the aspirants and probationers in the world manifest the shorter cyclic conditions in which many of their younger brothers must live. Many of the obstacles of the beginner were laid at his feet by the little-knowing, would-be disciple.

My brothers, guard your speech. Study its effect upon others and learn another lesson in harm-less-ness. You cannot advance upon the path until this lesson is learned.

C. EMOTIONS

This subject has posed a problem during this particular age, for the average teacher of the Wisdom. The beginner and the majority of probationers have little or no understanding of the emotions. Emotion is a name given to his feelings, and what is a feeling? Lack of proper terminology further complicates the task, and hence the lack of clear teaching anent this subject during the past.

Emotion is the effect produced by the impact of astral force upon the sensory system of the physical body.

The astral plane is that area between the mental and

128

Lesson 12

the physical planes, where the energy of mind and the energy of substance are brought together, thereby producing substantial form. Astral energy is set into motion by thought, word or deed, at which time it becomes a powerful force. The vibratory impact of that force upon the sensory system produces what we call an emotion, according to its type, strength, and quality.

Herein lies a key. The registration of an emotion is an indication of a thought which has taken form within the astral body. It orbits around the individual, in the astral aura, feeding upon his own life energy, coloring his personality experiences, and often controlling his consciousness to the degree of dictating his every act.

For average humanity, the astral-emotional energy body is composed of many such forms which completely blind the mass to reality. Any vibratory impact upon the average man's sensory apparatus (of which the brain is a part) is colored by these forms so that its true meaning is distorted or disturbed by the astral content through which it must pass.

The astral plane contains the aggregate of forms created by humanity, plus the forces generated by such forms. Here are man's thoughts, his dreams, his wishlife, concretized and made manifest. Little wonder that this sphere of existence has been likened unto a miasma where the steaming fogs and vapors of man's making veil reality from our sensitivities.

An astral form will manifest in time and space in a cyclic pattern, according to the revitalization it receives from one or more members of humanity. Herein lies a key to one of the world's problems. As an individual accepts and entertains a form originated within the astral consciousness of the race, he gives it the power of his own astral force, and so strengthens its attraction to the physical plane.

The Nature of The Soul

Astral forms, or emotions, for the beginner, have a life of their own, manifest cyclically in time and space, and have an effect upon all other lives.

The student at this point realizes the need to clean up his emotional nature. He learns by observation and reason which of his emotions produce harmful effects upon others, and these he eliminates from his vibratory activity.

By taking a positive disciplinary action via the application of kindliness, friendliness, and the Law of Love in every instance, his astral vehicle becomes a tower of strength, healing, and finally an agent of transmutation for others.

"See to this part of yourself, O disciple, for it must become harmless as the dove before the door is opened."

D. PHYSICAL ACTS

Each act performed by the physical instrument carries a vibratory frequency, the impact of which exerts an influence upon the environment. Physical activity is the result of an expenditure of energy, and that energy once set into motion becomes the source of a series of effects, called reaction.

When the student ceases the outer activity for a sufficient length of time to contemplate the inner meaning of his instrument and its various parts, much revelation comes to him.

The first and most obvious fact is that his physical body not only houses him, but that it is his instrument of contact with the world in which he lives. Its constitution includes a sensory apparatus (cerebro-nervous system) for the registration of incoming vibration, as well as outlets for the release of outgoing vibration. It is a

130

receiving and sending instrument composed of those centers which are tuned to receive and send vibrations which fall within a certain frequency range. Thus he perceives via the five senses and is in turn perceived by others in the same way.

It is interesting to note here that as the vibratory frequency of the instrument is lifted or quickened, other senses are experienced, such as telepathy and various so-called "extra sensory" perceptions.

The next obvious fact is that he, as a state of consciousness functioning through a physical instrument, is intimately related to others. This relationship is most easily demonstrated in both his ability and his need to communicate. That he has something to communicate to others, and that he can be understood by them, is his first realization of relationship.

The average man's lack of belief, or faith in a life after death, or in the existence of a Soul, is based upon his inability to communicate with those who have passed over, or with the Soul. As soon as a way is found to perceive and communicate with these and other states of Being, the human entity will not only believe, he will know. An event approaches which will establish once and for all in the race mind the fact of planes of existence other than the physical. The "event" will, of course, concern a type of perception and communication.

The next realization the student experiences is the quality of his relationships, and that he himself determines that quality via his thought, words, feelings, and deeds.

A very good example of this is the individual who suddenly realizes that the quality of his relationships is deceit. He is lied to, lied about, misrepresented, mistrusted, and mistrusting. Through observation he

The Nature of The Soul

discovers that he is communicating this quality to others, and, in turn, evoking the same from them. Often he is thinking one thing while speaking another, or speaking one thing while feeling and acting something else. Thus, his own vibratory activity is out of harmony and the discordant note is taking the form of deceit.

After a consideration of this four-fold vibratory activity, the student begins to glimpse the type and quality of influence he has been exerting upon his environment; the obvious disciplinary measures are initiated, and gradually he controls his vibratory impact upon others. He applies every concept of Truth, which he has grasped, to the task of daily living, and thus brings all of his energies and affairs into intelligent activity.

Use the following seed-thought in your daily meditation:

"I am the Soul. I sound forth in time and space as an harmonic chord. I am the Word made Flesh."

As a written assignment, please formulate three disciplinary measures which you should take in the light of the above information. Hand the assignment in to your teacher before going on with the next lesson.

LESSON 13

The Nature of the Etheric Body:

The Three-Fold Instrument
(Mental, Astral, Etheric);
The Nature of the Etheric
and Its Relation to
the Physical Mechanism;
The Center System
(Location, Significance, Transfers);
Meditation and Alignment
as It Relates to The Center System

LESSON 13

Before proceeding to a study of the attributes of the Soul, we shall once again turn our attention to meditation technique. You are now ready for a somewhat more advanced form which utilizes certain of the centers, and a more conscious manipulation of energy.

It is wise at this point to reevaluate the entire subject. What are you attempting to do via meditation? What are the Purpose and goals of the meditation technique, and how does one master the technique in order to eventually get into that area of meditation which supersedes form?

The motivating purpose for entering into the activity must always be the aspiration to serve. Perhaps this is why meditation is so difficult for beginners. Those who are not motivated out of a somewhat selfless (Soul–impulsed) aspiration to be of service to humanity, seldom persevere past the point where meditation is no longer a discipline. In the beginning the activity bears so little apparent fruit that the persona, who is not well–oriented to the Soul, is unlikely to exercise this discipline over his form nature. He does not realize that interior adjustments have to be made before his meditations can produce outer results. If he is well–oriented, and if he truly aspires to take his place on the Path as a disciple (a world server), this is one of the areas in which he will demonstrate the Will of the Soul rather than the little will of the persona.

One must, at this point, have some knowledge of the instrumentality of the Soul in order to more perfectly reevaluate the meditation technique and its place, both in the training and the service of the disciple.

The instrument of the Soul is three-fold in nature, being composed of three energy bodies which are coexistent in time and space. These energy bodies are:

1. The mental

2. The astral

3. The etheric

The physical body is not listed because it is not a principle. It is a temporary effect of very short duration when observed from the perspective which sees the evolutionary scheme as a whole. It is an appearance or effect, a substratum in a sense of the etheric, in its imperfect manifestation. As the etheric vehicle, or principle, is perfected, the dense substance of the physical body will have been lifted in frequency to the frequency of what is now its etheric counterpart.

The etheric body is the vital-energy body which interpenetrates all so-called space-form, relating, feeding, and sustaining the many informing lives within the One Life.

We see it first in its general manifestation as the substantial body of God, a vast network of energies and forces within which we live, move, and have our being. It interpenetrates all substance, relates it, and holds it in form. It is electrical in nature, being composed of many tiny lines of force (tubelike in appearance to the clairvoyant) which form channels for the flow of energies throughout its entire system.

The energy of thought and emotion moves through these tubes to impact upon another mind and emotional nature, and in order to take on an outer manifestation.

Lesson 13

We all know that energy follows thought. It moves through the etheric network to its destination, whatever or wherever that destination might be.

In the human form these lines of force underlie and are peculiarly related to the cerebro-nervous system. From this major network, the etheric body interpenetrates every atom of the physical body, and extends out some inches from it, varying in distance according to the evolution of the indwelling consciousness.

Through the medium of the etheric network, the mind impresses the brain. Through this same medium, the astral body (desire nature) impresses the brain and nervous system, and, again, through this same medium, the force necessary to action is fed into the physical body via the nervous system and the endocrine glands. When the etheric body is sufficiently developed, the Soul utilizes it to dominate and control the outer form nature.

The etheric body contains within it certain force centers which can be defined as centers of transmission for incoming and outgoing energies. Of the many centers in the etheric network, we shall consider here the seven major centers and their functions. Please remember as you read and study the following, that these centers are formed in etheric substance, and do not actually exist in the dense physical, though they do interpenetrate and produce effects within it.

Each center is located from three to six inches outside of the physical, extending into it in the form of an inverted spiral.

    1.   The Head center is located at the top of the head. This center puts the imprisoned consciousness (persona) in touch with the Overshadowing Spiritual Soul. It is quiescent until the man takes the upward way.

2. The Ajna center is located between the brows. It is relatively quiescent until such time as the three-fold persona becomes more or less integrated and can be consciously focused on the mental plane. At this time the ajna plays an important part in the alignment of Soul, mind and brain. It relates the three in awareness and aids in the creation of that magnetic field of Mind which is so important to the growth and development of the consciousness.

Later, the ajna serves as the center of control over the lower form nature. As the probationer disciple nears the third initiation, an interplay of energy is established between the ajna and the head centers which compels the entire system to reorientation.

This last statement is important to those of you who find yourselves in the process of becoming adjusted to a head polarization.

3. The Throat center is located about midway in the neck, finding its point of entry into the physical in the spinal column. This center is very active in the case of the intellectual. It is the center of contact with the lower concrete mind, the creative energies of sound, and it is the recipient in cases of mind-to-mind telepathy.

4. The Heart center is located between the shoulder blades and finds its point of entry into the physical in the spinal column. This center feeds the physical with vital life energy via the physical heart and the blood stream. It also relates the individual to his higher astral body, and puts him in first touch with the Love of God. Energies pouring in via this center impel the individual to seek, to establish relationships, and to aspire.

Lesson 13

A very interesting correspondence can be drawn here. The heart center in the spine corresponds to the physical sun which provides the conditions conducive to growth.

This center, like all the others, must be dominated by the head center, and coordinated with the ajna to be effective in service. When an alignment between the head, ajna, throat, and heart centers takes place, man becomes a conscious creator. In the creative artist today, the predominate centers are usually the head, throat, and heart. When the ajna becomes the coordinator, we shall see creative works which will surpass anything known today, insofar as influence is concerned.

5. The Solar Plexus center is located just above the waist, finding its point of entry into the physical via the spinal column. This center is the predominate center today insofar as humanity is concerned. It is very active in all emotional types, being the center of contact with the astral–emotional body. It has eventually to be dominated and superseded by the heart center.

6. The Sacral center is located about three inches below the waist, finding its point of entry into the physical in the spinal column. This center transmits the creative energies to the reproductive organs, and has eventually to be superseded by the throat center.

7. The Kundalini center is located just above the coccyx, finding its point of entry into the physical at the base of the spine. This center is the last to be awakened. Its energies are lifted into the ajna at the third initiation. Very little can be given anent the Kundalini at this time, for its mystery is revealed to the disciple only after a certain

evolutionary development has been attained.

The etheric body with its system of centers is the substantial form of the Soul, being a vehicle for the three major classifications of Soul consciousness. These are:

A. The Spiritual Soul consciousness which is focused into the head center. The persona then contacts his own "higher self" via the head center. The "higher self" or Overshadowing Spiritual Soul impresses the brain with Its Wisdom via the head center and etheric network as inspiration.

B. The human Soul consciousness which is focused into the heart and related centers. Here contact with the group, and both the mental and astral consciousness of the human family, is made, that contact being impressed upon the brain via the etheric network as intuition.

C. The animal Soul which is focused into the solar plexus and related centers. This center of consciousness relates man to the animal and to his past. Contact via this center and the etheric network is impressed upon the brain as instinct.

These three levels of consciousness within the individual and the mass have to be synthesized before man can enter into the kingdom of heaven. The work of synthesis cannot continue until man has integrated his three-fold persona, so-called physical, astral, and mental natures, into a working unit which is responsive to the Soul.

This is the first goal of his meditation: integration of the personality unit. As he focuses his consciousness in the mind via the ajna center, and endeavors from there to dominate the physical and emotional responses, he consciously or unconsciously directs the flow of energies within his lower centers upward into an integrated focus in the ajna. Thus, the consciousness imprisoned within the lower form nature, physical and astral, is lifted in frequency and gradually integrated into a working unit focused in the mind.

Thus, the persona takes up its residence in the ajna where he can put himself in touch with his Spiritual Soul via his mind, and still maintain a contact with, and control over, the lower form nature.

As soon as a certain degree of "residence" has been established in the ajna, the persona is given a meditation technique which withdraws or abstracts him even further from the world of form, placing him in more conscious touch with his higher self. From here, the cave (brain cavity) in the center of the head, he carries out his meditations, endeavoring to become responsive as a unit to his Overshadowing Spiritual Soul.

At this point, then, he has added to the goal of personality integration that of conscious Soul contact and response to that contact.

The Spiritual Soul "in meditation deep" sets into motion those Divine ideas it would have incorporated into its instrumentality.

The persona, in meditation deep, receives, interprets, and responds to these same ideas, setting them into the motion of manifestation via his etheric network and its system of centers.

Thus, the meditation proceeds in three stages.

1. The approach or ascent, that period in which the disciple aligns, integrates, and lifts his consciousness into a frequency which is receptive to the Spiritual Soul.

2. Meditation deep.

    a. The concentrated focus of receptivity which awaits an inflowing Divine Idea from the Soul via the head center.

    b. The interpretation and formulation of the idea into concrete knowledge. At this point the incarnating consciousness, identified as Soul, relates the received idea to himself and his environment. He interprets it according to the need of his time and locale.

3. Descent or embodiment.

After having received an overshadowing idea or concept, and after having interpreted it, it is then built into the lower response mechanism from a focus in the ajna. The incarnate consciousness, still identified as Soul, impresses the concrete knowledge upon the mind, astral-emotional nature, and the physical brain and nervous system. He does this via the projection of thought and sound (focusing of intent) through certain of his centers. Thus, embodiment of the higher ideal becomes possible.

In each stage of the meditation process, a triangle of centers is consciously used.

In the case of the lower alignment, the attention is turned to the bodies rather than the centers. This avoids dangers and unnecessary delays.

The lower bodies are aligned as quickly as possible as follows:

    a. become physically relaxed and comfortable;
    b. become emotionally calm and serene;
    c. become mentally poised and alert.

Lesson 13

At this point the persona is ready to begin the ascent and the integration process.

    a. he focuses the consciousness in the ajna, realizing that he is polarized in his mind.

    b. he then takes three deep breaths, realizing with each that he as a positive pole of magnetic attraction is drawing the:

        (1) consciousness imprisoned within the physical sensory apparatus into an integrated focus in the ajna center,

        (2) consciousness imprisoned in the emotional nature into an integrated focus in the ajna center,

        (3) consciousness imprisoned in the lower mind nature into an integrated focus in the ajna.

He then very softly sounds the OM, realizing these three aspects of himself to be integrated into a unit which is aspiring to the Spiritual Soul.

He then aspires, turning his attention inward. Visualizing a line of light extending back from the ajna into the cave in the center of the head, and another line of light extending upward from the cave to the head center, he endeavors to move back into the cave where he will be in direct alignment with the Overshadowing Soul.

Thus, three centers are brought into active play:

1. The ajna,

2. the cave in the center of the head, that place which is midway between the Soul and persona and does not become a center until it is consciously used,

3. the head center.

The Nature of The Soul

As soon as a focus in the cave has been achieved, he is ready for deep meditation.

Remembering that his Overshadowing Soul is in meditation deep, he endeavors to lift his frequency and so align himself that an interplay of energy is set up between himself in meditation, and his Soul in meditation.

Being directly under the head center, and connected to it via the line of light, he enters into receptivity, using a seed-thought as that attractive power which will command the attention of his Soul.

The first seed-thought the student uses with this meditation form is that of identity. He identifies as Soul, realizing that he is an extension of the Overshadowing Spiritual Soul. He is both incarnate in form, and above, free of form.

> *"And having pervaded this instrument with a bit of myself, I remain. I am."*

With as full a realization of this seed-thought as is possible, he awaits the "touch" of the Soul. He is attentive via the line of light and the head center, to his Overshadowing Self.

After having received the "touch" or impact, he then formulates it into concrete knowledge, relating it to himself and his environment. Here the Plan for his instrument (disciplines to be exercised, qualities to be built in, etc.) and the Plan of service to his environment (relationship of Soul identification to environment) are formulated. He is now building thought-forms.

Thus, again, three major centers are aligned and active: head center, cave, and ajna, for the line of light remains intact from cave to ajna throughout the entire process.

144

He is now ready for the descent, the embodying process. He remains in the cave and projects his formulated intent into the ajna upon the sounding of the OM.

"I, the Soul, appropriate the integrated three-fold persona in service to the Plan." OM

He moves out again into the ajna, and maintaining his focus there, but directing his attention to and through the following centers, he completes the descent.

1. AJNA CENTER — *"Let there be Light within the mind." OM*

2. HEART CENTER — *"Let there manifest self-less love within the emotional nature." OM*

3. THROAT CENTER — *"Let there manifest right activity within the physical body and its environment." OM*

Thus, the ajna (focused third eye), heart, and throat are aligned and active.

He completes his meditation by radiating Love from the etheric vehicle into and through his environment to humanity.

The Nature of The Soul

LESSON 14

The Ray Constitution of Humanity
and Effects of Fourth Ray:

The Rays of Attribute
and their Relationship to
the Three Primary Rays;
Individual Ray Make-up
and a Hypothetical Example
of Rays Working Through a Disciple
and an Average Human Being;
The Use of the Fourth Ray
as it Harmonizes the Opposites
and the Law of Paradox

LESSON 14

We come now to the attributes of the Soul, which are four types of energy made available to the incarnating consciousness as minor tones of the major three: Will, Love, and Intelligence. In other words, these four attributes are derived from the basic triangle of causative energies, and are then differentiated expressions of them. They are defined as:

1. The Fourth Ray of Harmony through Conflict, which is derived from, and is a differentiated expression of, the Second Ray of Love-Wisdom.

2. The Fifth Ray of Concrete Science and Knowledge, which is derived from and is a differentiated expression of the Third Ray of Intelligent Activity.

3. The Sixth Ray of Devotion, which is derived from and is a differentiated expression of Love-Wisdom.

4. The Seventh Ray of Ceremonial Magic or Divine Law and Order, which is derived from, and is a differentiated expression of, the First Ray of Will and Power.

These four energy expressions are created as the major three impact upon substance via the consciousness aspect. They are the expressions given to the major three by the Logoic consciousness as He works out His Purpose via the instrument of time and space. Thus, we call them the attributes of the Soul or consciousness aspect, meaning that they are the expressive qualities derived from the causative energies of the Soul.

149

The Nature of The Soul

These energies can be more easily expressed in time and space to produce a specific effect, than can the major three, since their frequencies are more easily appropriated and wielded by the incarnating consciousness.

Thus, the First Ray is more often expressed via its stepped–down or differentiated expression of Ceremony and Order, than as Pure Will and Power. The Second Ray is more often expressed as Harmony and Devotion, than as Divine Love-Wisdom or Pure Reason, and the Third Ray finds its expression more often in Concrete Science and Knowledge rather than pure Creativity.

The seven manifesting at the peak of their potentials sound forth in time and space as an harmonic chord which expresses perfectly as Logoic Purpose, thus manifesting perfection in form.

A man is an aggregate of energies, held together in time and space, via his etheric network, informed by an individualized spark of Logoic consciousness, and with all other men is a center or focal point through which Logoic Purpose is finally worked out into manifestation. Thus, we say humanity in its sum total is the Planetary throat center through which the Word of God sounds forth in time and space.

The individualized spark of Logoic consciousness identified as a persona, and evolving toward full Soul consciousness within the aggregate of energies otherwise defined as His vehicles or bodies, has to ascertain the type, strength and quality of these energies in order to consciously wield them in service to the Plan.

He learns through occult study that his Soul expression is colored by a predominate ray energy, one of the Planetary seven, and that each of the three vehicles is colored by one or another of the seven subtones of the Soul expression. In addition to these four rays, his

150

persona as a sum total functions on one of the sub-rays of his Soul, so that the consciousness has readily available to him five specific energies with which to work in the world of affairs. These five energies constitute his equipment during any incarnating cycle. An understanding of them reveals his talents, his abilities, his psychology, and his particular life problem. According to his use of these energies can be determined his point of development, and the karmic pattern of necessity built into the very substance of his bodies.

Thus, a teacher of the Wisdom can truly know his student, and in that knowing serve his Soul in Its relationship to the Plan, rather than the persona with its wants, its likes and its dislikes.

Let us now consider this information via an hypothetical aggregate of energies involving a disciple on the Path.

Ray of the Soul . . . .   Second Ray of Love-Wisdom

Integrating ray of persona   First Ray of Will or Power

Ray of the mental body . . .   Fourth Ray of Harmony

Ray of the astral body . . . .   Sixth Ray of Devotion

Ray of the physical body . .   Seventh Ray of Order

This Soul functioning on the second Planetary ray of Divine Love-Wisdom which expresses, remember, as the Love of Wisdom, has available to him two paths of least resistance into outer expression via the mental and the astral bodies. It will not be difficult for him to express his Love of Wisdom via a Fourth Ray mental body which can see into, and work with, the Law of Harmony, nor through an astral feeling nature which is highly colored with devotion, in this case devotion to the ideal of Wisdom; but the persona in its sum total and the etheric-physical body present the Soul with its specific problem during this incarnation.

The Nature of The Soul

The integrated ray of the persona is that of Will and Power, meaning that the energies of the three-fold vehicle can only be mobilized and consciously directed into manifestation via an inner, dynamic focusing of the Will. In the etheric-physical body, the vehicle through which the energies must pass into outer manifestation, we find a reflection or stepped down expression of the Will as Order.

Thus, this Second Ray Soul with its natural Love of Wisdom, its mental insight into the harmony of God, and its devotion to Wisdom on a feeling level, a natural mystic, has to become the occultist. He is faced with the karmic necessity of mobilizing all of these energies and forces into ordered action on the physical plane of appearance, and for him this is no easy task.

Thus, his Soul Purpose during this incarnation, his path of Service, and his karmic necessity lead him out of the tendency toward passive acceptance for all is well, into a path of dynamic activity in which Wisdom is made out-flowing rather than inflowing.

In the case of a lesser–evolved Soul, these same energies would have presented an entirely different set of conditions.

This particular Soul has available to him three rays of attribute, three minor tones, with which to work out his purpose in his time and place. These three rays, Harmony, Devotion, and Order, give him a set of frequencies easily adaptive to the physical plane of appearances, easily understood in their expressions by humanity. Thus, his persona could easily fit into its environment via harmony, devotion, and order, with one exception. The integrating ray of the persona is that of the First Ray of Will and Power, and even though it is a sub-ray of Love-Wisdom, until carefully controlled, it would present this persona with problems in relationship. He would have to Will to Love on personality levels, to express that Love outwardly toward others, while his whole tendency would be the expression of Love inwardly toward Wisdom to the exclusion of others.

Thus, we begin to grasp some measure of the significance of the rays. At a later date meditation techniques will be made available to you for the purpose of ascertaining your own ray makeup. In the meantime, attempt to absorb a growing understanding of these energies as each is considered in its turn.

The Fourth Ray of Harmony is one of the most interesting energies of the minor four, and one of the most important during this phase of human evolution. It is not the ray which produces the creative arts, as is most commonly believed, but in its positive expression produces a dynamic system of balance which tunes and harmonizes the many frequencies in the instrument to the frequency of the Soul.

In the case of the probationer on the path, this energy manifests first as an observation of the pairs of opposites. This is true to greater or lesser degree, depending upon his particular ray makeup. If the energy is not predominate somewhere in his makeup, it is still there in lesser degree, since these minor four are the attributes of the Soul, and part of Its nature.

This is an important point, for there is a great misunderstanding in the minds of many students anent this subject of available characteristics and attributes. Many believe that if they do not have a particular ray energy predominant in their makeup that they lack in this quality—that it is not available to them. This need not be true, since the seven ray qualities constitute the nature of the Soul. One particular quality may or may not be predominant, but it is nonetheless available, and upon full Soul development all qualities, the seven-fold nature of the

The Nature of The Soul

Soul, will be expressing perfectly in time and space.

As the aspirant becomes a probationer disciple, he begins to observe and to recognize the pairs of opposites as they are manifesting within his consciousness and its instrument.

He observes how he fluctuates from the so-called good to the so-called bad, how he swings with the pendulum from one extreme to the other, and gradually he realizes that in order to balance the opposites, he must take the middle path, swinging neither to the right nor to the left.

As this concept makes its impression upon him, it is usually misinterpreted to mean a path of non-action — of passivity. This is a glamour of the astral plane, one of the astral vapors which so distort Truth that it becomes non-recognizable in its appearance.

This harmonizing energy is anything but passive in quality. It is essentially dynamic, for it fuses the pairs of opposites together in such a way as to render them whole, thus producing a whole tone in the sounding Word of God.

For some time, then, the probationer attempts to become passive, to take the path of least resistance, and this does serve a purpose since it renders him more easily the observer.

Moving along what he considers to be the middle way, he observes the pairs of opposites, endeavoring to balance them from his central point of focus.

> *"Alone I stand upon the scales, and reaching out I bring into all relationships that peculiar motion which results in balance."*

"That peculiar motion" is the expression of the Fourth Ray of Harmony, which enables the probationer to move from passivity into action — to reach out and bring the opposites into that central point of focus where balance is restored, where the so-called bad is transmuted into good.

At this point the probationer begins to comprehend the Law of Paradox. He learns that all concepts, all systems of thought, must be based upon a causal truth. Anything that is must have its foundation in reality or it could not be. At the same time everything that is must be false for it is confined in a form. Thus, he applies the Law of Paradox to every concept, every form, every experience with which he is familiar, learning to understand the polar opposites, the so-called good and bad as "essence" and "form." Nothing is strictly true or false, good or bad, everything is both, and through a recognition of this, the essence or reality and the form or substance can be so fused as to produce the whole tone, which in its magical effect tunes or harmonizes all other frequencies within its range of influence.

This is Harmony—a differentiated expression of Love-Wisdom. It produces that understanding which is a prerequisite to right relationship, whether it be with the One Life, a situation, or among peoples.

During the coming week let your seed-thought for meditation be:

> *"The Sound of the Overshadowing Spiritual Soul.*
> *Aspire to sense the frequency of that silent sound,*
> *to understand its meaning, and then to reproduce*
> *it harmonically within the world of the persona,*
> *realizing that this vibration, this harmony is an*
> *attribute of the Soul."*

Please bring a written summary of your understanding of the Fourth Ray of Harmony to the next class, using both the lesson and meditation to expand your consciousness anent the subject.

The Nature of The Soul

LESSON 15

The Fourth Ray and the Ashramic Group Life:

Fourth Ray as Esoteric
Sound, Color, and Vibration;
The Ability to Harmonize
as a Prerequisite for Access
Into Conscious Awareness
of the Ashramic Life;
An Ashram Described

LESSON 15

In considering the Fourth Ray of Harmony, the student must realize that it is in essence the inner esoteric sound or vibration of God indwelling the manifest Cosmos. This vibration is present within all forms, inherent within all consciousness, and available to disciples as both an energy and a Law to be wielded in service to the Plan.

Thus harmony, whether recondite or outwardly visible, is an integral part, an essential ingredient of everything that is. It is not necessary to look away from or beyond discord to find harmony. It is everywhere equally present in essence, and is made visable via recognition and invocation.

The probationer-disciple learns to invoke harmony into outer manifestation via the invocation of it as an attribute of the Soul, first into his own brain awareness, then into the vehicles of appearance, and, finally, into his outer environment. Thus, he gradually produces that auric influence which is characteristic of the accepted disciple and successfully passes initiation, i.e., gains entry into the ashramic group life.

This subject of Hierarchial ashrams is one with which most of you are more or less familiar, but only in a vague and intangible sense. Its lack of clarity in the minds of probationers produces such a distortion of glamour in the astral body, that very little is truly known about it in the exoteric world. However, since we have entered into a new period in the growth and development of the human consciousness, much that has necessarily been esoteric is being made exoteric to the brain awareness of those members of humanity who stand within the periphery of the Hierarchial Light. Thus, a clear enunciation of certain facts in nature is being made to probationers to both speed up, and render more easily completed, that phase of development in which they now find themselves.

In the past, probationers have had to more or less struggle through this period of growth with little or no apparent aid from their seniors. Gradually, over a period of many incarnations, apparently alone and unaided, the probationer acquired via a trial-and-error method, those experiences in consciousness which made it possible for him to gain entry, or to initiate himself into, the realm of accepted discipleship in one or two remaining incarnations.

Today many disciples turn their attention to the group of probationers in the world, aiding, and in one sense, almost lifting them up into a new spiral of achievement. Thus, the Path is rendered, at one and the same time, more readily available, more easily grasped, and yet more difficult to tread, since it is being telescoped to fit the need of the time. Probationers are presented with the opportunity to accept greater responsibilities than heretofore, and are given the esoteric wherewithal to meet those responsibilities. Those who can seize the opportunity and at the same time affect that steady growth which is derived from character building, will have established a new Path of Return within the body of humanity.

The probationer, then, is recipient of certain facts in nature which, as they are unfolded in the consciousness, place him in more conscious touch with his Soul purpose.

An ashram, while it is a fact in nature, exists in consciousness only. This is the first major concept to impact upon the brain awareness of the applicant to the initiation, which gives him birth within the ashramic group life.

In his consideration of an ashram, he has visualized it as being composed of a focal point (usually a master of The Wisdom decked out in robes and jeweled turban) with a group of bewitched and benumbed disciples bowing in adoration at his feet. This ashram he places somewhere in the heavens, and desires greatly to become a part of it.

Such a picture couldn't be further from the reality; yet this is the major thought-form which attracts the astral and even lower mental consciousness of many probationers in the world today.

The ashram exists within the consciousness of its membership and is a group awareness. Each member partakes of, and contributes to, the overall consciousness of the group. Each member, then, is in conscious touch with each other member, and to some degree with the central directing life of the ashram. The plans and purposes of the group are focused into it via the central directing life, each member relating himself according to developed talents, fitness, and karmic necessity, to the working out into manifestation of those plans and purposes.

The Overshadowing Spiritual Soul, on its own level, has Its particular life and affairs which are in, and a part of, the ashramic group life.

This is the second major concept anent this subject to impact upon the brain awareness of the probationer.

His Spiritual Soul, that higher, Divine Self which he is in reality, is now functioning within the ashram. It is not waiting to be admitted into the group life; it already is a part of that life.

The Nature of The Soul

What does the initiation entail, then, for the Spiritual Soul? It involves the integration, illumination, and control of the persona which leads to its inclusion in the ashramic group life. This, the Overshadowing Spiritual Soul proposes to do. This then, is an immediate goal designed to serve Its higher Purpose.

The higher Purpose, often referred to as Soul Purpose, has to do with the relationship between the Soul on Its own level and the Christ consciousness of which It is becoming aware. The ashramic group life is a focus of that Christ consciousness into a group Soul through the Hierarchial member acting as Its central directing life.

The Divine Plan as held in focus by The Christ is precipitated into the ashram where the membership can, as a group consciousness, ensoul it, and via that ensouling, relate it to the need of humanity in any time and place.

The Divine Plan is a state of consciousness referred to as The Christ. This is the Plan for humanity, the evolution of each individual member of humanity into conscious identification with The Christ, the development or unfoldment via experience and self-initiated effort of every separated unit of consciousness into the Being of Christ.

The Soul's own realized Purpose has to do with Its specific relationship to that Plan—a series of Divine Acts (or states of consciousness) to be made manifest throughout a series of incarnations called the Path of Discipleship, which shall contribute to and see the working out of the Plan. Thus, the Spiritual Soul is concerned with humanity, both in a collective sense and in an individual one, rather than with its so-called self. In other words, the Soul's Purpose has to do with both the humanity focused into the whole family and the individual brother, rather than with its own attainment.

162

Lesson 15

This is the third major concept anent this subject to impact upon the brain awareness of the probationer. His Soul Purpose is concerned with the Plan for humanity and how he can best serve that Plan in his particular time and place.

Such Divine Purpose is contained within the ashramic group life. The probationer gains entry as he becomes an instrumentality in the three worlds of endeavor, through which the ashramic group consciousness can express its share of the Plan. His job is not so much to lift up into the ashram (though this he does do during high moments of meditation) as it is to make himself available to the ashram, both in consciousness and in instrument, for a job of work to be done. He permits the ashram to work through him, to gain entry via an interior vertical alignment within himself, to manifest its group awareness within his brain consciousness, and outwardly into the world of affairs. Thus is an accepted disciple but an accepting disciple, an outpost of the Master's consciousness.

The Fourth Ray of Harmony is invoked specifically as the probationer enters the above described stage of growth. Realizing that the Fourth Ray is esoteric sound, and that sound produces color, the probationer invokes that silent sound of his Soul as the attribute of Harmony, producing its color (quality) within his own brain awareness and its thought life.

He endeavors via meditation to sense the tonal quality of the Soul, which is harmony, and to become so aligned with this vibratory frequency that it can impact upon his brain via the head center, cave, and the ajna.

Then, as he begins to sense this tone, this frequency which is harmony, during his meditations, (and such sensitivity is at first very subtle, being little more than an abstract feeling or intuition), he endeavors to reproduce

The Nature of The Soul

its color within his inner thought life.

Esoteric color has to do with quality. The quality of the
Fourth Ray in the mind is a kind of insight which is so
broad and so inclusive as to wash away all prejudice, all
criticism, all pet rules and standards of behaviorism.
Thus, the inner thought life is cleansed of any discordant sound, so that its radiant color is the golden color
of understanding. It is at peace with God and His world.

It is during this stage that the probationer applies the
Law of Paradox over and over again, seeing Truth in its
many facets, its many sides, as a whole, and as a relative, so that condemnation of any man or situation is not
possible, but only that golden understanding which is
Wisdom. Thus, the Fourth Ray of Harmony, an attribute of the Soul, tunes the many frequencies within
the brain awareness to the frequency of wisdom, and the
man discovers peace of mind.

After having reproduced the Soul tone of harmony
within the brain awareness, the probationer then sets
out to reproduce it within the substance of his vehicles.

Please note: This is done after the dynamic frequency of
this energy has been imposed upon the brain awareness,
and not before. It must have produced its results here
before it is invoked into the vehicles.

This invocation of the Fourth Ray into the vehicles is a
magical operation which I shall not clarify at this point,
for to do so would only serve to endanger you. However,
know this: "When the student is ready, the teacher, or
the teaching appears." If and when you have successfully accomplished the development described in the
preceding, you will surely become recipient of whatever
knowledge is necessary to complete the next stage of
this growth.

Lesson 15

When the Fourth Ray is invoked into the substance of the vehicles, those vehicles are lifted in frequency to such a pitch that the ashramic group life can pour into and through them. The bodies are not only purified, they are literally rebuilt through the magical application of esoteric sound to them. This is the period wherein old karmic patterns of disease and disability are completely eliminated, and the flesh is cast to a new mold.

The probationer, literally with a new consciousness and a new instrument, is now ready to recreate his environment, to produce that auric influence which completes his initiation into the new life.

What can be said about such an event at this time, other than that which is general and abstruse? Such a one has become an accepted disciple through his acceptance of the way, the life, and the consciousness of the disciple. Hence, he lives in the world as such, his auric influence is such that it produces obvious growth within all units of consciousness which it touches. Here is a young Christ, not as yet full grown perhaps, but conscious of his Christhood and productive of the good, the true, and the beautiful for his brothers. He has become a Power in the world, an influence for The Christ, an agent of the Divine Plan for humanity.

Please continue with the same seed-thought for meditation and learn the true meaning of peace.

The Nature of The Soul

LESSON 16

Fifth Ray
and the Sequential Unfolding
of the Divine Plan in Time and Space

Our "Reality" as an Outpicturing
of Our Inner State of Consciousness;
The "Outpicturing" of the Divine Plan
in the Coming Age, and
Details of the Work to be Done;
Third and Fifth Ray Related;
Fifth Ray as the Divine Equation

168

LESSON 16

In his study of the attributes of the Soul, the probationer soon discovers that here are tangible realities which he can more readily understand and apply than the rays of aspect. They make up both his seen and unseen world in a close and real sense, are the very basis of the civilization in which he lives, and account for almost all of his developed talents and abilities.

These are the energies which underlie his inner state of consciousness, and constitute the forms his outer experiences take. An experience is but the pictorial manifestation (an outpicturing in dense substance) of the inner state of consciousness. That "state of consciousness" is the combination of characteristics, attributes, qualities, etc., which, in their sum total, constitute the inner (incarnating) man. When this combination is somewhat integrated into a focus, and identified with its experiences (of which the bodies are a part), we call it a persona. When the integrated focus has detached its identification from its experiences (detached from its own effect in substance) and reidentified as a focal point within the One Life, we call it a Conscious Soul Incarnate. The consciousness has then become identified as consciousness, and realizes that while it lends itself to its effect in substance, nonetheless the creator is not its own creation.

Through this process of de-identification and reidentification, the Soul evolves into the Christ, the Christ being the only begotten Son, i.e., the consciousness of the many focused into a One! The Father, then, is the consciousness of the One focused into the many, while the persona is conscious of neither the One or the many, but only of that illusion called self.

Of what is the Soul conscious? What does its awareness include that can be defined as goals to the aspiring probationer?

The Soul on its own plane is conscious of the group life, hence its participation within the ashram. Its awareness includes the consciousness of its group in an ever—widening sphere of identification which gradually includes the many.

This means that the brain awareness becomes but an instrument through which the group life (Soul) expresses itself in service to its brothers (other group souls).

Its particular service has to do with its relationship to the Plan, and that of course, is determined by the type, strength, and quality of its energy potential, i.e., the ray of the Soul.

What is the Divine Plan for humanity? We have defined it in numerous ways, speaking in generalities rather than in specifics, and this has been necessary, for each must interpret the Plan according to his relationship to it.

In this lesson, however, we shall be somewhat more specific by relating it generally to this particular time in space, this cyclic period of growth within which humanity now finds itself.

The Divine Plan for humanity in this cycle includes the following growth and development:

A. Identification, both individually and collectively, of the mass consciousness with the Soul via:

    1. Conclusive proof, in several scientific fields of

endeavor, of the existence of the Soul as the causal factor of manifestation:

a. through psychological findings anent reincarnation, life after death, and the incarnating entity or Soul.

b. through the instrumental perception of the etheric network and its final discovery as the substantial body of the One Life, thus relating and leading to new discoveries anent the Life aspect.

c. through instrumental contact with the astral plane, and groups of disciples working within that sphere.

d. through instrumental contact with the mental plane, the perception and recording of thought-forms, and the tracing of energies released and directed into manifestation by those thought-forms.

e. through data gathered via contact with outer space.

Thus, science itself will force a complete reevaluation of all religious and philosophical systems of thought, lifting humanity up out of its apparent lethargy into a new, dynamic, spiritual endeavor.

B. Realization by the mass consciousness of the Purpose of life in the three worlds as being the growth and development of the Soul via:

1. The forced shift by science of human consciousness from an astral to a mental focus.

2. The intensive effort of disciples to re-educate the mass to the new ideas and ideals.

3. The emergence, out of the ruins of the outmoded structure of organized religions, of a new World Religion which cannot be confined within, or limited to, any outer organization. It will be of such strength and purpose, of such universality, as to break the bonds of any attempted organization of it! This will truly be a World Religion because it will spring forth from the fountainhead of the mass mind and heart.

C. A new culture and civilization created in an endeavor to aid the growth and development of the consciousness aspect.

1. The development of a new and valid science called Occultology.

2. The building of a new economic structure whose purpose is to manifest the growth and development of consciousness. This economy will convert all natural resources to the Spiritual betterment of humanity, meeting the common need whenever and wherever it is focused.

3. A new educational system designed to aid in the growth of the Soul within the child, and to develop the Soul purpose from a potential into an active expression.

4. The end of the political regime and the beginning of the true function of the New Group of World Servers within the body of humanity.

5. The advance of medicine into the science of regeneration and rejuvenation of substance.

Lesson 16

This is but a bare outline containing only a few of the changes the Divine Plan holds for humanity now, but these few indicate much more clearly the fields of service into which probationers may enter as a part of their own initiatory activity.

In the light of the above, consider what humanity has yet to experience prior to, and as a part of the mass initiation. The impact of the Fifth Ray alone, via the various fields of science upon the consciousness of humanity, will demand an intensive effort of all probationers and disciples in the field to stabilize that impact into an ordered, steady, progressive growth. Here is the field of service dictated by the Divine Plan. How shall you relate to it?

The Fifth Ray of concrete knowledge and science is that energy which properly equates Spirit, matter, and consciousness—defines them into a manifesting picture. Hence this lesson, which brings into a focus this energy of the Fifth Ray, clarifies somewhat the Divine Plan for humanity in its relationship to the world of affairs here and now.

Thus, we see that this energy is concerned with time and space. It is the concretizing aspect of the Third Ray, that energy which makes possible the clothing of a universal abstraction with concrete mental substance, thus producing the specific thought-form in a sequential manner. The abstraction is precipitated into concrete form, and the sequence of the manifesting form creates so-called time and space.

The Third Ray is the form building aspect — the energy and substance of intelligence—the matter aspect. The Fifth Ray is that frequency of the substantial intelligence which produces the final form in its outer structure—that which moves into appearance, the movement itself creating time.

The Nature of The Soul

While it is realized that this is a somewhat difficult concept to grasp at the onset, it is nonetheless important to your development at this point. Try to visualize the idea in its timeless sense, being precipitated into that frequency which produces its movement through a series or sequence of defined forms, thus creating the manifestation of its evolution in time and space.

This is the connotation of the Fifth Ray as seen from the perspective of the Overshadowing Spiritual Soul. Its Purpose, then, or its Divine Intent, is to produce the equation of Spirit, matter, and consciousness into such movement as to result in an experiencing (which we call evolution), by every atom of consciousness, of all that is possible to the sum total. Thus, the consciousness knows not only in theory, but in actuality, all that is possible to it from the lowest to the highest state of Being.

What does all of this mean to the probationer who is caught up in time and space? Whose consciousness is imprisoned, so to speak, in the movement of the form building aspect?

The probationer is learning the art and science of form building; he is endeavoring to become the builder in a creative sense, rather than the building. An understanding of the Fifth Ray of concrete science and knowledge will not only place him in consciousness in the world of ideas, which is above the frequency of form, but it will teach him how to use time and space to the advantage of the Plan.

Knowing this, the initiate disciple moves into his own manifestations in the three worlds of human endeavor. He not only places them in time and space, but he creates his own time and space as well.

Thus, he masters the form nature, and the form building aspect, the substantial intelligence which is his

174

negative pole of manifestation. He rises out of it, a Conscious Soul Incarnate, to finally become the Christ, and go unto the Father.

We have defined the frequency of the Fourth Ray as sound. How do we define the frequency of the Fifth Ray? What can be told to you at this point which will render you receptive to an understanding of this energy potential which is available to you as an attribute of the Soul?

I can only state that the frequency of this energy is that of movement. It is the steady motion of the Soul which produces a moving picture, so to speak, of its growth.

The probationer, who is also an applicant to initiation, endeavors to sense this motion, this intelligent activity, before it creates time.

> Let your new seed-thought for meditation be a *receptivity to that downward and outward movement of the Soul which produces its inward and upward growth.*

Please write your understanding of the Fifth Ray of concrete knowledge and science, using both the lesson material and meditation technique in an approach to it. Bring this paper with you to the next class.

The Nature of The Soul

LESSON 17

Fifth Ray Related to Evolution and Initiation:

The Path of Return
and Self-Initiated Growth;
The Relation of Fifth and First Ray
in Terms of Three Motivations of Will
Related to the Three Initiations;
The Problems of Separation,
Discrimination, and Alignment as
Fifth Ray Impacts the Instrument

LESSON 17

The probationer disciple is endeavoring to take up his residence within his mental body, to achieve control of the forces which constitute his emotional nature, and in some measure, to control the motion of that substance which has coalesced to produce his bodies.

Evolution itself brings him to this cycle of opportunity, placing him within the necessity of the situation somewhat prematurely, to all outward appearances. He is then faced with this three-fold task prior to his understanding of it, and so, for some period of time, deals with it almost unconsciously. He does not know what he is trying to do or why, but only that he must do something. Here is the driving force of evolution itself impulsing him in a certain direction almost in spite of his will. This is a period which is fraught with much real, inner pain.

Finally, evolution brings him to that place where self-conscious and self-initiated growth is seen as a possibility. Speaking in occult symbols, he stands neck deep in the battle being waged between the forces of the Soul as they are brought to bear upon the persona, and the forces of the many forms with which he as a persona is identified. Here is a gigantic conflict raging within his own ring-pass-not, and within which he is submerged up to his head.

Realizing that he can bring it to an end only from a head polarization, and hence from a position within his mind, this one faces a major decision in the evolutionary process. Will he, for the sake of his own liberation, cooperate with the forces of evolution, and initiate the beginning of the end of conflict?

179

The Nature of The Soul

In that moment of clear seeing, the individual will either seize the opportunity and maintain himself in the head, via decision, or he will ignore it to go down again into the midst of conflicting forces for yet another period of time.

Sooner or later, during one or another of the cycles of opportunity, the individual will grasp the connotations of this reappearing moment, wield the energy of decision, and place his feet for the first time upon the path of initiation as a probationer.

Consider the tremendous significance of this act. He must place his feet upon the path from a position within his mind. The only expendable energy available to him which will cut through the conflict to move him onto the path is the energy of Will.

This is the moment, when finally despairing of the attractive pull of the form nature, he states: "I will arise and go unto the Father."

This is his first conscious effort toward liberation, his first conscious cooperation with the Divine energy of Will as transmitted to him from the Monad through the medium of his Spiritual Soul. Thus, Monadic forces are brought directly to bear upon the conflict taking place within his ring-pass-not.

This first impact does in no way lessen the conflict, but it will maintain him in the head, above and almost free of it.

That phase of the path which we call probationary discipleship is characterized by three motivations of the Will.

1. The will toward individual and personal liberation from pain. This is the beginning of self-initiated growth.

2. The will toward union with the One Life. This is the advance toward a known spiritual attainment.

3. The will toward humanity's liberation from pain. This is the real beginning of active discipleship, and finally places the probationer within his own ashram.

Thus, we see that the first statement "I will arise and go unto the Father" is but the beginning, and that it is necessarily selfish. It concerns the separated self, and his suddenly realized necessity to escape pain.

We find the mass of humanity today approaching this stage, which is the completion of the first initiation (the realized son-ship which can will to arise and go unto the Father) and the approach toward the second initiation.

Thus, humanity again approaches the reappearing moment, when from a sudden experience of clear seeing, the mass, individually and collectively, realizes that only from a focus in the mind as the son can liberation from pain be achieved. Those who can be considered the leadership of the mass will see a way out which leads from the valley of pain to the mountaintop of freedom, and that way out will be cognized as self-initiated growth toward spiritual maturity. The leadership will in turn transfer the concept to the mass, and humanity will consciously place its feet upon the path.

If, in this new age of many new concepts and ideas, one is more important than any other, it is this concept of self-initiated growth. Here is an idea which is not new in itself, and yet has never before made its impact upon other than a few minds at any given time. Consider the spiritual significance of the concept. Consider its many implications and their effects upon humanity.

Man grows because it is a basic law of consciousness

that he does so. Regardless of how little, mean, or petty he may appear, each incarnation will see his growth toward the positive side of his nature. This is evolution and it appears as a long, slow process with which man has very little to do. Growth is something which naturally happens to him, and deep within every man's consciousness is knowledge of this.

Now, suddenly, he discovers that he can, through his own effort, initiate a new growth and development! He can conceive a goal of spiritual maturity within himself, and initiate the experiences which will produce an embodiment of that goal. Hence, every man can become a Christ because he wills to do so. No longer is he hampered by fate or karma, for he has reached that place wherein he sees himself as the creator of his own fate. Via the creative process of thought, he can become that which he would be. He is no longer held prisoner to his heredity, environment, or built-in response mechanism. Here is the real vision of freedom which humanity en masse now approaches.

Thus, we see the Divine Plan again, from a somewhat different perspective, as it relates to the consciousness of humanity today. We see the field of service, into which the probationer can enter, with a growing clarity which gradually erases all doubt as to what constitutes right action in any given instance.

We also see man's separative point of view as a tool which we can use in service to the Plan. This concept of self-initiated growth, which is to make its impact upon the whole of humanity, has a natural path of approach already created for it. That path can be put into right use as the appeal for liberation from pain, and the way of that liberation is placed upon it to impact upon the minds and brains of men. Despair not that the mass motive concerns the separated self, for this is evolution. Rejoice, in that the direction upward, "I will arise and go unto my Father," can be taken, even if from a separated need to escape pain.

The second motivation of the Will toward union with the One Life will come after the first step is taken, and it will constitute the second initiation.

In the meantime, where do you find yourselves? All of those who are sincerely and seriously attracted to this course of instruction will find themselves in the third and final phase of probationary discipleship where the Will motivation is concerned with humanity as a whole. Here the probationer initiates that service which will place him within the ashram as an accepted disciple. He is taking the third initiation wherein his realized need to be of service is concerned with (1) the fitting of his instrument for increased service, and (2) active contribution to the One Life via the present imperfect vehicle.

It is during this stage that the probationer consciously works with the Fifth Ray of concrete knowledge and science. This energy makes it possible for him to use his mind to develop that knowledge of the Plan with which to do the following:

1. discriminate between the real, and the non-real;

2. discriminate between the essential and the non-essential;

3. discriminate between the important and the lesser important.

His use of Fifth Ray from a realized point of Soul consciousness develops his mind into a tool of keen discriminative perception.

The meditation form, regardless of the predominant ray of the seed-thought, is basically and technically an expression of the Fifth Ray. That is, the form itself, which is a process of mathematical alignment, is a Fifth Ray activity. Thus, we see that the probationer appropriates and directs this energy into activity, as he aligns his persona and its vehicles with his Spiritual Soul via a mediating focus.

His point of identified focus becomes the mediator between Spirit (as seen from the level of the Spiritual Soul), and matter. Thus, he equates Spirit, matter, and consciousness from his particular level of activity.

In this way he:

1. maintains his residence in the head;

2. controls the forces of his astral-emotional nature;

3. controls, somewhat, the motion of that substance which has coalesced to produce his bodies.

It is now that the probationer realizes in full the need to consciously create the forms his energies shall take as they make their appearance in the Light of Day. Up to this point, he has been content to let evolution, his unconscious, his environment, his neighbors, and finally the Divine Plan as a vague and unknowable something, dictate his experiences, and hence the direction of his energies.

Now he realizes that not only must he submit his will to the Divine Will, but that he must ascertain that Divine Will as well. It becomes his business to know the Divine Plan, and to cooperate with it in full waking consciousness of what he is doing. Thus does he become the manipulator rather than the manipulated.

He achieves this as he aligns (a) Spirit, as his

Lesson 17

Overshadowing Spiritual Soul, with (b) matter, as the substantial force within:

1. his vehicles;

2. his environment;

3. his experience;

through himself as a mediating (meditating) focus.

He draws a line of energy from his Spiritual Soul, to and through himself as a focus in the mental body, to whatever form (be it his bodies, a situation, or condition) with which he is momentarily concerned, thus establishing the perfect alignment between Spirit and matter. In this way, he arrives at a knowledge, and an understanding, of the Purpose of that form; and as he meditates, he impresses Purpose upon the form to alter its appearance according to the Divine Plan.

Using this Fifth Ray technique the probationer learns to create his own time and space, contributes to the One Life in service to Its Plan, and takes the third initiation, passing into the ashram as an accepted disciple.

Continue with the same seed-thought for meditation, and as an assignment please carry out the following technique:

A. First Week

Consciously align the substantial forces of the three-fold instrument with the Overshadowing Spiritual Soul via an identified focus in the mind as the Son. Carry this alignment with you throughout the entire day, endeavoring to cognize and realize it as often as is possible.

B. Second Week

Choose a situation of a negative nature within your environment and align the substantial forces of that situation with the Overshadowing Spiritual Soul via an identified focus in the mind as the Son. Carry the alignment with you through the entire day, endeavoring to cognize and realize it as often as is possible.

C. Third Week

Use the same technique, this time working with a situation of a positive (pleasing) nature within the environment.

D. Fourth Week

Choose a negative condition manifesting within the body of humanity as a whole, and align the substantial forces of that condition with the Divine Plan via an identified focus in the world of mind as the Son. Carry the alignment with you throughout the entire day, endeavoring to cognize and realize it as often as is possible.

At the end of each week write a brief report of the activity.

LESSON 18

The Sixth Ray of Devotion and Ideation:

The Sixth Ray Conditioning of the Past Age;
The Role of the Idea and
its Counterparts of Ideal and Idol;
The Soul as an Idea Unfolding
via Seven Stages of Growth;
Building Right Relationship
with the Sixth Ray as it
Passes Out of Manifestation

LESSON 18

As we look out upon our world today, which is in reality an aggregate of many energies and forces held together in certain fixed relationships by the etheric network of the human family, we see evidence of one particularly predominant ray which colors, and substantiates the whole moving picture of our present civilization. This energy, while it is no longer the major impacting influence, since other energies have overshadowed it, is none the less the major substance and frequency within which humanity moves. Every materialized form is colored by it since the thought–form presentation of the Wisdom which came into being through the Greek philosophers, and by which the experiences of humanity since that time have been determined, was created out of it. This energy, that of the Sixth Ray of Devotion, can almost be called the substantial stuff of which all things in the present period have been made.

Thus, we see that the probationer is concerned with certain impacting energies which are responsible for bringing in the new systems of thought, and hence a new world of form; he is concerned with those energies as they impact upon the already established frequency of the Sixth Ray. This is a most important concept to grasp and understand, for there is a great deal of misunderstanding among students and probationers anent this subject. The so-called passing of the Sixth Ray from the position of major impacting influence does not mean the death of its activity, nor the elimination of it from today's scene. It means only that this energy has created its major effect, both in consciousness and in substance, and can then be added to by other influences as humanity proceeds along the evolutionary way. That already established effect must be dealt with in such a way as to maintain, without distortion, the evolutionary development produced by the impact of the Sixth Ray during the past age.

Thus, the probationer and the disciple in the world of affairs is very much concerned with this energy as a frequency already built into the consciousness of humanity and its many forms.

We tend to think, as the old gives way to the new, that that which already is, must be eliminated; it becomes unwanted and scorned because it is of the past. We fail to realize that it is the past and the future which, in their conjunction, produce the present moment. Therefore, the individual who, in his blindness, fails to take that which is into consideration, and who would too quickly pass from and disregard the realities of the past, moves foolishly in his own little sphere of glamour, being of little use to the Plan he thinks he seeks to serve.

There is a tremendous lesson in this for all those who find themselves consciously taking part in the present crisis of opportunity. While the influence of the Sixth Ray produced a kind of fanaticism, and astralism, which is disgusting to the modern disciple, it also produced a good, and a truth which is beyond description in its beauty. Look into and through the outer crystallization of its negative aspect and observe that beauty if you would understand this energy expression.

The Sixth Ray of Devotion is in its highest aspect the energy of the idea, or ideal of Divinity which is conceived in the consciousness of the Soul. Thus is the Soul endowed with the ability to ideate, i.e., to create a form in consciousness which is an expression of Divine Being.

Plato brought us the concept of Truth in its purity as being found only in the idea, and all manifestations below that level were but distortions or shades of Truth. The energy content of this concept was that of the Sixth

190

Lesson 18

Ray, and Plato, along with others of his group, brought into being the thought–form presentation, which was created by the Lord of that ray to act as the guiding energy for the growth and development of humanity during the past age.

That pure truth can be found only in the idea, cannot be denied by the earnest seeker after it. Beauty is really perceived in the idea of beauty; the truth of the rose is found in the idea of the rose, because that idea is its Soul, the very essence of its form. Thus, all seekers are advised to seek within, if they would truly enter into the Kingdom of God.

We begin to see the Soul itself from a somewhat different light as we make an approach to it via the Sixth Ray of Ideation. We have defined the Soul in many terms in an effort to understand what it is. We have called it the Second Logos, the consciousness aspect, the magnetic field created between the polar opposites of Divinity, etc.

Now we say that the Soul is the idea of Spirit conceived within the womb of matter and born forth into the world of form as the consciousness of God, in seven stages of growth.

1.	Infancy	animal man	individualization
2.	Childhood	astral man	completely emotional in nature
3.	Puberty	mental man	the partially integrated self-conscious unit
4.	Adolescence	devotional aspirational man	Soul-infused persona
5.	Youth	group conscious	mastery - Christ
6.	Middle Age	Planetary and Solar consciousness	Logoic
7.	Spiritual maturity	Solar and Cosmic Consciousness	Centered Logoic

The Nature of The Soul

As the personality unit becomes Soul conscious, or Soul impressed, he finds himself perceiving the world of ideas, i.e., the truths he has long been seeking, oft'times called the Ageless Wisdom. To these ideas, or ideals as they later become, he directs his devotion, attempting to embody them into a living manifestation of truth. Thus, he makes his conscious approach to God via the Sixth Ray of Devotion to an ideal.

Later, as the personality unit is merged with the consciousness of the Overshadowing Spiritual Soul, he perceives these ideas as being in, and of, that Soul.

The Soul evolves as it ideates the overshadowing impression of the Christ into its own consciousness, setting into motion those Divine Ideas which are its radiatory activity. As that radiatory activity expands, as it gains in spiritual potency, it catches or lifts the personality unit up into the periphery of its own sphere, where the two are merged (Soul and persona, or idea and its expression) to re-incarnate again into the brain as a whole being—the self-conscious (group conscious) son or unit of God.

Thus, the Sixth Ray is concerned with that which can only be defined as the idea of wisdom. Here is wisdom in its essence, a differentiated expression of the Second Ray of Divine Love-Wisdom.

Here also is the great philosopher, the seeker after truth, who, perceiving the idea, moves into a world so vastly different from that of form that he is truly in, but not of, the form.

Would we pass too quickly from this energy expression? Would we fail to perceive and carry with us that which it has built into the consciousness of humanity during the past age? The very idea of God, and Gods, of beauty, harmony, and truth itself, is basically an expression of the Sixth Ray. Humanity has perceived the idea of the good, the true, and the beautiful, and has responded to that idea. God help us to maintain it during this next era of logic and reason, of magic and order. Let it be the foundation from which our logic, reason, magic, and order may proceed.

As these new energies impact upon that which is already built in, they naturally produce a conflict in which the old form is disintegrated. This is a necessary manifestation in the evolutionary process, and it could be a painless one if the consciousness involved would detach sufficiently from the form to maintain the idea which is Truth. When the form is seen as the importance, the idea is lost as the form goes down in the face of the new impact.

We look about us in the world today and we see many appearances, some loved, others hated. These appearances are of such a fast changing countenance that we hardly know them from one year to the next. Many are disintegrating, disappearing before our very eyes. As we watch all of this, we tend to react in one of two ways:

1. to mourn the lost form, seeking solace in grief,

2. or to scorn it as being old and outworn, a false thing of the past.

Either way is a manifestation of personal attachment to the form, and in both the idea is lost.

We see this taking place particularly in the religious world as the conflict between the new energies of Science and the older, more stable energy of Religion destroy the form.

What can the probationer do to be of service during this crucial period in the growth and development of humanity?

The Nature of The Soul

Above all, he can understand. He can observe the truths which were the motivations behind the present religious structure, and which are again the same motivations behind the new era of science. He can see these truths in their essential reality and make his peace with both energy expressions of them. Thus, he becomes a peacemaker in an era of conflict; a custodian of Light, of Wisdom. His thoughts, his feelings, and his words can carry the energy of healing, which again is the energy of Wisdom, and so seal the cleavage, heal the breach between Science and Religion.

The disciple who is wise never speaks out against a religious form truth has taken, but rather he breathes forth that truth in such purity that the old form is not mourned. He points out and reveals that synthesis which is the same truth in both the old and the new and so points the way of progress.

Such are needed in this time of conflict when the minds and hearts of humanity are sorely troubled. There are many young disciples in the world today; many probationers who seek entry into the Fifth kingdom. Their task is clearly set forth for them. The need of their time is obvious, for they can, in a united effort, so seek for and enunciate Truth, as to pierce the veil of confusion blinding the eyes of humanity.

As you move in the world of form, and as you observe both the old and the new, seek truth in the idea. Look past the form to that idea which is its Soul, its cause, in order to preserve and perpetuate the good, the true, and the beautiful gained in the past. Thus is that error which sends humanity into the experience of the dark ages avoided during a new cycle.

> Let your new seed-thought for meditation be a *receptivity to the Divine Ideas of the overshadowing Soul, before they have taken form.*

194

Lesson 18

As an assignment, please write your understanding of the Sixth Ray of devotion, using both the lesson material and the meditation technique in an approach to it. Bring this paper with you to the next class.

The Nature of The Soul

LESSON 19

The Opposites of Sixth Ray
and its Impact on The Instrument:

The Opposites as Seen in
Present World Religions;
The Energy of One-Pointedness
vs. Fanaticism;
Glamours of the Sixth Ray

LESSON 19

The pairs of opposites, as we see them manifest in the world today, are largely the result of the Sixth Ray as it has worked out into expression via humanity, the Planetary throat center.

Jesus, the Lord of the Sixth Ray, brought the idea of love down into a focus within the body of humanity, where it could be seized upon and consciously wielded for the betterment of mankind. He translated the idea into a doctrine of love, which, if rightly interpreted and applied, would take the self-conscious personality unit up to the portals of initiation. The consciousness of humanity has been given both the energy and the technique which will expand it from a separated self, into an all inclusive, conscious part of the One Life.

Christianity, the great advocate and follower of Master Jesus, has done very little actually, to further this goal. It has pursued a course of devotion to the ideal which it translated from the idea, but that ideal has been largely a misinterpretation, producing the polar opposite of love in the minds and hearts of its persons.

Thus, we find that mass of humanity which calls itself Christian and accepts Jesus, The Christ, as its Savior, expressing hate and prejudice, even today, in its attempt to dominate the world with its religion. Here the would-be disciples of The Christ perpetuated wars (both cold and hot), inflicted untold and uncounted cruelties upon their own kin and others, and poisoned the multitudes with a hatred so evil as to endanger the very life of humanity itself. And all of this in the Name of The Christ, who is the very Being of Love.

The Nature of The Soul

If these words seem harsh, it is because they speak a truth which is difficult to face. This thought–form presentation of The Wisdom is particularly related to Christianity, and many of those who find themselves karmically related to it have contributed to the Christian way of life. Christianity itself cannot be blamed, but only those of us who have made, and continue to make it, what it is.

This religious form will not, and is not meant to, break up and disintegrate before our eyes. It yet has a mission to fulfill, and must right the wrongs it has committed before that mission can even be realized. Many of its antiquated forms will disappear, but Christianity itself is destined for a rebirth which will manifest the doctrine of Love as the Master Jesus gave it.

Many of you who are attracted to this course of instruction as probationers will reenter the field of Christianity as serving disciples in this life or the next. Thus will the Sixth Ray of Devotion demonstrate its true expression as a built-in quality of the human consciousness and instrument.

Let us observe more closely both the positive and negative expressions of this energy for further clarification.

The Sixth Ray produces a devotion to an ideal, which in its positive manifestation is a one-pointed direction toward spiritual enlightenment and embodiment. It is the energy of Buddha, of Light, as that Light seeks its source via the curve from matter to Spirit. Thus, the seeker lifts the Light of matter into a frequency which is in harmony with the Light of Spirit in order to know Truth.

Such a one is in love with wisdom. His whole nature yearns toward spiritual understanding, and will not permit him rest until that understanding is attained.

200

Lesson 19

Thus is the philosopher born to travel the byways of mind until the path is seen and taken which leads away from form into the very heart of consciousness.

It is little wonder that the world, and even the bodies, have been neglected by seekers of the past age. The influence of the Sixth Ray was such as to give man the perfect way of, and justification for, his desire to escape. The form was seen as a prison which must be left behind before truth could really be known. Socrates, one of the focal points through which this energy made its impact upon humanity, demonstrated this expression of it in his welcome of death, and his pronouncement of the body as "the enemy of the philosopher."

Christianity, with its condemnation of sex, its puritanism, and its many distortions as to what constitutes good and bad, demonstrated this particular expression of the Sixth Ray on an even lower level of emotional interpretation.

The eastern world responded with a rigid system of self-denial, which led to such a decadence in the world of affairs that only violent revolution could manifest as the new energies impacted upon the crystallized energies within the present form.

The new truth to impact upon the consciousness of humanity, as the Seventh Ray comes into prominence, will be formulated as follows:

1. Truth is in the idea which is the Soul of form (Sixth Ray),

2. But that truth must be brought down into appearance in order to manifest *perfection in form* (Seventh Ray).

The modern philosopher will advocate a system of

thought which is designed to bring heaven to earth, while the philosopher of the past advocated a system of thought designed to escape the earth and its forms for an indefinable heaven elsewhere.

In this way two facets of Truth are brought together to reveal a more perfect goal of attainment. The form, as well as the Soul, is seen as being endowed with a Divine Purpose, which can only be revealed as the duality of Soul and form is fused into a oneness. The form then, is but a vehicle within and through which the idea can be expressed.

The bodily senses are seen as having been divinely created, and when properly aligned with the Soul they will become the outpicturing of the Soul's perceptive faculty, rather than a snare and a delusion from which the Soul must escape.

As the energy of the Sixth Ray, the attribute of ideation on Soul levels, impacts upon the probationer disciple, his devotional nature is stimulated and he begins to build his ideal of the Soul.

Looking about for a pattern after which to fashion his ideal, he will usually discover some individual who personifies his subconscious picture of that ideal. This individual, as a personality, then becomes the object of his devotion and he wants more than anything else in the world to be like the idealized one. Incidentally, he also desires, with great intensity, to be accepted by the individual and will do all that is in his power to bring about such acceptance.

We find many probationers, particularly in the past, patterned this ideal after Jesus of Nazareth. In doing this, they became devoted to the personality rather than to the Christ of Jesus, and so were lost to Truth.

Lesson 19

Others pattern their ideal after a teacher or friend, and in so doing build such a glamour around the whole subject that it becomes their goal of attainment. It is then necessary for the probationer to undergo the painful experience of disillusion before Truth can be approached via an undistorted ideal.

Probationers must learn not to expect and demand perfection from their teachers, for the form aspect is not yet perfect, and cannot be, until the total substance of the three planes of human endeavor has been lifted far higher than its present frequency. Even Jesus of Nazareth, in the form aspect, made mistakes. His persona was not perfect, though many believe it was. This failure to recognize and accept the imperfection of a leader not only leads to glamour, but leads as well to an inability to seek beyond that glamour for a higher truth. The masses justified their Holy Wars by an act of violence in which Jesus beat the money changers out of the temple. This was a mistake and He knew it was, but the mass, who could not accept an imperfection within their Saviour, closed their eyes to the Truth of His message. That message was one of Love, of forgiveness, of non-violence.

In fashioning your ideal, pattern it after the idea. Build your own form, that which most perfectly conveys and reveals the idea. This is your contribution to the Divine Plan in this time and place.

The probationer builds his ideal of the Soul as a state of consciousness on mental levels, as a condition or quality on astral levels, and as an expression in activity on physical levels.

The state of consciousness will contain those ideas which are the Truths he has attained via his focus in the mental body and his alignment with his higher Self, the formulation of those ideas into thoughts, and the assemblage of the thought-forms into a planned service activity.

The condition or quality on astral levels will be a particular tone (according to his ray makeup) of Love. It will not, and must not, be expected to be the same for all individuals, and probationers must realize and accept this fact. One's tonal quality of Love may manifest as a quiet strength in times of trouble, or as a brilliance of radiating beauty, or an expression of affection and understanding.

The expression in activity will consist of the service plan, and will manifest in all of the outer affairs of the persona. It will also be stamped into and upon the form itself, be carried in the voice and gesture, and be revealed in the inner response mechanism.

The modern probationer must learn to direct his devotion to the Plan, rather than the focal points through which the Plan is brought into relation with humanity. Therefore, do not make the mistake of becoming devoted to a teacher, a member of the Hierarchy, or even one of the Great Ones, but rather devote yourself to the manifestation of the Divine Plan.

Please continue with the same seed-thought for meditation.

LESSON 20

The Incoming Seventh Ray of Divine Law & Order:

The Meaning of the "New Age" Clarified;
The Conflict Between the Outgoing
Sixth Ray "Thought-Forms" and the
Incoming Seventh Ray "Thought-Forms";
The Polar Opposites of Seventh Ray Energy;
White vs. Black Magic and the Temptation
to Create from a Separated Point of View

LESSON 20

The rapidly integrating new group of conscious serving disciples in the world today is faced with facilitating one of the major evolutionary changes to be brought about in the growth and development of humanity. Truly, in this present moment does the future meet the past to produce a crisis of opportunity unparalleled in human history.

The crisis is one of transition, in which those decisions are made, and those patterns constructed, which will determine the experiences of the next twenty–five hundred years.

There are many who look toward the "New Age" with hope that its coming will bring the spiritual values so lacking in the human consciousness today. They await this "New Age" as they would await a miracle, failing to realize that it is upon us now and that the changes it brings are opportunities.

This is a point which demands clarification, for to await a miracle is to compress the lips, shake the head, and refuse to accept the opportunity proffered.

The New Age is. We have already entered into it, and its meaning is simply this: that new energies and forces are impacting upon the mass consciousness and its many forms of expression, which, as they impact, produce a condition of instability within the consciousness, the form, and hence the world of affairs. This condition of instability can be likened unto the first two years of a child's life, in which the mold is set for the directional flow of his energies throughout the life experience of this incarnation.

The Nature of The Soul

In other words, the so-called New Age has incarnated, and is now in that phase of growth which will determine its characteristics and qualities for the twenty–five hundred years that are its life cycle.

This means that humanity stands at the crossroads, the forked path of decision, with the responsibility as the Planetary throat center, of making those decisions which will manifest God's plan on earth during this New Age.

If the higher spiritual values are to be worked out in human affairs, if the path of return is to be taken which leads back to God, and if The Christ is to make His Reappearance during this cycle, it will have been because humanity seized the opportunity to build into this transitory period the mold of the long–awaited Golden Age.

Thus is the new group of conscious, serving disciples faced with a tremendous challenge, for upon them falls the task of awakening, guiding, and inspiring humanity to the spiritual facts of life. The fact of the crossroads, the choices confronting them, and the way of Light has to be so clearly enunciated and placed before humanity that the mass consciousness can build in the necessary new response mechanism.

Contrary to the condition of the past, we find human consciousness today demonstrating a fluidity which renders the mass receptive to almost any new pattern of thought which might be inflicted upon it. Change is a constant reality, and receptivity to change is the present reality. All too soon this transitory period will pass, and the forms created will become the guiding factors for the experiences to come. The fluidic and unstable consciousness of the young child (New Age) will have been molded to a pattern, and his growth and development affected via that pattern.

Lesson 20

The new group of disciples can be likened unto the parents of the child who dictate the pattern of the mold according to their response to the environment (in this case the world of affairs) and their treatment of the child within that environment.

The disciple, then, is concerned not only with the pairs of opposites as they have been built into the consciousness via the energies of the past, but with the pairs of opposites which are potential within the newly impacting energies.

The energy of the Sixth Ray brought the philosopher, the man of God, into being during the past age. It also brought into being the fanatic, the devotee who would escape the form and hence his spiritual obligation for the sake of the separated self.

Consider the potential pairs of opposites of the Seventh Ray which necessitates attention to form.

The Sixth Ray necessitates attention to Spirit, while the seventh redirects that attention back into the world of matter.

The Seventh Ray is the energy of Spirit, of Will, as that Will seeks manifestation via the curve from Spirit to matter.

The Seventh Ray is, in its higher aspect, the reflection of Spirit in matter.

Right use of this energy, then, works out into manifestation via Divine Law and Order, and Ceremonial Magic, the Will of God. The result is perfection in form.

The polar opposite of this, i.e., misuse of Seventh Ray, is the working out into manifestation via ceremonial

The Nature of The Soul

magic of the personal will of the separated persona. The result is the manifestation of desired forms with no thought as to what God's Will might intend.

The discovery by humanity, which is rapidly developing, of mental substance as being the prime matter, and of the Will as the magical force which directs that matter into a specific appearance in form, will bring the forked path of decision out into the open.

In addition to the above, discovery will immediately follow of the knowledge of techniques, i.e., the way in which Spirit and matter, or will and mind, are manipulated by the consciousness to produce a predetermined effect in the world of affairs. Hence, we are moving into an age of magic in which all effects will be consciously created via white or black magic.

This brings one to a moment of pause and deep consideration. If the mass consciousness is now living in terror of such a threat as the bomb, think of what its terror, its hopelessness, would be if a like threat could be produced by the manipulation of will and mind. This will be the nature of the battle of Armageddon at the end of this New Age, unless the balance of power can be shifted from the dark forces of ignorance and materialism to the Light forces of Wisdom and Spiritualism.

The Seventh Ray as an attribute of the Soul is simply the ability of consciousness to precipitate its intent into form.

This energy in its right use, i.e., when rightly motivated, invokes Divine Law into activity to produce Divine Order in manifestation.

The probationer disciple is faced with one of the major trials of initiation as this energy begins to impact upon him. The very secrets of God, speaking occultly, become known to him, and the forces of creation are made

210

available to him. To what use shall he put them?

Here is the great moment of temptation symbolized by the story of Jesus as he was tempted by Satan.

Who and what is this devil who would dare to tempt The Christ? He was the Dweller on the Threshold, the sum total of consciousness identified with form who would pursue the nature of that form.

This so-called devil rose up from within the personality of Jesus to do battle with the Christ, and Jesus said, "Get thee behind me, Satan," meaning, I, the conscious Son of God, will lead the way, you must follow.

Such temptation comes when the whole consciousness, spiritually and materially identified, is faced with the realization of Power. No matter how oriented to the Divine Plan, or how rightly motivated, such a realization arouses that sleeping Dweller (separated self) with its silent voice of temptation.

The man suddenly realizes that he is a creator, that by a simple manipulation of Will and Intelligence, he can produce what-so-ever form he will choose.

Consider the effect upon the subconscious wish-life, upon the past ambitions and dreams which have yet to be fulfilled, upon the sense of ego itself.

It is easy to renounce ambitions and desires which have little hope of fulfillment insofar as the consciousness is concerned. But what of the moment when that consciousness realizes that it can carry out any course of action, any ambition or desire it may choose, when the world is offered as its toy, its pleasure?

The inflow of Seventh Ray always brings into manifestation such a crisis, which is the crisis of opportunity, for it offers the opportunity of initiation, initiation into the White or the Black Lodge.

Every probationer faces this trial, and humanity en-masse faces it on a lower level of the spiral, as the Seventh Ray comes into incarnation as the predominating energy of the Age.

Therefore, we see this period in human history as one which is of great importance, where the experience pattern by which the growth and development of consciousness is affected, can undergo a shift from negative to positive.

If humanity can choose the right–hand path which is the way of the disciple, if the world of affairs can be made to reflect the spiritual values, humanity will no longer need to know anguish and pain in order to grow. The experience pattern which produces growth can shift from hate to love, from war to peace, from an era of conflict to one of harmony.

The deep cleavages in consciousness, the psychological maladjustments, the environmental imprisonments of individuals and groups, all can be healed and a Golden Age of the Soul truly appear on the face of the earth.

Between now and the end of this century, humanity will invoke or reject the appearance of The Christ by its choice.

Actually, the Hierarchy and its group of conscious, serving disciples see no choice. The decision has already been made by them, and the work goes forward. But, for the probationer, and the mass, the energy of decision yet remains to be wielded and the work to be initiated.

As you invoke the energy of the Seventh Ray into your consciousness and instrument during the coming week, keep in mind this crisis of opportunity.

212

Lesson 20

The Seventh Ray of Divine Law and Order is the precipitation of Spirit (Will) into matter (mind). Thus is told the whole story of this remarkable energy.

> Let your seed-thought for meditation be a *receptivity to that precipitating Will from the level of the Overshadowing Spiritual Soul into your consciousness, and in turn a further precipitation of Divine Will into the substantial forces of your bodies via your mind.*

Please bring a written copy of your understanding of the Seventh Ray to the next class.

The Nature of The Soul

LESSON 21

The Seventh Ray and Ceremonial Magic:

Ceremonial Magic as it Works
in the Three Lower Worlds
as Energy, Force, and Substance;
The Appropriation of Energy and
Direction of Force
as it Impacts Substance;
Diseases of Disciples
due to Misuse of this Process;
The Use of Will in Relation to
Seventh Ray Form Building;
Seventh Ray as it Impacts
the Instrument

LESSON 21

As the Seventh Ray comes into predominance in the world of affairs, disciples will find themselves recipient of an energy so potent and so powerful that unless care is taken its impact will produce great disturbance within the inner psyche, the bodies, and the environment. The disciple must learn to direct this energy as a power potential into a force which is in perfect harmony with the Plan he seeks to serve.

In order to better understand this, let us apparently digress for a few moments to the consideration of energy, force, and substance.

Energy, force, and substance are terms used to define the same essence in varying stages of activity. Because of the lack of better terminology we shall define this essence as Life.

The Life Essence in its free state is defined as Energy, i.e., potential power, potential activity, potential expression.

It is derived from the Will to Be and in one sense can be said to be the Will of The Logos sounding forth within His ring-pass-not.

Energy, then, in its highest aspect is potential Life or the Will to Be.

It is then differentiated into seven potential expressions which are defined as the seven rays. These seven rays in their energy forms are seven potencies, or seven power potentials for the expression of Life or the Will to Be in Love or Reason.

When this same Life Essence is appropriated and directed along a path of least resistance into manifestation, i.e., imprisoned within form, it has become force. Force is that potential which has been excited into expression.

When this same Life Essence coalesces and liquifies, we have substance, which is energy and force in its most dense state in any frequency range; thus, the three worlds of human endeavor make their appearance in mental, astral, and so-called physical substance.

Any appearance in form is constructed of the energy, force, and substance which characterize the frequency ranges upon which it (the form) is found. There are then within any form:

1. Energy or Potential . . . . . uninitiated cause
2. Force . . . . cause in expression
3. Substance . . . . appearance or effect.

Energies in the strict sense of the word are either overshadowing or latent potentials, the impulses of which activate the consciousness into a greater awareness. When a man, acting under such an impulse, seizes available energy in order to perform some activity, he consciously or unconsciously:

1. Invokes a higher law which directs free energy into a specific pattern (path of least resistance) through his own vehicles.

   This energy, immediately upon entering the path of least resistance through his bodies, becomes force.

2. With the focused third eye, he maintains the steady flow of force in its predetermined pattern

throughout the vehicles, thus producing in time and space

3. An effect in substance, i.e., the manifestation of energy and force into substantial form.

It is interesting to note here that the ills of disciples are the result of three major causes:

1. Misappropriated energy as a result of wrong motivation, thus precipitating into the vehicles force which cannot be safely handled.

2. Appropriated, but not rightly directed energy, which creates an erroneous flow of force throughout the system, bringing imbalance into the center system, the glands, and finally the organic functions of the body.

3. The inability to complete the path of least resistance for the flow of force into final manifestation (due to an undeveloped third eye), thus creating what is erroneously referred to as energy blocks. They are actually force blocks which dam the flow of force in one or another of the bodies, producing congestion in time and space.

The Seventh Ray is a reflection of Spirit (The Divine Will) in substance. As an energy, it is that potential which makes possible the creative act of the will to produce a specific form in time and space. Thus, the disciple, and the humanity who is recipient of an inflow of Seventh Ray energy, find themselves in possession of a creative will. This is their Power potential.

As a force, the Seventh Ray has become a powerful activity which moves cyclically to produce the manifestation or appearance of all forms which find existence within the consciousness.

Remember, this expression as an attribute of the Soul is the ability of consciousness to manifest its intent in form. Hence, the impact of this energy gives will power, or intent, to all forms the consciousness entertains, which then moves as a powerful force within the bodies to produce its effect in substance.

Consider the consciousness of the average probationer. It is filled with contradictions and conflicts. Forms exist within the subconscious which are in direct opposition to those truths the probationer is attempting to embody. Both are given the potential power of expression as the Seventh Ray makes its impact, and the result is a manifestation of both in conflict in the outer life and affairs.

The poor, bewildered probationer is beset with every kind of a manifestation he has ever imagined, and many he is not consciously aware of having even considered. The more persistently he attempts to discipline his form-nature, the more violent its opposition as it receives the power to manifest its responses. The more persistently he attempts to manifest the Plan as he sees it, the more opposition to that Plan he sets into motion without consciously realizing that he does so. He manifests most of his own obstacles to successful service out of an ignorance of the Law.

This continues until such time as his consciousness can be illumined with the fact that as he seeks to serve the Plan, he is recipient of the precipitating energies of the Plan, and as those energies impact upon him, he directs them into his vehicles as force via all that lies formulated within his consciousness.

A man thinks, and according to his thought, he directs those energies and forces which are his to control into a specific pattern which we call a thought–form.

A man feels, and according to his feeling, he releases

into the form he has created the power to manifest.

A man speaks, and according to his spoken word, the empowered form is directed into time and space.

When this three-fold activity is entered into consciously, with intent to manifest a specific effect in the world of affairs, it is called ceremonial magic. Whether it is white or black magic is dependent upon the man's motive, the reason why he creates.

This Seventh Ray activity is consciously initiated as a man becomes mentally polarized; as he realizes the positive and negative polarity of his constitution; and as he ascertains the purpose of his three-fold instrument.

His will, which is analogous to and is an extension of Spirit, is positive to his mind, which is analogous to and is an extension of prime matter. The will in the mind, or Spirit in matter, is positive to the substantial forces of the three-fold instrument.

Thus, the manipulation of will and mind results in outer manifestation; is the key to the creative process; and is the activity entered into by all mentally polarized persons.

The purpose of the three-fold instrument is very easily seen once its polarity is understood. It constitutes the matter aspect and is negative to the Will in the following pattern:

Positive		Negative
Will	—	Mind or mental body
Will in the mind	—	Astral - emotional
		Etheric - physical
		Outer sphere of influence

The Nature of The Soul

Will in the mind then becomes:

Force or Power in the astral,

Life; activity; or the movement of force in the etheric and appearance in form.

Thus, we see the purpose of the three-fold instrument as being the vehicles through which the creative process of the consciousness can take place. These bodies enable the Soul to create a specific effect in substance.

The probationer disciple learns that his mental, astral, and etheric bodies are for the purpose of manifesting God's Plan on earth via the creative act of embodiment.

As the probationer becomes conscious of the Seventh Ray crisis, the disturbance described in the foregoing, he sets out to discover what he can do about it; and he very quickly learns that he must begin to assert his mastery over his own form-nature via an act of the creative will.

It is at this period in his development that he becomes painfully aware of the dark forces, and their active opposition to the Plan he seeks to serve. He is conscious of being the recipient of so-called attacks, little realizing that in many cases he is the source of his own attack, and at times a focal point through which the dark forces work.

This is a subject of great importance to him, one about which there is much confusion, glamour, and misinterpretation. He has to undergo a rather hurried and marked expansion of consciousness before light can illumine the dark areas of his awareness. In the meantime, he is sorely in need of techniques with which to calm the disturbances and protect himself from the effects of black magic, whether of his own making or that of another.

He may seek to enter into the protection of his ashram by visualizing himself within the auric radiation of its light, plus an invocation in times of crisis, of pure white light from Hierarchial levels into his bodies via his head center.

This will afford him protection from outside impact, but the most important technique for him to use during this period is that which will protect others, as well as the Plan he seeks to serve, from any mistakes which he might be making, and from the harmful effects of his own form nature which he has not yet brought under control.

When the probationer experiences intense emotional reactions, such as resentment, condemnatory criticism, depression, futility, etc., he is a focal point through which the dark forces attack his brothers. He is for that moment a part of the opposition to the very Plan he seeks to serve.

Since probationers have not as yet perfected their consciousness or their bodies, they should proceed with caution to receive and give direction to the inflowing energies.

Here are a few protective techniques the probationer can use effectively whenever he realizes a need for them.

1. When you are experiencing an emotional reaction which you cannot for the moment control—

   Flood the aura with Light and Love which will transmute the forces as they leave your ring-pass-not. This is exceedingly important. While you may not be able to work directly with that pattern within the response mechanism which is giving you difficulty, you can eliminate its harmful effects upon others in this way.

At the same time, try to maintain a cheerful countenance to others, even though the battle rages within. Recognize that battle and deal with it when and as you can, but do everything within your power to protect those with whom you have a subjective and an objective relationship.

If necessary invoke the will of the Soul to manifest harm-less-ness in your vibratory impacts.

2. When you are formulating a specific plan of activity —

Realize that you are not yet fully trained in the science of impression, and, therefore, you may, or may not, be correctly interpreting the Plan. Always qualify any meditation which is entered into for the purpose of manifesting an effect in substance (any effect in the outer world of affairs) with the following mantric statement:

"If this be according to Divine Intent, then let it manifest in Divine Law and Order."

3. When you are broadcasting concepts of truth on mental levels —

Your realization may or may not be correctly interpreted, therefore permeate it with light. If it is a truth it will stand; if not, it will disintegrate and cannot then mislead another.

It is wisdom to do this with all opinions you may have formulated, as a general practice.

4. As a general early morning practice to be carried out either before or after your regular meditation, you may *invoke the Divine Will of the Soul to guide you in the path of harm-less-ness and to protect your associates from any harmful influence you might unknowingly wield.*

The probationer who is sincere in his conscious aspiration to be of service will practice the above techniques as a matter of course.

More information on this subject of magic will follow. In the meantime, please continue with the same seed–thought for meditation.

The Nature of The Soul

LESSON 22

Service and Its Relationship to the Ashrams:

Specifications of Service Activities
as they Relate to the Seven Ray Ashrams;
Power Potential to Serve Based on
your "Position" Within
the Ashramic Group Life;
The "Offices" of Ashramic Auric Influence
and Peripheral Manifestation

LESSON 22

As the probationer disciple consciously prepares himself for initiation, three subjects of great importance to him at this point demand his attention almost simultaneously. These subjects appear at first to be unrelated and almost incomprehensible to his present brain awareness, yet they are placed before him as the next field of knowledge which he must explore and master in order to attain further growth. They are:

1. His peculiar ray makeup, and hence his group relationship to the Plan.

2. His chosen field of service.

3. The Art and Science of Magic, providing him with those techniques which make his chosen service possible.

Since each of these subjects is a vast field of knowledge in itself, we shall consider them consecutively in the order of their importance to the probationer, covering as much as is possible in so short a work.

He must discover first the ray upon which his Soul is functioning. This will clarify to him his potentials insofar as Purpose, Power, and Will are concerned.

His purpose as a Soul is linked to the ray group of which he is a member, revealing, therefore, that aspect of the Plan with which he is generally related.

The ray groups are related to the Plan in the following manner:

The Nature of The Soul

1. The First Ray—via Government

2. The Second Ray—via Education and more specifically the teaching of the Wisdom

3. The Third Ray—via civilization through
   a. inventive and creative genius
   b. the economic structure
   c. organization at top levels

4. The Fourth Ray—via the balance of Power through
   a. culture
   b. international relationships including peace and war
   c. social standards and behaviorisms

5. The Fifth Ray—via Science

6. The Sixth Ray—via Religion and Philosophy, or in the coming age via attitude and ideation

7. The Seventh Ray—via civilization through the wise manipulation of the form in the fields of
   a. Law and Government
   b. Education
   c. Organization and Economy   *culture*
   d. Sociology
   e. Occultology
   f. Religion and Philosophy
   g. Parapsychology, Psychiatry, and Spiritual Alchemy

A disciple's power potential is released to him, according to his particular place within his ray group, as he assumes the responsibility of that place and cooperates with the group.

In other words, his service activity is dependent upon his position within the ashramic group life and not upon his personality likes and dislikes. His power potential to be of service as a conscious disciple is released to him only as he accepts that particular position and sets out to serve his ashramic office.

This is a most important concept and one which is oft overlooked by the would-be disciple. Each has built up a glamour around the concept of service according to his emotional evaluation of it. He considers what he shall or shall not do; arrives at what he thinks he is particularly fitted to do from an astral polarization based upon his likes or dislikes. He forgets that his Soul has evolved to a specific point of development which may or may not be apparent in the persona, and that according to that point of development will be determined his position in the ashramic group life, i.e., the office of service for which he is responsible in relationship to that aspect of the Plan shared by the group membership.

Is this not a somewhat new and different concept of discipleship than the one contemplated by most of you? And does it not reveal a glimpse of a plan so vast and yet so perfect that each individual tone and color of the One Life finds its perfect expression within its particular field of relationships?

An ashramic group life exists in the consciousness of its membership, yet it is a reality. Each member holds a particular office in relationship to each other member and the humanity they collectively serve. Each moves, as his point of development evolves, from the aura of the ashram into and through its periphery, from its periphery through its sphere and into its center and through that center into the Hierarchy itself. Each member then moves from office to office assuming the responsibility of each consecutively until his karmic debt to humanity has been absolved and he stands free to choose his path of service to the Cosmic Christ.

What are some of these offices?

Only two in their generalities concern you at the moment. These are:

1. The office of Ashramic Auric Influence.

This office is held by all those probationers, each in his specific place, who constitute the aura of the ashram. In other words, they have been attracted into the magnetic radiatory field of the ashram, and as they orbit in that field outside of the periphery, they constitute its auric influence in the three lower worlds. Their task is mainly to carry and transmit the tonal quality of the ashram into their own particular sphere of influence. They do so via their right aspiration to be of service, their established alignment with the ashram, and their application of its principles in their daily lives.

Probationers who hold this office are consciously preparing themselves for the third initiation.

2. The office of Peripheral Manifestation.

This office is held by all of those probationers who are in the process of piercing the periphery. Their task is to transmit, via the aura, those higher potencies both in energy and concept form with which they are being impacted, into the etheric network of humanity. They are in the process of taking the third initiation, completing it as they successfully initiate their chosen service activity and move inside of the periphery as an accepted disciple of the Hierarchy. They must, via their subjective and objective service, manifest from the periphery some little aspect of the Plan in the life and affairs of humanity.

A disciple's creative will, that is the Divine Will of his Soul, is released to him as he develops that invocative strength which invokes into his consciousness the relationship of the group service potential to a specific time and place.

Here again is a somewhat new concept as regards service, yet it has been stated often that the disciple responds to the need of his times.

Not all of the service potential of an ashramic group, or of a disciple, can be made manifest at any one time, except in periods of extreme human crisis, for much of that potential would be premature.

The disciple has, then, to cooperate with the Plan by activating that creative potential which is relative to the point of development achieved by humanity in his time and place.

This the Master Jesus so well demonstrated in His life on earth as Jesus of Nazareth. Much of His creative potential had to be held in check until humanity could safely respond and cooperate with it.

One other point here in regard to the creative will. This potential is gradually released as the disciple in the brain begins to invoke into his personality expression the point of development achieved by the Soul in Its own sphere.

As we recapitulate the foregoing, we realize that much new knowledge, actually in the nature of a minor illumination, is released into the brain awareness with the discovery of the ray of the Soul.

With that knowledge comes the Soul Purpose as it relates to Group Purpose. The probationer discovers the general field of service toward which his Soul has long been preparing to enter, and within which he will work incarnation after incarnation until he has finally achieved to mastery. At long last he knows, and he can begin to see from that perspective which envisions a service plan from its end to its beginning, over a whole cycle of incarnations. He is planning a contribution which will require not just one short lifetime to complete, but many. He is initiating a contribution to the One Life which will evolve with his own consciousness, with that of his group, and with humanity.

He will be illumined with his point of Soul development, and begin to realize the invocation of that development (the incarnation of his Spiritual Soul) into his persona. He will not only become aware of his ashramic group, but of his place within that group. He will realize his relationship to, and, therefore, his alignment with, the Hierarchy, and can begin to cooperate with it.

His power potential for service will be released to him as he assumes the responsibility of his particular office. He will then be enabled to manifest an influence for good within the body of humanity.

His brain will be flooded with illumination in regard to the need of humanity in this time and place, enabling him by an act of the will to relate the Plan to that need. His will has become the Divine Will because it is perfectly aligned with and oriented to the focused will of the Plan.

This brings us to the realization that a technique whereby the ray of the Soul can be ascertained, is necessary before the probationer can advance very far into a realized manifestation of all the foregoing. We shall discuss such a technique in the next lesson. In the

Lesson 22

meantime, use the following seed–thought in your daily meditation.

> "Build an altar in the form of a cross in the cave in the center of the head, and there place the persona, as an indication of your willingness to accept the Divine Intent of your Soul. Do not, in this preparatory work, attempt to discover that Intent, but rather meditate upon the act of willingness symbolized in the sacrificial ceremony above."

A complete sacrifice of conscious reservation is a prerequisite to the illumination described in the foregoing.

The Nature of The Soul

LESSON 23

Creation of the Ashrams and Alignment:

The Appearance of the Planetary Logos
in Time and Space;
The "Birth" (or Individualization)
of the Seven Kingdoms;
The "Birth" of the Ashrams;
The "Birth" of Humanity
and the Evolutionary Process
of Identification;
The Role and Use of Alignment
in Determining Your Soul Ray

2 Ray
LOVE/Wisdom

1 2 3 4 5 6 7

238

LESSON 23

We have stated elsewhere in this course of instruction that the Father of our Christian Bible is the Planetary Logos; that a man's will is an extension of God's Will; that his purpose is contained within the larger Purpose; and that his power is the power of Logoic Intent.

It is via an understanding of this concept, and a consequent alignment with the Source of the Spiritual Soul, that the applicant to initiation is enabled to reach an awareness of that Intent which has empowered him into being; the Purpose originating on Logoic levels for his appearance in time and space.

The Planetary Logos, functioning from His level of identified focus, differentiates the ray of light upon which He is evolving into seven energy expressions via His own seven-fold consciousness.

In order to clearly understand this concept, the student must clear his mind of all preconceived or limiting ideas he may be entertaining in regard to the meaning underlying such terms as identified focus, consciousness, Planetary Logos, etc. We tend to define, and thus limit, a concept in those terms which express a familiar experience within our own tiny sphere of awareness.

The Planetary Logos functioning within His own level of identified focus is not one person (if I might use so inadequate a term), but seven persons in one. This is what is meant by His seven-fold consciousness. And incidentally, this same reference applies to "The Seven Spirits before the Throne." Any Logoic Consciousness, whether it be that of a Monadic, Planetary, or Solar Life is seven-fold in nature. These seven Divine Persons, Divine because Their Nature includes somewhat the seven-fold expression of God (the One About Whom Naught May be Said), are defined as the seven Logoi. The sum total of this group consciousness equals Logos; Shamballa, Head Center.

Out of Themselves each of the Logoi reproduce their own kind, and the seven egoic (Soul) groups are born into expression within the Buddhic sphere. These are the seven ray groups, represented by seven major ashrams, held together and in right relationship by the seven Lords of the rays, who in their sum total equal Christ, Hierarchy, Heart Center.

Out of themselves each of the egoic groups reproduce their own kind, and the seven types of persona (mask) are born into expression in the three planes of human endeavor. These are the seven sub-tones of each of the seven egoic groups equaling, then, forty-nine distinct energy expressions, who in their sum total equal World Persona, Humanity, Throat Center.

Thus the Logoic Intent is carried into the lowest frequency of the Cosmic Physical Plane, via the process of Spiritual reproduction, i.e., the reproduction of the consciousness aspect, or its involution into the human form. Thus Logoic consciousness involves, via reproduction, into the depths of Its own substantial form and from that point evolves all of Itself into a higher degree of perfected awareness.

This may seem somewhat abstract and abstruse to you now, yet it carries within it the mystery of the whole process of involution and evolution, and the Purpose of humanity in the scheme of things.

What do we mean when we say that every Being, whether sub-human, or a so-called God far beyond the

240

human state, either has been, is now, or will be a human being?

The individualized Overshadowing Spiritual Soul did not evolve through the lower kingdoms in nature to finally reach individualization into the human kingdom, though this is the interpretation given by many.

Actually, a spark of Logoic fire descended into the realms of matter, united with units of the consciousness imprisoned therein, and individualized the totality into a human being. Thus, a human is a composite of the Soular life of the mineral, vegetable, animal, and higher kingdoms in nature. Humanity, then, is the vehicle of synthesis for the consciousness of all kingdoms in nature, or for all of the consciousness of the Planetary Logos. It is via humanity that He is enabled to integrate all of his consciousness into a unit responsive to his Divine Prototype.

This means that you, the conscious thinking I, while you may be imprisoned within an animal form, and express at times an animal nature, have never truly been such. You, the conscious thinking I, capable of creativity, are a direct descendent of God, in that you are the spark of Logoic Fire which descended into matter and individualized the sum total of consciousness you now are.

Evolution of the total consciousness is possible only because of the descent and burial into matter of that Logoic spark. Its magnetic quality is such as to integrate into a whole, the units of consciousness from the mineral, vegetable, and animal kingdoms which orbit within its ring-pass-not. Thus do all kingdoms in nature meet and merge within humanity, and thus does the Planetary Logos lift into a higher state of perfected awareness the very depths of his own lower consciousness. This, in turn, lifts in frequency the substance of his cosmic physical body until at the height of its perfection there are no distortions or sub-planes of it.

The evolutionary process is actually a process of identification. When the Logoic Spark made Its descent and individualized the group consciousness or Soul which gave it house, so to speak, it identified at the lowest level of its individualization, that is, as unevolved animal man. It then manifested the consciousness of unevolved animal man, and the experiences necessary to the growth of the identified focus. Gradually such experience, plus the magnetic quality of the Logoic spark of fire, integrated the mineral consciousness with that of the animal man. Man and his body became one.

At the height of this development, the Logoic spark began to identify with his emotions, and to manifest the experience necessary to the growth of the identified focus within the astral sphere. Gradually such experience, plus the magnetic quality of the Logoic fire, integrated the vegetable consciousness with that of the animal man. Man, his body, and his feeling nature became one.

Thus the Soular life of the mineral and vegetable kingdoms in nature, into which the Logoic Spark had made its descent, was integrated with the animal Soul, and man became what he is today, an emotionally polarized persona.

The process of identification proceeds from this point with the Logoic Spark identifying with his thought-life, becoming more mental in nature; lifting the integrated mineral, vegetable, and animal aspects of his nature up into a focused unit of consciousness within his mind where he can begin to identify as a Soul.

The individualization proceeds, then, from the level of animal man to the level of incarnating Soul. The

Lesson 23

identified focus, the I consciousness, begins to exert its control over the form-nature via its residence in the mental body, gradually realizing its true identity and its Divine Heritage.

Relate this to the collective body of humanity, and you begin to realize the internal process manifesting within the consciousness and the instrumentality of the Planetary Logos via humanity, the cellular life of His physical brain.

When the Logoic Spark, identified as a self-conscious persona, half emotional, half mental in nature, begins to grasp his true identity, when he begins to realize that he is a consciousness inhabiting the bodies, that he is Divine in nature, he then begins to seek inwardly and upwardly for that Divine Prototype which precipitated him into incarnation. At first this is a half instinctual, half intuitional act, of which he is only vaguely conscious, but it serves to establish a tentative alignment with the overshadowing realization of what he is, in reality.

Via this interior, vertical alignment, more and more of his Divine Nature is impressed upon his brain awareness, until finally the fact of his ashramic group life makes its impact, and he begins to cognize, vaguely at first, his Spiritual relationships.

I know of no other words in which to clothe this concept for your understanding, yet I know, also, how meaningless it is to you. You are so caught up in the environment of time and space, so inclined to believe only that which is presently perceivable to the five physical senses, yet this is but a minute fraction of the sum total of your life and affairs. Your life in the Ashram is not only of much greater influence to the growth and development of human and even Logoic consciousness, but it is also of much greater "degree," if I may use that term.

243

The Nature of The Soul

Here, within a magnetic field of Spiritual relationships, both of an horizontal and a vertical nature, you live, move, and have your being. Here, according to the point of Soul development (Spiritual Age), the Purpose of the whole incarnating cycle in the three worlds is known. And here, within that egoic group of brothers, some younger, some older than you, is your Spiritual security, your relationship to the Father.

It is awareness and perception of all this described above that you are working toward now. How is such awareness achieved? It appears a stupendous undertaking to the man whose focus of consciousness includes so little at present. Yet relatively speaking, it is not so stupendous nor so difficult as that growth which he has already made. Consider the vast expansion which you have experienced from that dim, dark past in which the Logoic Spark was literally buried, to the present, where it burns with a steady expanding flame.

The concepts contained within this lesson are put into intelligent activity within the consciousness via two new meditation techniques which are utilized, one in the morning, and one at night. Much of its success will depend upon

1. Your degree of rightly motivated aspiration;

2. Your perseverance with meditation forms previously given;

3. And the degree of invocative strength developed via your past application of truth as you have known it.

This meditation technique is an advanced one in which you begin to move from the confines of the meditation form and hence from the limitations of your own form-nature.

244

Lesson 23

A. Establish the three-fold lower alignment as quickly as possible without the use of a word form. This is important. Do not formulate the activity in words, but rather put the concept into action.

   1. Become physically relaxed and comfortable without saying or thinking the words.

   2. Become emotionally calm and serene without saying or thinking the words.

   3. Become mentally alert without saying or thinking the words.

B. In the same way establish the focus of consciousness:

   1. First in the ajna where the three-fold persona is integrated into a unit aspiring to the Soul—without saying or thinking the words.

   2. Then, along a line of light, withdraw the focus from the ajna into the cave, all the time aspiring with Love to the Soul — without saying or thinking the words.

C. Identify as the Soul, again without word form, and then enter into a meditative contemplation.

   Retrace the involutionary and evolutionary path you have taken as a Spark of Logoic fire. Use the creative imagination, tracing your descent from Logoic levels into an egoic group, from there into incarnation individualizing a Group Soul consisting of units of consciousness from the mineral, vegetable, and animal kingdoms, into animal man, with yourself the Divine Spark buried in the very heart of the totality of consciousness. Endeavor to sense this act of individualization, and then carefully retrace the evolution of that individualized group Soul from its beginnings to its present point of development—always with yourself as the Divine Spark of Logoic fire residing at the very heart of the total consciousness.

Then, as you reach the present point of development, again using the creative imagination, realize that you are the Logoic Spark, the Son of one of the seven Planetary Logoi, and that you are residing within the heart of the Spiritual Soul. Then, via a line of light extending upward through the head center, make your alignment with the Planetary head center via:

1. Your ray group (ashram)

2. The Master of your ashram

3. The Lord of your ray group

4. The Logoi Who is your Divine Father

Become then still, poised and alert, wholly receptive to the Divine Intent of your Being.

D. Make your descent via the sounding of the OM — visualizing yourself as the Divine Spark—slowly forming a small golden sun in the center of the head which gently, yet with strength, radiates its Light into the mind and brain.

Sound the OM through the ajna center, pouring Light out upon your world.

LESSON 23B

The following is an exercise to be used each night upon retiring. It is suggested that every student who is seriously endeavoring to dedicate himself to the service of the Plan for humanity, and who has been seriously attracted to this thought-form presentation, use the exercise without fail.

Each of you has some little realization of the fact that the consciousness is very much alive and functioning elsewhere when the brain and body are sleeping. Sometimes knowledge of this is impressed upon the brain via dream experiences which are usually vague distortions of the reality.

As the probationer begins to fit himself for service, and to consciously prepare himself for initiation, his consciousness is gathered into a closer relationship with his ashram during the period of sleep. Here he is impressed with the particular Wisdom of his ashram, its plans and purposes, etc.

At a certain point in his development, via some senior disciple, he is instructed to enter into this relationship consciously upon going to sleep, and to endeavor to impress upon his brain that Wisdom of which he is partaking via the relationship while out of the body. This hastens, somewhat, his development, expanding his consciousness and permitting a more perfect sub-conscious absorption of truth than when the awareness is focused in the brain as a censor.

With this in mind, you may carry out the following:

As you go to sleep, slowly and easily, without

creating too great a point of tension, upon a line of light withdraw the consciousness from the ajna center into the cave in the center of the head. Look outward for a moment to the ajna, ascertaining that the line of light remains intact, and then turn your attention to the line of light extending upward via the head center to loose itself in a sphere of light which is the relationship with your ashram. Realize that that overshadowing light is placed there for you by the ashram and place your consciousness within it upon going to sleep. Endeavor to remain there, with no other thought in mind than your relationship (as an incarnating Soul) to the ashram, until you go to sleep.

Keep a paper and pen handy and upon waking write the thought uppermost in mind, and any other impression of Wisdom or Truth that you have been able to impress upon the brain. At a later date you will be given a more advanced technique to use in this regard.

LESSON 24

The Relationship Between
Soul and Persona Rays:

The Overshadowing Soul
and the Persona Redefined;
The Process of Soul Infusion;
The Use of the Seventh Ray
in Aiding This Process;
The Role of the Persona Ray
in the Service Activity,
With an Example
of Rays Two and Four

LESSON 24

In lesson 22 of this series of instruction it is stated:

"As the probationer disciple consciously prepares himself for initiation, three subjects of great importance to him at this point, demand his attention almost simultaneously. They are:

1. His peculiar ray makeup, and hence his group relationship to the Plan.

2. His chosen field of service.

3. The Art and Science of Magic, providing him with those techniques which make his chosen service possible.

"Since each of these subjects is a vast field of knowledge in itself, we shall consider them consecutively in the order of their importance to the probationer, covering as much as is possible in so short a work."

In our last two lessons, we have been considering the ray of the Soul, and are now ready to proceed to a consideration of the rays of the persona and its three fold vehicle of manifestation. This also brings us to the chosen field of service initiated by the probationer.

There is much confusion, even yet, in the minds of most of you regarding the differentiation between Overshadowing Soul and persona. We have discussed this in numerous ways using various terminologies and definitions for your clarification. Once more in this series we shall turn our attention specifically to this subject, for

251

its understanding is a vital prerequisite to initiation. I would suggest that after this lesson you go through the series, searching for and copying in a special notebook every reference to this distinction. Study that which you find, using the technique of meditative contemplation, recording each realization you receive in your notebook. Turn the notebook in to your teacher when you have completed the series. Your final grade, and you will be given one, will be based largely upon this special assignment, and your meditation record, which will be requested at the same time. The final grade will be important to you, should you choose to take a more advanced course of instruction at a later date with any teacher or school serving this thought-form presentation of the Wisdom.

We have defined the Soul as the consciousness aspect, and in so far as humanity is concerned, we have given it three classifications, namely:

1. Sub-human—including mineral, vegetable, and animal;

2. Human—this is the persona;

3. Super-human or Spiritual—this is the Overshadowing Soul.

Both the persona and the Overshadowing Spiritual Soul are consciousness then. One, the persona, is an extension of the other—the overshadowing. They are separated only by time and space, or form. The persona, a part of the Soul, is incarnate and imprisoned within the form-nature. The Overshadowing Spiritual Soul is that aspect of the consciousness which has maintained itself in identity, above the frequency and, therefore, free of the limitation of form.

That which overshadows is connected (if I may use so

poor a term) to the persona by a consciousness thread, which enters the form nature via the head center and the etheric network, and is anchored to the form in the region of the pineal gland. The Spiritual Soul is reflected into the cave in the center of the head via this thread of consciousness as the persona gives its attention to it. In other words, when the incarnating consciousness, otherwise known as the persona, the conscious thinking I, begins to aspire to the Spiritual Soul (its own identification with Spirit) and to turn its attention upward via an alignment which uses the consciousness thread, the interplay of energy between that which overshadows the form and that which indwells it creates a magnetic field of light in the cave in the center of the head. The persona then attempts to place himself, to focus his consciousness within that light; and as he does so, the Spiritual Soul is reflected downward into the light, where the two, Soul and persona, are merged in awareness. The mergence takes place only momentarily at first, during his moments of meditation, until finally a polarity has been established (a brilliant focus of light) which locks the mergence, so to speak; and the man in the brain (now actually the man in the heart, for this center is the heart of his being) becomes the Conscious Soul Incarnate.

The persona has freed itself from form, is no longer identified with it, and the Spiritual Soul no longer overshadows. He has incarnated into the form, which is no longer a prison, but has become an instrument of service, a vehicle through which the Spiritual Soul makes its appearance in the light of day, as we know it on earth.

It is interesting to note here that this information is to be released, with ever-increasing clarity, by science as well as religion and philosophy, during this New Age when the Seventh Ray of magic, of Divine Law and Order, comes into dominance.

The Nature of The Soul

The Seventh Ray is, remember, the reflection of Spirit into matter. Here, then, is that great cycle of opportunity which not only renders the above readily attainable to all who are ready, but also renders it knowable as concrete knowledge to all of humanity. This shall be known as a part of the evolutionary development toward which mankind is moving. It shall be demonstrated as an established fact in nature, toward the end of this century, by those now taking initiation, and shall become a fixed ideal or goal in the minds of all men.

I would have you consider the vast connotations of this fact. What has been the Spiritual goal for humanity during the past age? A vague concept of an indefinable heaven, attainable only through Jesus Christ as a persona to be worshipped rather than through the teaching He presented, with an everlasting hell of fire as the only alternative.

What a tremendous change this new concept (new insofar as the consciousness of present day humanity is concerned) holds for mankind. Contemplate that change, and soak up its meaning, for this is the Divine Plan with which you seek to relate. This is the Truth that shall make men free, the cause toward which you are dedicated, and the work of this wonderful new energy (new insofar as its present impact is concerned), which we call the Seventh Ray. This is its magic, the effect it shall create in substance via the consciousness who appropriates and puts into right use its meaning. Grasp the meaning implanted into these words and much shall be revealed that has hitherto remained hidden. Do you realize the glory of that to which you have aligned your aspiration and dedicated yourselves to serve?

The integrating ray of the persona is that undertone of the Soul ray with which the incarnating consciousness has identified. It is a sub-ray of the Overshadowing

254

Soul, and since it is the ray upon which the consciousness in the three worlds functions, it is the most important of the sub-rays.

This ray indicates the specific field of service for which the persona has been "best fitted" by its long cycle of incarnations.

For instance, let us consider the hypothetical case of a Second Ray soul with a Fourth Ray persona, whose evolutionary status is that of probationer disciple.

The Second Ray soul relates this disciple generally to the field of teaching.

The Fourth Ray persona relates him specifically to serve in one of three fields, namely:

Via the balance of power through

1. Culture

2. International relationships including peace and war

3. Social standards and behaviorisms

Let us say that his choice is the field of culture because of past training. He is first of all a teacher of the Wisdom. He will, then, endeavor to bring into the culture of the present civilization those new ideas and ideals which will make of it an instrument through which the Divine Plan is enabled to manifest.

He will, undoubtedly, enter the field of teaching, gradually becoming an expert as an inspirational art teacher. He may confine his activity to the present educational system, seeking from within to adapt it to the Plan; or he may serve in one of the occult schools, or function independently in an attempt to establish his profession "as such" in the world of affairs.

In any of these events he will be attempting to balance the power of materialism with the Power of Light in the field of culture. Thus, he is stepping the ray of his Soul down into the frequency of Harmony in order to balance the pairs of opposites within his chosen field of service.

Regardless of this one's station in life, his daily routine, or his apparent karmic necessities, he will not find himself, nor take initiation, until he himself initiates that service, via a planned activity, toward which he is best fitted, and has been long trained by his Overshadowing Soul.

There is a common misinterpretation in the minds of many aspirants and young probationers in the world today anent the initiation of a service activity.

Too many are prone to believe that in whatever field they might find themselves lies their service karma. Would that it were true.

Do not forget that initiating a planned activity which will "precipitate" (and I use this word advisedly) his service karma is a part of a major initiation being taken by the probationer.

Do not forget, also, that most probationers in the world today find themselves in jobs which are not at all to their liking (nor do such jobs call forth and activate their true potentials), simply because of the necessity of caring for themselves and their families.

This necessity is a karmic necessity of a personality nature, and it must be met. However, it must not only be met by a probationer, it must be resolved, so that it does not conflict with his service karma.

If this seems contradictory to other teaching which has been projected to you, please reserve judgment until it has been adequately clarified for you, for we shall go into it more specifically in our next lesson.

In the meantime, suffice it to say that this problem, which is so much a part of the world problem, is a part of the test and trials of initiation, and as it is solved by the probationer in this day and age, it will be solved for the whole of humanity.

The probationer in any age is faced with a world problem which, as he arrives at and manifests its solution, lifts the whole of humanity into a higher standard of living, thus providing the group of probationers in the world with a group service karma. They serve, not only each in his own field, but as a group, in the very act of taking initiation in a specific time and place.

The Nature of The Soul

LESSON 25

Hindrances to the Manifestation
of One's Service Activity:

The Problem of Detachment from Past Life Forms;
Right Handling of Personal Karma
via the Assumption of Service Karma;
The Problems of Self-Importance, of Fear,
and of Balance in personal and Service Obligations
when Initiating a Service Activity;
Right Orientation to Service
by Affiliating with a Service Group,
by Sacrificing Personal Ambition
to the Good of the Divine Plan,
and by the Elimination of Self-Importance

LESSON 25

Any initiation is a new beginning. It involves an expansion of consciousness into an hitherto unrealized field of Spiritual knowledge; a reorientation of the entire persona to that which has been newly realized; and a precipitation of the truth into the daily life and affairs.

How many times this has been stated, yet how little of its meaning makes an impact upon the brain. An initiation is literally a new birth, involving a renewal of the life within the form. It is a new birth which is taken consciously, by the Soul, without benefit of discarnating, in order to break the karmic patterns already established within the persona.

Ordinarily, when a life in the body has served its purpose, i.e., when it has worked out a sufficient degree of karma, and effected a pre-determined degree of growth, the Soul brings about an abstraction of the persona from its physical body, and that transition known as death ensues. The consciousness is removed from the karmic limitations of its physical environment in order to suffer new ones.

Consider what takes place in the life and affairs of the persona at the time of the transition. He is removed from his family, from his friends, from his home and place of work, and from his particular station in life.

He undergoes, then, after passing over, a period of reorientation in which he detaches from the forms his past life has taken. The karmic relationships of father, mother, life partner, children, etc., are gradually removed from his consciousness as such, so that his former mother or son are no longer mother and son, but rather brother Souls.

All the while that he is engaged in this reorientation, he extracts the wisdom gained from his experiences via a review of the past life. He sees it in retrospect, gaining a new understanding of its lessons through observation, and gradually he is enabled to detach from the forms that life took.

The length of this period will be determined by the age of the Soul, and the relative unfoldment of the Soul within the persona, so that some spend the equivalent of centuries in this devachanic experience, some the equivalent of a few years or even moments, after which they go on to higher forms of learning and other paths of experience while out of the body, and still others are so unable to detach, so earthbound, that they seek reincarnation prematurely into a like environmental condition.

The detachment from the forms the past life has taken makes possible the rebirth of the persona into a new and different environment, a new and different set of coordinates which will provide the karmic limitations the new life shall take, and render possible another expansion or growth of consciousness and the balancing of another aspect of the total karma.

Consider how necessary this is to the evolutionary process. What would happen if a man carried over from one life to another his old loves, his old enemies, his old likes and dislikes, which were created largely by the childhood environment, rather than his intelligent choices, or his former status in life. Even his talents must change, or the painter should always be the painter, the statesman the statesman, and the thief the thief, etc.; and the Soul would never achieve a rounded–out development.

Yet, when it is suggested to the probationer that he must initiate his own service activity, he is stunned, shocked, and frightened as he begins to grasp the meaning of that statement.

So, let us look again at the path of Initiation. What does it mean? What are its connotations?

The path of Initiation is a process which enables the Soul to master its own form-nature and free itself from the Wheel of Rebirth. What does this process involve?

Each initiation involves the expansion of the personality consciousness to include some degree of the Wisdom of the Soul, and to that degree, via a reorientation of the whole persona, to detach from the illusions of the form without benefit of death.

Since we are concerned with the third initiation, which is the illumination of the total consciousness and the transfiguration of the form, we shall consider some of the general detachments which take place at the time of this particular initiation.

Karmic Obligation of a Personal Nature

This is one of the most difficult concepts to impress upon the probationer; and it may take many lifetimes before the Overshadowing Spiritual Soul can impress it upon the persona sufficiently to render initiation attainable in any one incarnation.

Personal karma is resolved into, and balanced by, the conscious acceptance of service karma. This in no way means that a probationer's personal karma can be eliminated like an old glove. It does not mean that a man is justified in shirking or failing to meet his present responsibilities. It means, simply, that those responsibilities are met via the acceptance of a greater burden of karma.

Does this not appear paradoxical? Yet all truth is a paradox; an inability, or a refusal, to see the paradox indicates that a man's thought is an opinion rather than a truth.

A general lack of understanding anent this concept, plus a certain apathy on the part of the consciousness in regards to service, holds so many today from entry through the door of initiation. It is a deplorable condition to observe in a world where the need of humanity shouts for the service activity of thousands of probationers who stand at the very gates of illumination, but who see not the open way.

It is often an undue illusion of self importance that renders a potential disciple karmically not free to serve the Plan according to his relationship to it.

I speak now to many of you, who, in your present job or work, waste your talents and your energies upon a world condition that you alone could solve.

How many of you are completely satisfied with the way in which you earn bread for your families? How many of you love your work, would not change it if the opportunity to do so were presented? And how many of you consider the daily routine to be the service for which you are best fitted to render the Plan?

For those of you who answer in the affirmative, this is not written for you, except as a general truth which will give you an understanding of your brothers.

For those whose answers are negative, this is written directly to you, and your numbers in the world today are many.

There is a new profession being established within the present civilization. Many of you have incarnated for the express purpose of helping to establish it, while many others of you have incarnated for the opportunity it presents in regard to your own growth, if you can and will seize that opportunity.

The new profession is the Practice of the Wisdom in the various fields of human endeavor. It makes its entry more easily into the body of humanity via the fields of teaching, healing, the creative arts, business, and vocational guidance, so that we find most disciples who are directly related to this aspect of the Plan particularly fitted to serve in one or another of these fields.

Probationers, even after realizing their specific relationship to the Plan, and after having formulated in meditation a planned service activity, fear initiating that activity if it takes them from the means by which they have been earning their livelihood. The probationer becomes confused, undergoes a most uncomfortable period of conflict in which he feels pulled between two obligations, his obligation to the Plan and his obligation to his dependents. If his daily routine necessitates his constant violation of those basic concepts of truth which he has accepted as being the Path, his conflict is increased, and often he suffers psychological and physical dis-ease as a result of that conflict.

This is a most difficult problem and its resolution demands the development of the discriminative faculty, plus a subjective effort to manifest Divine Adjustment to the Divine Plan.

The probationer is not justified in failing to provide for those who are karmically dependent upon him; therefore, he cannot, with wisdom, move prematurely from one activity, which does provide him with a measure of material security, into another which does not. His move can be made only after it has been thoroughly worked out according to the Plan, and after a karmic adjustment has been made that provides for his personal obligations.

Regardless of how impossible the situation may appear, that adjustment can be made if the probationer is rightly oriented to the Plan. Right orientation entails the following:

1. His affiliation with a service group whose members are united in a common purpose and goal. This may surprise you somewhat. No probationer initiates a service activity in this cyclic period of opportunity alone and unaided. Hierarchial effort today moves into the body of humanity via a group movement rather than through selected individuals working alone with some aspect of the Plan. Thus, if the probationer is rightly oriented he will find his place within a service group, and his relationship to the Plan will be from within a group in relationship to it. More will be given anent this particular subject later in this series.

2. His complete dedication to the Divine Plan for humanity. That Plan, the evolution of the Soul, has taken the first place of importance in his life. It is, in fact, his life, his cause for being in the three worlds; and he is willing to make the complete sacrifice for it, the sacrifice of all personal ambition and desire to the working out of the Plan.

Thus, he is enabled, as he sets out subjectively, to establish Divine adjustment in his life and affairs, to ask nothing for the personal self. This, of course, constitutes the supreme test for the probationer, for who does not come into a service group in the beginning with conscious and unconscious self-motivations? All do, for that is where they are in the evolutionary process, and if they had purified their motives, they would have taken the initiation long since.

The probationer, then, must accept himself as he is. He must be able to look into his own mind and emotions, seeing here a personal ambition, and there a personal desire, and with a divine sense of humor place them upon the altar.

The man who fools himself at this point and tells himself that he is without personal motivation fails to pass the test, and must continue another period of preparation for initiation.

3. His conscious effort to eliminate his illusion of self-importance. This is perhaps the most difficult of all for it demands a detachment from the karmic form of all relationships and the establishment of right relationship, which is essentially brotherhood, with all associates.

Let us, for example, consider the probationer who is a husband, and a father. His task is to detach, without benefit of the transition known as death, from his sense of husbandship and fatherhood, which are in most cases a subconscious dictatorship or ownership, and to reattach as a brother whose relationships are all within the One Life. The effects are of so subtle a nature that, unless one is very careful, a glamour can be built in here which would serve as a pitfall or bypath for incarnations.

The probationer does not desert his obligations. He does not leave his loved ones or his dependents, but he realizes that his sense of importance in relationship to them is false. The true Father is God, and He is the only real security upon which humanity can rely.

The probationer then goes even further and considers just how important is he to his family? What would happen to them if he were to suddenly discarnate? This enables him to look at these relationships from a new perspective, as being within the One Life; and while he continues outwardly to manifest as husband and father, he does so inwardly detached from a sense of self-importance. Thus, he places his and his family's security in the Plan. He realizes that his dedication is to the greatest good for the greatest number, and this includes all of humanity. Thus, the probationer shifts his sense of responsibility from family to humanity, which includes family, and manifests the Plan for all.

In this way the probationer resolves personal karma by accepting his service karma, realizing as he does so that the Plan includes every member of humanity. His obligation is to the whole.

We shall proceed with this subject in the next lesson. In the meantime, please write as an assignment your understanding of the above concept.

LESSON 26

Creating a Body Receptive for Your Service Activity:

Deciding Whether Your Service Activity
will be an Avocation or a Vocation,
Based on Karma and the Body Receptive;
The Body Receptive as it Relates to
the Profession of The Wisdom;
Adjusting Personal Karma to Allow
your Service Activity to be Full Time

LESSON 26

As a probationer arrives at that point in time and space wherein he is setting into motion a planned service activity, several choices confront him.

First, he must decide whether he shall initiate the activity as an avocation or as a vocation, and this will be dependent upon two major factors:

1. The relation of his karmic situation to his chosen field of service. In other words, will his present karmic obligations permit his entry into the field on a full-time basis?

2. The point of evolutionary development achieved by humanity as a whole in relation to that aspect of the Plan he seeks to serve. In other words, has a sufficient field of magnetic receptivity to this aspect of the Plan been built into the body of humanity to permit his full-time objective occupation therein?

In answer to both of these questions, if the probationer is a young man or woman who finds his service within the present fields of either psychology or education, among many others, and has the means of attaining a suitable education, he would find no difficulty in entering his chosen field on a full-time basis.

If, however, his chosen field should be that of teaching the Wisdom or of Spiritual Healing, or Right Human Relations, etc., he might find it necessary to initiate the activity as an avocation until such time as he and the group to which he belongs awakens, stimulates and activates the "body receptive" to his field within the

271

body of humanity. This is a most important concept and should be given much contemplation.

There is, within the body of humanity, a state of consciousness composed of many persons throughout the world, which is specifically related to that aspect of the Plan you seek to serve. This state of consciousness, or world group of personae, we call the "body receptive". They are karmically receptive, either potentially or actively, to a particular aspect of the Plan, and it is through them that the disciple precipitates his share of that Plan into the world of affairs. They constitute his lower alignment with humanity, just as his ashram constitutes his higher alignment with the Hierarchy.

The "body receptive" to psychology, for example, is sufficiently active to permit disciples in that field to function on a professional basis, while the "body receptive" to the teaching of The Wisdom has not yet permitted disciples to function therein on a professional basis.

Those disciples who are specifically related to the new thought–form presentation of The Wisdom find themselves faced with the task not only of initiating a planned service activity, but also of pioneering a new profession within the body of humanity. They not only have to teach those who are sufficiently receptive, but they also have to awaken, stimulate, and activate those who are subjectively ready for, but not yet magnetically receptive to, the teaching.

Observe the pioneering work going forward in the field of parapsychology for a greater understanding of what yet has to be initiated in the field of The Wisdom.

I should like to say just a few words here in regard to The Wisdom as a profession, for most of you who respond to this series of instructions are related to it in one specific or another.

Lesson 26

The Wisdom is not religion, though it is applicable to it; it is not education, nor science, nor psychology, nor healing, nor government, etc., though it is applicable to, and within, all of these. It is, then, a profession in itself, which will, when adequately developed, express itself in many specialized aspects.

Its purpose will be to synthesize, through its magnetic quality of Light, the consciousness of the many into a One, i.e., to attract, relate, and integrate the separative consciousness of human beings into a living totality of One Humanity.

Its immediate goal is to awaken the "body receptive" to it so that it can be given birth within the world of affairs as a recognized profession. This period in time is the opportunity for its cycle of emergence. Contained within the larger cycle of emergence are three major high points, if I might call them that, which are particularly advantageous to the precipitation of The Wisdom into world affairs. Two of these three high points manifested from the years 1960 to 1963, or 1964, and on or about 1975. The third point will manifest toward the end of the century.

Disciples and probationers are urged to take advantage of these high points of opportunity and, particularly, to prepare for the coming one.

You might well ask, how can I best prepare to be of service in this way?

The Wisdom makes its entry as a profession first in the specialized field of teaching. Many probationers initiating their planned service activities at this time find themselves specifically related to this aspect of the Plan.

[An aside note may be inserted here: In 1975 The Wisdom, already established somewhat as a profession, entered the specialized field of healing, uniting,

273

as it did so, the many different organizations dedicated to the better health of man into an integrated effort toward his Spiritual, mental, emotional and physical well-being.]

At present the majority of probationers will establish teaching centers throughout the world where The Wisdom, as such, will be made available to humanity.

This must begin on a small scale, of course, but if it is established properly, it will expand rapidly and anchor itself within the body of humanity as a recognized fulfillment of a specific need.

This calls for an immediate expansion of consciousness on the part of the probationer. Remember, The Wisdom is not a Religion. Most probationers tend to think of it in those terms and this is a major mistake, and a major hindrance to its precipitation. It is applicable to and within religion, but it must not be confined or limited therein. It must not be established *as* Religion.

It is The Wisdom, applicable in *all* departments of human living, and probationers would do well to meditate upon the concept.

As a young teacher initiates his activity; that is, as he begins to actually teach The Wisdom to his first students, he must be very careful to do just that. He does not take them from their present religious affiliation, but urges them to look for, find, and enunciate, as well as to practice, the truth present within their respective churches.

He will arrange his classes so as not to interfere with and demand a choice between their present church affiliation and their new study. He must be very, very careful in this respect, for if he does not establish right relationship with every religion, and particularly with orthodox Christianity, he will defeat the Purpose of his service activity.

Lesson 26

The young teacher does not call The Wisdom psychology, or parapsychology, or even occultism, for it is not these, though it is applicable to, and within, them. He calls it The Wisdom and urges the practice of The Wisdom by his students in their daily life and affairs.

I cannot over-emphasize this point, for it is one which gives the Hierarchy great concern at this time. So many probationers in the world today are confused as to what The Wisdom is, and, in their efforts to make of it something which it is not, they are thwarting Hierarchial effort rather than aiding it.

If you are endeavoring to teach The Wisdom, or to practice it, then by all means call it that. The concept of The Wisdom should be impacting humanity today with a tremendous force, yet that force has been diffused and scattered by the misguided efforts of many.

Learn to speak of The Wisdom often, refer to it in your conversation, and if asked for an explanation of it, why, then, give that explanation, for this is an opportunity to awaken, stimulate, and activate the "body receptive" to it.

The probationer who is related to this specific activity will usually initiate his service first on a part-time basis, teaching one or two classes a week until such time as he has activated his share of the "body receptive." As he initiates whatever objective measures he formulates to activate the "body receptive," he also initiates an intensive subjective effort toward the same end. This will be as follows:

He becomes a focus in consciousness via an established meditative state of mind, through which the energies and concepts, on a subjective level, can pass from Hierarchial levels via his ashram, into the etheric network of humanity via the "body receptive." He pays particular attention to the "body receptive," endeavoring to awaken a response from within it to The Wisdom with which it is specifically related.

Eventually, in some one incarnation or another, the probationer initiates his service activity on a full-time basis and completes the third initiation. In order to do this he must bring Divine Adjustment to the Divine Plan in his life and affairs, resolving all karma of a personal nature that stands between himself and his service.

This brings him to another and most difficult choice. When and where that is in time and space, and in what degree shall he precipitate the remainder of his outstanding personal karma so it can be adjusted?

This brings us to a place in the initiatory process which is almost heartbreaking and often terrifying to the probationer in its connotations.

What man at this point upon the path knows the karma he has engendered in the past which yet must be resolved or balanced before he can give himself to the Plan? He knows not whether it will bring apparent pleasure or pain, whether it will take a relatively short or long time to resolve. He only knows that it is there and must be consciously precipitated to be resolved.

This, again, is one of the sacrifices and the tests of initiation. At the third initiation the man deliberately, and in full waking consciousness, precipitates the remainder of that personal karma which stands between himself and his chosen field of service.

What can be said anent this subject that will bring clarity and yet give the assurance and courage which is so necessary to the committing of the act?

It is a part of this specific initiation. Each and every one who reaches this point goes through this experience and grows thereby. It is the sacrifice of the separative self to the Plan.

These are statements which have little meaning to the man who has not made them a part of his consciousness via experience, yet, the Truth within them, and his response to that truth, give him the courage and the perception to complete the initiation.

The probationer who is faced with this necessity must put his faith, his trust, in God, and in all of those higher Spiritual relationships in God, who have, through their own sacrifice, aligned with him to help him through this period.

He must realize that no Soul is burdened with more than It can, via Its persona, carry and resolve according to Divine Law. He then sacrifices the separated self in the following manner. After having established his own meditative focus, and alignment with the Plan via his ashram, he evokes from within himself Love for that Plan.

When the Love within him reaches its height, he then pours it out upon humanity, and meditates upon the following invocation:

> "I stand willing to serve the Divine Plan. Make of me a whole consciousness and a whole instrument so that Light may pour through me to light the way of men. Whatsoever karma I may have engendered in the past which stands between myself and my presently potential service, precipitate in that order which will, under Divine Accommodation, open my eye to the way of the Disciple. Guide me that I might adjust whatsoever karma is precipitated according to the greatest good of the greatest number. Give me knowledge of the Law of Love. I stand willing to serve the Divine Plan."

The Nature of The Soul

LESSON 27

The Soul's Ideation of a Plan of Action:

The Relationship of the Soul as Mediator
Between the Monad and the Persona;
The Christ as "Perfect Action Within the One Life";
The Plan of Action to Become Christ-like via Identifica-
tion as Soul aspiring to be the Christ,
and by Expressing this Through the Persona;
The Karmic Relationship of the State of your Equip-
ment when it Expresses itself Negatively;
The Law of Grace

LESSON 27

It is the nature of the Soul to manifest itself in form, i.e., to reflect its "condition" or "state" upon the substance of the vibratory plane into which it is focused, in such a way as to arrange that substance into the appearance of an organized form. Thus, consciousness inhabits a body, and via that body produces an environment with a resulting series of experiences.

Experience reveals the Soul to itself. It out-pictures the consciousness in substance, which reflects back into the center of perception its own state of being. Since the Soul is in potential the expression of Wisdom, it evolves or unfolds that Wisdom via its ability to perceive its own appearance in form, and to cognize the meaning of that form. In other words, as the Soul looks into the reflection of itself in the mirror of experience, which is actually a moving picture of its state of development, it intuits its own mistakes and grows in Wisdom.

The Over-Soul of Humanity, focused into the three worlds of human endeavor, reflects its "state of being" upon the substance of the three-fold vehicle of appearance. This organized form we call the body of humanity. The Over-Soul then inhabits that body via its many members and produces an environment which we call the world of affairs. Its experience in that world of affairs reflects back into its own center of perception, via its many members, its state of being, and the Over-Soul then unfolds the necessary Wisdom to produce an evolution of itself.

The unfoldment of Wisdom within the Soul itself then takes place as the Soul ideates a Divine Plan of Action.

The Nature of The Soul

This ideation of a Divine Plan ensues when the Soul compares, or reflects back into comparison, its present reflection with that Monadic impulse which has moved it into being.

The Monad, which is the archetype of the Soul, assumes the stature of Christ; the Divine Son; consciousness of, and sacrificial action within, the One Life.

The persona, that part of the Soul, remember, which is imprisoned via reflection in the form, aspires to the Overshadowing Soul, which is a growing expression of Wisdom. The Overshadowing Soul aspires to the Monad, i.e., The Christ, which can be defined for the moment as perfect action within the One Life.

The persona aspires via discipline.

The Soul aspires via ideation.

At the time of the third initiation, as the secrets of that initiation are revealed, and these constitute the expansion of consciousness which characterizes initiation itself, the persona merges its awareness with that of the Overshadowing Soul via identification; and the sense of duality between the two disappears. The Overshadowing is no longer overshadowing, but moves within the brain because the consciousness therein is identified as the Spiritual Soul.

This is an act of magic in itself, carried out by the creative Will. It produces a specific change in awareness. The man gains awareness of himself as a Soul, and there is no longer a division between Soul and persona. That division is healed, the apparent gap in consciousness closed, and the persona takes its intended place: the revealing mask or appearance of the Soul in the three worlds.

Lesson 27

The man who is now the incarnating Soul shifts his level of aspiration onto a higher turn of the Spiral and via ideation aspires to The Christ. This takes the form, in appearance or experience, of service to the Plan. Interiorly the Soul now ideates the Divine Plan, and outwardly he serves that Plan in an endeavor to manifest perfect action within the One Life.

What does this mean to you?

1. It means that you have reached that point of development wherein via identification you are to become in awareness the incarnating Soul. No longer are you to aspire as a persona to a Soul which overshadows. Identify within the cave in the center of your head as the Soul, and endeavor to remain there throughout the twenty-four hours. Each time you think or say "I," do so from this center, cognizing the meaning of the "I" as Soul.

   As you look out upon your world, look through the ajna center from your residence in the cave as the Soul, and do not permit yourself to be pulled down or out, either from that position or that identification.

"I am the Soul here and now."

2. It means that you have reached that point of development wherein your aspiration is directed to The Christ. From this time forward, identify as the Soul and aspire to The Christ.

   As the Soul in the center of the head, ideate the Divine Plan as it is held in focus for you by The Christ.

   This you do by becoming so perfectly aligned

with The Christ that you are receptive only to His impact in this center.

Do not align negatively with thought–forms on mental levels, or feelings on astral levels, or situations and circumstances on physical levels. That is, do not permit yourself to be attracted— and therefore influenced—by them. Remain positive to all horizontal effects, and positively negative, alerted to and attracted by The Christ via your vertical alignment.

"I am That I am."

Thus, you are enabled to ideate (give form within your consciousness) to the Divine Plan.

3. It means that you are ready to put the Divine Plan into action within and through the substance of your own vehicles.

All substance in the three worlds is impressed, that is, colored or conditioned, by one or another of the seven rays. Thus is substance given its Divine Intent by Spirit.

That substance which has coalesced to produce your bodies, mental, astral and etheric–physical, is, then, already impressed with a Divine Intent according to its predominant ray energy.

You, the Soul, have chosen the ray type of substance through which you shall make an appearance in the three worlds, and conditioned that substance further, via reflection, with your karmic intent.

Your equipment: mental, astral and etheric–physical bodies, reveals the karmic necessity which brought you into incarnation. This is your karma, and its effects manifest as experience patterns in your life and affairs.

Lesson 27

The way you think, feel, and act are all the effects of the karmic necessity built into the substance of your bodies.

A karmic necessity always manifests as a choice, so that the effect in experience may be the adjustment of karma, or the building of new karma to be worked out in another life. Since there are few who have arrived at the possibility of the perfect act, which is the balance of karma with no further creation of it, most persons either balance the old via a building of new, in your case, service karma; or fail to make an adjustment which necessitates a return to a like experience; or place an additional burden of karma onto that which has already been engendered.

If the probationer is prone to criticism, this indicates the karmic necessity to build into the substance of his mental body an understanding which supersedes criticism. In other words, the Soul observing this reflection of its consciousness in the experience of the persona, will, as that reflection is thrown back into its own center of perception, see it in comparison with the Monadic Impulse which is the motivation for Being. *Spiritual*

The Soul ideates the Divine Plan as held in focus by The Christ, which, in this case, takes the form of loving understanding. As that loving understanding grows or unfolds within the Soul, the Soul then endeavors to reflect it, via the mind, into the brain awareness of the man, and the man gradually develops the quality of compassion.

This is a somewhat new concept of karma and can easily be related to Evolution as one of its great laws.

We see the law working in the world of the persona as a harvest in experience of that which the persona sows in experience. We also see the inner meaning of karma as it relates to the Soul and its growth.

The Nature of The Soul

When the man begins to think as the Soul, he is then enabled to adjust those karmic causes and effects within himself without going through the long, slow, outer process of action and reaction. He adjusts the karmic necessity within himself to the Divine Plan as he ideates that Plan, and invokes the Law of Grace or Mercy.

This has always been a subject of interest to probationers, for once a man becomes aware of the law of karma, it is difficult to see how something which has been set into motion can be offset or superseded. Yet, the Law of Love teaches a Law of Grace or Mercy, and it is so.

Let us look at a probationer who does have this tendency to criticize, along with other companion qualities of a negative nature. Obviously he has engendered quite an overlay of personal karma, as he has expressed these qualities in the past. Yet, now he is applying for initiation, seeks to serve the Plan, and is gradually overcoming the negativity within himself. Must he spend years or even incarnations reaping the effects of seeds sown in the past before he is free to be of service?

No, it is not necessary that he do so, for once he overcomes the karmic cause of such effects within himself, the Law of Grace begins to operate. The overlay of personal karma created in the past by these karmic causes is transmuted as he takes up his service in the three worlds.

Please note: this is possible only as the man overcomes the cause within himself, and not before.

Even then there is a short cycle of manifesting negativity as the law already in motion fulfills itself, but if the probationer maintains his equilibrium (manifests compassion in the face of an experience which would have—in the past—evoked an expression of criticism) through the completion of the cycle, it will not reappear as another obstacle to service.

It is wise at this point for the probationer to consider these karmic necessities that have been built into his instrument.

Wherever he is manifesting a condition of negativity within his own expression, here is indicated the necessity to expand his consciousness, via ideation, to understand its polar opposite, and via that understanding, to re-condition the substance of his bodies to manifest that polar opposite. Thus are the karmic effects created in the past offset and transmuted, and the man gradually liberated from the prison of the form.

What is the prison of the form but those forms we build for ourselves, which call us back into incarnation over and over again?

The Nature of The Soul

LESSON 28

The Form's Role in the Soul's Use of Magic:

The Brain as Necessary to Form Building;
Meditation as an Alchemical Process of
Altering the Brain's Cellular Construction;
The Function of the Brain in Form Building
and the Practice of Projection;
The Science of Impression as Used by the Soul
to Train the Response Mechanism of the Brain

LESSON 28

The Art and Science of Magic, which we might also accurately define as the art and science of service, operates according to fixed laws which the probationer is learning to manipulate. These laws control the movement of energy, force, and substance into predetermined patterns, which we call forms.

As the Soul comprehends the Law, and manipulates it in cooperation with Divine Purpose and Plan, He masters the form nature and not only liberates himself from its prison, but uses it (the form nature) in service to The Christ.

It might be well at this point to consider the form nature for further clarification. A form is any arrangement of energy, force, and substance that is perceivable to the consciousness. For instance, a thought which can be perceived and known as thought by the consciousness is a thought-form. If that thought sets up a vibration within the astral body, and is perceived from an emotional polarization, it has clothed itself in astral substance and is an astral form. If this same thought is brought down into appearance in the Light of Day, i.e., made manifest to the five physical senses, it has become a physical form.

A form is but the appearance of reality, it is not the reality itself. This is a concept which gives rise to some problems in comprehension, because the consciousness of the probationer is still imprisoned within the brain, which is not only a form, but *the* form-making instrument insofar as the three lower worlds are concerned.

The Nature of The Soul

If we are to understand in any way, man as a Soul and his supremacy over the world of appearance, we must understand the brain and its occult function. Here is the instrument which produces the phenomenon of magic, or form building, in the three worlds. Its final secrets are known only at the completion of the third initiation, but an approach to such revelation can be made now.

The brain is in actuality a focus in substance of the incarnating consciousness. We say "the man in the brain." What we mean is "the focus of the Soul in substance, the man in his house." The brain is a condensation of mental, astral, and etheric matter, created by a focus of these three frequencies of matter through the cave in the center of the head. The pineal and pituitary glands are the positive and negative polarities, which set up an interplay of force resulting in the birth of consciousness within, or its reflection upon this condensed matter that we call the brain.

The cave in the center of the head is occultly defined as that place where land, air and water meet, because this is the center in which etheric, mental, and astral substance is focused (in that order) for condensation into form. The brain might be called the master-form, the instrument through which the focused substance is condensed into intelligible appearance in the lower mental, astral, and etheric-physical worlds.

The consciousness imprisoned within the brain sees the outer world according to the forms impressed (or condensed) there. In other words, he sees an outer appearance through its form or formulae within his own brain, and interprets it accordingly. Thus is he limited by his own form-making instrument.

A very good example of this is the student who perceived the phenomenon of occult light for the first time. In the middle of her meditation, she suddenly found

Lesson 28

herself (in her imagination) opening the door of her refrigerator. The light flashed on as the door opened and flooded the inside of her head with its brilliance.

When this same student realized that she had perceived this phenomenon through an acceptable form within her own brain, and that the perception of the "light in the head" was by no means uncommon, she no longer needed the refrigerator in order to perceive the light.

As the probationer practices the daily meditation, he lifts the frequency of his brain, changing the cellular construction of it in such a way as to alter the forms already impressed upon it. This is possible because his meditations act upon the etheric, mental, and astral substance being focused into and through the cave. He can alter his own brain because he is working from that center which is its cause. The substance of the vehicles is conditioned through the brain itself from the center (the cave), which brings it (the substance) into first focus. Thus is the cave (a part of the head center) the heart of a man's being. It is the very center of his three vehicles and is constructed of etheric light substance in all three frequencies of the lower worlds. In other words, it is here that land, air, and water meet, and in just that order.

Several points of extreme occult importance are indicated in this instruction:

1. That the brain is necessary to the building of form in lower mental and astral planes, as well as the physical. This has been veiled heretofore to safeguard humanity from the works of premature magicians, but such safeguarding is no longer possible with the incoming Seventh Ray. The great occult secrets having to do with magic, and the brain as the instrument of it, are revealed as the Seventh Ray makes its influence felt.

2. That once the man has freed himself from the limitations of his own form (the brain) and stands within the cave in the center of the head, he is in the position of master, i.e., he can control substance.

3. That the way of becoming the magician is clearly defined as:

   a. meditation
   b. practice in form-building
   c. practice in projection

It is unusually simple. The man frees himself from the confines of form through his attention to meditation. In meditation he gradually places himself, his own focus of consciousness, in the cave in the center of the head, where he becomes the manipulator. He then practices form-building, molding substance into those forms that he wishes to manifest. Over a long period of time, he evolves his consciousness into an identification with the Soul, and as the Soul, with the One Life, until the final secrets of projection are made known to him. These relate to the focused third eye, the brain, and the ajna and throat centers.

The mental, etheric and astral substance necessary to the building of an intended form is appropriated by the consciousness in the cave. This is important; the magician does not appropriate from an astral polarization via the energy of desire. He appropriates needed substance from a Soul polarization in the cave via the energy of Divine Intent.

He then brings that substance into proper focus via the focused third eye, and molds it into shape, impressing the shape upon the physical brain for condensation into form. The condensed form is then projected from the brain into time and space via the ajna and throat centers.

Lesson 28

Let us consider this in its practical application insofar as the probationer is concerned.

The probationer is attempting to live in the world as the Soul. This is the purpose behind all of his disciplinary action. He is endeavoring to lift himself from a separated personality focus into a Soul focus, from which he will know himself to be, and to function within his daily life and affairs, as a part of the One Humanity.

As he ascertains the secrets of magic, he employs them to this end. The forms he builds will all relate to *this* goal until such time as it has become a manifest reality in the three worlds.

First, he achieves a momentary cyclic polarization via repeated meditation exercises in which he focuses his consciousness in the cave in the center of the head, and identifies as the Soul.

Later, he stabilizes the cyclic polarization into a permanent one via a steady and constant Soul identification in this center. He takes up his residence here.

At this time he is so identified with the Soul, that he views the vehicles from an entirely different perspective. These three vehicles have become his three-fold instrument of contact with the three worlds of human endeavor. They are seen as a necessary instrument of service to the One Life. As the Soul, he then endeavors to appropriate and control them, i.e., to assert his mastery over this form nature.

He must clearly differentiate between the form nature and his own intent. It is at this stage that he seriously studies that form nature, learning particularly that sensation is a characteristic of the form, and not of consciousness. The consciousness who is identified with, and limited within, the form nature perceives via, evaluates according to, and bases his decisions upon, this sensational response of the form to stimuli.

A very good example of this distinction between form and consciousness is the Soul's attitude toward food. The Soul will permit the body to take into itself only that food which is necessary to its health. It is not the consciousness who is hungry. It is not the consciousness who likes or dislikes a particular kind of food. The response of the form nature itself to the act of eating is a sensational response.

The probationer, newly identified as the Soul, asserts his mastery over the form nature through these distinctions and the training of the vehicles to newer and more effective tastes. In other words, knowing that it is the nature of the form to respond via sensation, he trains it to like that which he intends for it. He refines its sensational response to stimuli.

In the same way he trains the vehicles to permit, or to carry through into manifestation, his intended expressions of Love, Compassion, Harmony, Beauty, etc. He is refining the form nature via his alteration of its sensational response. He trains it to enjoy via sensory experience these higher qualities which he himself enjoys from a higher correspondence of sensation. That higher correspondence might be defined as inner knowing, Wisdom, or pure reason, the very nature of consciousness.

In other words, consciousness knows, it cognizes pure reason, while the form senses.

It is important at this time to point out that it is the nature of form to respond via sensation. The Soul does not attempt to kill or stamp out this nature, but rather to train its sensational response toward a positive reaction to the higher qualities. Thus, he is impressing substance itself with a new condition, a new natural response.

Lesson 28

From his polarization in the cave he determines the new response to be impressed; builds its form (habit); focuses that form into the brain for condensation; and from there projects it into time and space (*now* in the bodies as a part of the built-in response mechanism) via the ajna center and the throat center. As the visualized form (in this case the new response) is projected via the ajna, its note or vibration is sounded in the throat center. The OM, which is the magic word of the Soul, is sounded on that note which is the vibratory frequency of the constructed form. This note is intuited by the Soul.

After this work has been completed via a formal meditation, the Soul maintains via the focused third eye, his attention to it until well after the vehicles automatically respond via the new impress.

In other words, he maintains the vision in the ajna and continues to sound the note in the throat center, via the tonal quality of his voice, as he goes about the task of daily living.

If this is done properly, the entire work can be completed in a seven-day cycle. For six days the attention is maintained upon the effort. On the seventh day, the consciousness relaxes his attention knowing the work is complete and the effect in substance is *good*.

The connotations of this lesson cannot be grasped in one reading or even in one class discussion. They demand deep contemplation. For those whose sincerity of motive is such that the intuitive faculty is functioning, real illumination can be had from the foregoing.

The Nature of The Soul

LESSON 29

The Soul's Role as Magician,
and the Breaking and
Rebuilding of the *Antahkarana*:

The Nature of the Soul to Create Forms;
The Veiling of the Secrets of Conscious
Creativity Due to the Atlantean Episode;
The Atlantean Violation of the Plan;
The Great Invocation;
The Laws of the Creative Process;
The Use of Esoteric Light,
Sound, Color, and Vibration

LESSON 29

The appearance of form on any plane of existence pre-supposes that its creator has consciously or uncon-sciously cooperated with the law, and that working under and with that law, he has followed a certain process which we call magic. The process results in an appearance of form, where before there was no form. It molds substance (and I refer now to prime matter) into a vehicle for Spirit and/or consciousness, whichever the case may be; and after condensation of that prime mat-ter into its desired frequency, it maintains the sub-stance in a coherent whole within a ring-pass-not. This is true whether the form be a thought or a physical body.

Because there has been a necessary veiling of this sub-ject since the Atlantean period, we find that it is misin-terpreted by almost all students and probationer disci-ples working in the world today.

A clear enunciation of Truth is demanded as the new cycle of opportunity comes into being. It is with that enunciation, primarily anent this subject, that this treatise deals. Why then is this course of instruction entitled "The Nature of the Soul"? Because it is the nature of the Soul to create form. Because the Soul is the mediator between Spirit and matter. Because the Soul *is* the magician.

Before it would be wise to proceed with the unveiling of truth anent the creative process, some consideration of the cause of its present condition is vitally necessary.

There was a time in the history of mankind when this

subject was not shrouded in mystery, when all children were taught the steps of the creative process as naturally and as systematically as they are now taught the fundamentals of arithmetic.

And why not? This is man's Divine heritage. It is the reason for his being, the Logoic Purpose underlying humanity's place in the scheme of things. Man was *born to create*, to build the forms into which the consciousness of God could manifest.

In the long passage of time and history, what could have happened to have caused mankind to lose his Divine Right? How was it that he could have been denied his place in the life and affairs of the Logos of which he is an inseparable part? He must have committed an almost unpardonable crime against that Life, and this he did.

We see the karmic consequences of such an act all about us today. We see a humanity utterly lost to knowledge of its identity, of its Divine Purpose, and of its inmost natural creativeness. We see humankind steeped in fear of the monster it has created out of substance, a lonely, suffering humanity at the mercy of that monster, denied the golden key of Wisdom, which is its only hope for freedom.

Only a few words are permitted regarding the Atlantean episode, but these few will suffice.

When a man creates a form out of substance, he is using the economy of the Life in which he lives. He does not alter the composition of it, but he does alter the relationships of Spirit, matter, and consciousness. When he does this in violation of the Plan of the One Life, he naturally sets up a disturbance within the whole sphere (Planetary and even Solar), which puts it out of tone (so to speak) with the Life in which it lives. Thus, its own relativity is disturbed, its purpose thwarted, and its growth momentarily delayed. Is this Planetary Karma? It must be so, yet we have to look at the part humanity has played in this karmic precipitation in order to bring about a balance of it.

Let us look again at humanity's place in the scheme of things, in order to clearly ascertain his Purpose and the violation of that Purpose. Humanity, as we have said many times, is the Planetary throat center, the center through which the Logoic Word sounds forth. That word (the Soul and later the Monad on its own plane) is creative. It creates the forms within which our God shall appear.

Looking at it from another perspective, we see humanity as the brain of the Logos. Each human being is, then, a brain cell within the One Life. The Logos, or directing will, transfers His Purpose and Plan, via the heart of His Being, the Hierarchy, into this brain for condensation into form. Humanity then takes into itself that Purpose and Plan, recreates it into form, and gives it appearance in the Light of Day.

During the Atlantean period when all human beings were *conscious magicians according to Plan*, humanity, for an inexplicable reason (except that it be karmic), denied the Logoic Plan for one of its own. That is, men conceived and created according to their own separative purposes. In so doing, the economy of the Planetary Life was misused, the relationship of Spirit, matter, and consciousness altered, and the antakarana between man and his own Soul broken. As the word sounded in time and space, it took on a destructive tone because it was sounded in violation of the One Life.

The breaking of the antakarana resulted in an upheaval within the consciousness of the Planetary Life, and man set himself adrift from the Logoic Purpose which had brought him into being, i.e., he broke off his own relationship with God.

It was not a vengeful God who denied man his Divine heritage. It was man himself who destroyed his own awareness of himself as Soul, and consequently shut the door upon his creative genius.

The outer results of this act came in the form of a cataclysm which wiped out the Atlantean civilization. The violent changing of the earth's surfaces, the inundation of heavily populated areas with water, and the gradual decline of man's knowledge of the creative process, were but outer reflections of the terrible upheaval taking place within the consciousness of the Planet itself.

Since that time, humanity has gradually brought itself back to the reappearing cycle of opportunity. The antakarana, not only between man and his Soul, but between the Hierarchy and humanity, is being reconstructed by those disciples in the world who consciously serve the Plan. That Plan, which has to do with man as a creator, is once again being focused downward, and the redemption of both consciousness and substance for Logoic Purpose becomes possible.

Thus, the unveiling of the mysteries proceeds according to law, but with this specific warning: Let your creative genius be directed to the working out of God's Plan on earth.

It is suggested that the sincere student take The Great Invocation into meditation for further clarification in the light of the above.

"From the point of Light within the mind of God
Let Light stream forth into the minds of men.
Let Light descend on earth.

Lesson 29

From the point of Love within the Heart of God
Let Love stream forth into the hearts of men.
May Christ return to earth.

From the centre where the Will of God is known
Let Purpose guide the little wills of men,
The Purpose which the Masters Know and serve."

These first three stanzas have to do with the reconstruction of that triple strand of Light which is called
the antakarana. They refer, also, to the proper equation
of spirit, matter, and consciousness, which since At-
lantis has been out of balance.

"From the centre which we call the race of men
Let the Plan of Love and Light work out
And may it seal the door where evil dwells.

Let Light, and Love, and Power restore the Plan
on earth."

These last are self-explanatory in the consciousness
of one who has intuited the Truth from the above
text.

The laws which have to do with the creative process
concern:

    1. The illumination of the three.

We are concerned here with the equation of spirit, matter, and consciousness. Into what relationship must
these three be placed in order to produce a manifestation of the Plan?

This was the first law the Atlantean consciousness
violated, in that it disregarded the relationship completely. The same is true of the black magician of today

305

who creates for his own purposes. Remember that the Divine Purpose of humanity in the scheme of things is to create the forms into which the consciousness of God can manifest.

If you will recall, the first instruction in this series had to do with the triune cause back of all manifestation. The trinity of spirit, matter, and consciousness is the key formula, the *first* cause of all that is. The man who creates must, then, work with this cause if his creativity is to be in line with Divine Purpose.

As conscious Souls, we are the mediator between spirit and matter. We must then take our conscious place between the two in order to perform the Divine Miracle of creation.

This we do via our conscious alignment with, and focus within, the causal triangle of the manifest planet.

We become one with the consciousness of that Life in which we live, move and have our being, enter into His meditation, equate spirit to matter according to His Plan, and proceed from here with the building of the form into which such Plan shall manifest. Thus do we set up the necessary polarity into which the consciousness of God can manifest.

Volumes could be written anent this subject, yet it is necessary for our present purpose to touch briefly upon it in order to proceed with the text. Therefore, I urge each one of you to take this concept into meditation, to expand it until you cognize the depth and the breadth of its meaning.

Never attempt to build a form from within a separated focus of identification. Establish first in deep meditation your at-one-ment with the One Life. *Dare* to set aside your own separated identity, your own purpose and goal, and to ascertain the way in which you can *best* serve the Plan via your alignment with it, as an integral part of the One Life.

I here insert a warning. Do not attempt to become the One Life within yourself, but give up self in order to become a part of that One Life; and from this focus, learn to serve the many.

The first law with which the magician is concerned is the equation of spirit, matter and consciousness. Via this equation he is enabled to view the archetypal form, or in other words, to ascertain that aspect of the Plan for which he as Soul is responsible.

> 2. The appropriation of substance and its creation into devic form.

The building of the form proceeds in four frequencies of prime matter. This means that behind all form on *any* plane of existence are four frequencies, sometimes referred to as the *four elements of earth, air, fire and water.*

They are known by the occultist as

1 = esoteric light
2 = esoteric sound
3 = esoteric color
4 = esoteric vibration

These four frequencies of prime matter make up the substance of any plane of existence, and are the stuff out of which the devic form is constructed.

The magician must appropriate these four elements, and in their proper combination construct the devic form into which the Plan can be carried into outer manifestation.

The Nature of The Soul

Let us look at the manifest form itself. Behind the physical appearance is the physical-etheric devic form. Behind this deva are four frequencies of etheric matter called earth, air, fire, and water—or light, sound, color, and vibration—which have been combined in such a way as to produce an etheric deva of a certain type.

Yet as we look at this, we are seeing but the lowest appearance in substance of the quaternary. These four have been driven forth into manifestation. But before they took form in mental, astral, and etheric substance, they were created as the quaternary on Soul levels out of the four frequencies of prime matter. Thus does the construction of the form proceed above the three planes of human endeavor, in the Buddhic sphere of the Soul.

Once the form is constructed, it is driven downward by the Soul to pass into outer manifestation. We shall deal with this later. In the meantime, attempt to cognize the meaning of the instruction contained in this lesson, remembering that all work thus described so far is carried out by the Soul on its own plane of affairs.

LESSON 30

Becoming Receptive to Intuitive Realization:

Air's Relation to Esoteric
Breath and Sound;
Distinguishing Between
the White and Black Magician;
Earth's Relation to Light
or Primordial Blackness;
The Origin of Evil as Related
to the Previous Impress of Earth;
The Impact of "Air" on "Earth,"
and the Birth of the Opposites
as Devil and Christ

LESSON 30

The four frequencies of matter, sometimes referred to as the lower quaternary, have to do with the four spiritual principles into which prime matter (insofar as humanity is concerned) has been divided. This is a somewhat difficult subject, since we are dealing with a matter which has come out of the major three, and is the prime matter only of the physical body of our Planetary Logos. These are the frequencies which constitute the cosmic physical nature and limitation of our Logos, and by which He is related, in a physical sense, within His cosmic environment. They condition His influence in his own world of affairs, in that they underlie the radiatory activity which is peculiar to Him, and which has its effect in his Solar and Cosmic relationships.

In order to more clearly understand this subject, consider again the fact that Spirit and matter are but the two polarities of one energy or force. Spirit, matter, and consciousness make up the causal triangle of manifestation. Out of that first trinity is born a focus of consciousness which is Logoic, in that it is a precipitated synthesis of the three. This focus is numerically a four in consciousness, since it is the harmony of the three, which has been precipitated into a lower frequency of itself.

Thus, while Logos means One, it also means four, in that that which is behind Logos is sounding, i.e., breathing. Sound has to do with breath, the first harmonic movement of the major three into manifestation.

Thus, that frequency of matter that is defined as esoteric sound, or the so-called element of air, is numerically a One or a four, the living breath or Word of the Creator.

311

The Nature of The Soul

The Word, or breath, contains within itself Spirit, matter, and consciousness in a new frequency, which in its subjective focus is a One, and in its outer manifestation is a four. Thus, out of the three comes the lower quaternary of manifestation.

This frequency of prime matter is a principle, then, created out of the first movement of Will upon intelligence. The first motion of the Will moves forth from the One, who creates as a focus (breath) of the major three into a new synthesis of sound (the Word).

The Word or breath, the actual sound of God which we call Air, as a frequency of matter, is everywhere equally present within any form. Thus, this frequency of matter is the first to be appropriated by the creating Soul as he sets out to build a form into which the Plan is made manifest.

This is why the magician is concerned first with the equation of Spirit, matter, and consciousness. If he is to serve that Life in which he lives, he must ascertain such relationship before he can bring it into proper focus, i.e., sound the Word.

He must then, via repeated meditations, seek to enter into the meditation of the One Life until he can do so at will. Once he does achieve this awareness, the Plan becomes clear, as well as his relationship to that Plan. When he is identified as a consciousness with the One and the Many, he sees Spirit and matter in their relationship to the One Consciousness, and can then bring the three into the proper new focus for the manifestation of the Plan in time and space.

While it is impossible to make this perfectly clear to the student via any grouping of words, such clarity will come when the meditation described is reached. Then, and only then, will the student understand the instruction anent the illumination of the three, yet such instruction is preparatory and does aid the meditation process. Therefore, study it well, and take it into contemplative meditation.

This first movement of the will upon Intelligence is the first cause of the form-to-be, which is set into motion by the creating Soul. It is the Logoic movement into manifestation.

If the word, the sound, or the breath is analogous to Logos (that which is the precipitated frequencies of the major three into a synthetic harmony), then the element of Air, which is the first to be appropriated by the magician, must be so constructed by him as to carry the focus of consciousness of the form-to-be.

Contained within every form is its own created causal (Soul) consciousness, whether that form be man, or one which has been created by man. The creating Soul relates Spirit to matter via the newly created consciousness which is to manifest a new form. That consciousness must, then, be *of* the Plan and not of any separated identity.

It is this very point which differentiates the white magician from the black magician. The consciousness imprisoned in the form created by the black magician is of his own separated identity. It is created by his personal desire and ambition, while the white magician creates from the Soul level of the One Life, according to the Plan of that Life.

Via esoteric sound, the movement of the Spiritual breath, the consciousness of the form-to-be is given birth in light. Air is shaped into and sounded as the Word.

To proceed with a further unveiling of Truth, while the element of earth is defined esoterically as Light, it is in its essence the primordial black. That darkness or primordial no-thing becomes Light (consciousness in matter), or the element earth, as Logos, the Word, sounds within it.

Here is the second frequency of prime matter, a principle created out of the second movement of Will upon Intelligence. The first movement gave birth to consciousness as the Word, a focus of cause; the second movement gives birth to consciousness in form, the form which separates it, so to speak, from its creator.

Earth, then, is created out of no-thing, the primordial dark, that which is the polar opposite of Logos, inert intelligence. It is created by the action of consciousness upon no-thing, as that consciousness is breathed into its sphere. When consciousness radiates (via air) out into a sphere of no-thing, that no-thing or primordial dark becomes Light, and the element earth is born. Thus is the Word imprisoned within a ring-pass-not, its etheric Light body.

An aside note may be inserted here. The above presupposes that the Soul on its own plane, in order to take unto itself a form, had first to breathe itself forth into the void. It gave itself unto that void, where even the Father was lost, and awoke to find itself within its prison.

Herein is explained the mystery of the dark night of the Soul, when it again crosses the void, this time in full waking consciousness, to rejoin the Father.

We come now to an ancient mystery which has to do with the origin of evil upon this planet. While that primordial dark is truly a no-thing, it has already been impressed in a previous Solar system with a form nature. That form nature is dormant until Light moving within darkness awakens it into activity. Thus is the opposition to consciousness as a Divine Being born. The so-called devil is born along with the Christ in the first sheath of Light created. The Dweller on the Threshold resides in the causal sheath and is, therefore, the last opposition to be confronted by the applicant to the initiation of liberation.

Here is the major physical limitation of our Logos, His karmic equipment carried over from a former incarnation, and the reason why ours is not a sacred planet. That Light, which is the element earth, moves into a color dictated by a previous impression of substance, borning a form nature which is in opposition to the evolution of consciousness.

It is with this opposition that the Adept deals as he builds the forms designed to carry the consciousness of the Plan into manifestation.

How does all of this relate to the work of magic into which a probationer disciple enters in order to serve the Plan?

The first implications are those which have to do with the tremendous forces of creation itself, with which he is finally working. He has to appropriate the very breath of the One in Whom he lives in order to create at all. He must himself function as the One, and as that One, breathe forth into the primordial black the soul (consciousness) of the form-to-be, in such a way as to create out of nothing the element which gives shape or first body (light or earth) to that Soul.

He does this in full knowledge that harmony upon this planet is known through conflict. He must then ascertain the conflict which will be born into being with the newly-created form, and with wisdom, account for it.

That primordial no-thing which he must appropriate in order to create the element earth, contains within itself a dormant opposition, which will rise up as the consciousness of Planetary prime matter, to oppose the very Plan he seeks to serve. Yet, that consciousness will be a part of the newly-created Soul, wedded to it, as

The Nature of The Soul

Light irrevocably awakens and attracts it into being.

Why create at all, he wonders? Yet the realization must come that it is only in this way that Planetary karma can be resolved. This aspect of Logoic equipment must be redeemed before our planet takes its place among those sacred in the system.

The assurance of success lies in the name of Christ. Only in this Name do we propose to create; only in this Name is synthesis truly possible. The Word he sounds forth in time and space is the Name of Christ.

Let us now recapitulate the procedure thus far from a somewhat different perspective.

> *"The Soul in meditation deep, merges with the One and sees the Plan before him.*
> *The illumination of the three reveals the Word.*
>
> *The Soul in meditation deep, takes unto his heart that Word and sounds it there.*
> *The creator and his creations are one.*
>
> *The sounding word casts a shadow in the darkest night. The Soul with heartfelt Love sounds forth the Word to sound within the shadow, and Light is born within its sphere.*
>
> *Three colors merge and blend, and fire claims the Word. The creator and his creation are no longer one."*

The above is translated from an ancient work of teaching, long lost to humankind. Its finding, and its release, indicates the promise of this new cycle. It is given here as a seed-thought for meditation by the Soul who seeks to serve.

LESSON 31

What to do With Intuitive Realization:

The Relationship of Fire and Water
in the Creative Process;
Individualization of the Manasic Unit;
The Claiming of the Manasic Sheath;
The Birth of the Deva;
The Soul's Preparations for Driving
the Deva Down into "Birth"
in the Three Lower Worlds;
The Use of the Brain
in the Creative Process

318

LESSON 31

We come, now, to the most difficult stage of the creative process to reveal in word form. How is mind itself created? How does the Soul, through a manipulation of this frequency of prime matter, become an isolated ego?

Here, indeed, is a mystery which has troubled the thoughts of every serious student of alchemy down through the ages. For just as every form in the three worlds is indwelt by its own causal consciousness, so also is it indwelt by such consciousness through the medium of an isolated mind. That isolated mind is an effect, a radiation or emanation of the manasic unit created and contained within the causal sheath.

The Word, sounding within its sphere of light, produces three colors which merge and blend into one Fire. That Fire is manas, the principle of mind which blazes up to claim the Word.

The student must be very careful at this point to avoid a confusion which could result through misinterpretation of two apparently conflicting concepts. The element of earth or light comes before, and is in a higher frequency of prime matter than, that of fire. Earth, then, or the principle of light, which must not be confused with the physical plane of the planet earth, comes before fire or the principle of manas.

Light moves into three colors, which, as they blend, become fire or manas. The three colors are the spiritual forces or energies of Divine Will, Divine Love, and Intelligent Activity. One of them, insofar as this planet is concerned, becomes or takes on the nature of the

319

The Nature of The Soul

Dweller on the Threshold, as that opposition to the Plan, which is born within the light, moves into the frequency of prime matter which we call the principle of manas or mind.

In Lesson 30 it is stated:

> "That light which is the element earth, moves into a color dictated by a previous impression of substance, borning a form nature which is in opposition to the evolution of consciousness."

The color, one of three, gives manas, in this planetary system, a nature which is contradictory to the Purpose of the Soul, yet it is only via mind that the Soul can manifest his purpose. It is with this specific color or nature of mind that the Soul is concerned as he seeks liberation from his prison. It is this color which isolates him, via the principle of manas, from his brothers. It constitutes the illusion of the mental plane with which the initiate must deal as he seeks to serve the Plan.

The Soul or consciousness of the form-to-be, is swallowed up in fire, and its sound is lost. As that fire consumes the Word, its light is dimmed, gradually receding to a point, and the Soul is claimed by another sheath, the manasic unit. It has been given form: the creator and his creation are no longer one.

There is naught now but form. The Soul or Word within its form is silent until its creator awakens it to life.

The creator looks upon his creation and sounds that note which is its life.

The note is sensed, and the sleeping soul responds. The Word begins to vibrate, moving out upon a wave to join the myriads. Thus, is the fourth principle of vibration, or the element of water, created by the sound of the Word within its form.

The wave creates time and space, or a sphere of activity, within which the form relates to other forms.

Air, earth, fire, and water have been thus manipulated and the deva lives, a creation not yet born into appearance in the three worlds, but having causal place in the Buddhic sphere within its creator's aura.

Thus is a persona created prior to its birth in the three worlds of human endeavor.

Please remember that all four frequencies of prime matter thus described are above the three lower worlds. They make up the substantial body of the Buddhic plane, and in different equations, make up the substantial body of the mental, astral, and etheric planes as well.

The lower mental is a condensation into a lower frequency range of the four elements in an equation that gives fire the predominance.

The astral is a condensation of the four into an equation that gives water its predominance.

The etheric is a condensation of the four into an equation that gives earth the predominance.

Air is everywhere equally present.

The physical plane of appearances is produced by the Dweller on the threshold as a distortion of air, earth, fire, and water. When the Dweller is overcome or transmuted by the Angel of the Presence, the physical plane will be no longer.

For so long as the Soul is the victim of the Dweller, he is condemned to the Wheel of Rebirth in the Dweller's domain.

The creative process described thus far takes place on

The Nature of The Soul

Buddhic levels by the consciousness, who is functioning within and as the One Life. He is then operating above the brain and lower mind nature, unobstructed by the forms contained therein. He has yet to precipitate his created form into manifestation.

And now I tell you something of a secret which is of great importance to you at this time.

Those who read, study, and meditate upon these instructions are already engaged in this creative process during those hours when the body is sleeping. The new expansions of consciousness, which are achieved via experiences in consciousness, are conceived and given form by the Soul-centered student himself as he functions in the ashramic group life each night.

It is his task to drive these new experiences down into manifestation, to impact and impress the brain in such a way as to give them birth in physical, astral, and mental awareness.

The life experience of the accepted disciple in the three lower worlds is created in this way. The plan of service, which takes advantage of every opportunity in time and space, is conceived and molded into devic form by the Soul-centered disciple while his body sleeps, until continuity is achieved to the degree that he enters the ashramic group life during his meditations. Human karma, national, group, and individual karma are observed, and accounted for, i.e., made right use of in service to the Plan, as experiences are created which will resolve it all in Divine Law and Order.

Sooner or later each one of you will create in full waking consciousness, not only such experiences in this incarnation, but the total life experience of following incarnations, the total service plan which proceeds with continuity from one life to the next.

Lesson 31

In just this way, the initiate moves into his own manifestations in time and space, leaving nothing to karma or fate, but manipulating such karma to serve the Plan.

As you enter into meditation, do so with the realization that your immediate goal of development or unfoldment is to achieve that continuity between the Soul on its own plane and its life in the body, so there is no gap or break between.

At present your waking hours find you functioning in the brain as a recipient of higher impress when such reception is possible. Realize that you are moving toward such a union with the Soul on its own plane that you will function as the creating and impressing agent.

How is the created form driven downward into manifestation?

The Soul has now to impress the intangible (insofar as the three worlds are concerned) and subtle form, with its imprisoned consciousness, upon the form-making instrument in the three worlds, the physical brain. This he must do in such a way as to make possible its appearance in etheric, mental, and astral substance.

In Lesson 28 it is stated:

> "The brain is actually a focus in substance of the incarnating consciousness. We say, 'the man in the brain'. What we mean is, the focus of the Soul in substance, 'the man in his house'. The brain is a condensation of mental, astral, and etheric matter created by a focus of these three frequencies of matter through the cave in the center of the head. The pineal and pituitary glands are the positive and negative polarities which set up an interplay of force resulting in the birth of consciousness within, or its reflection upon, this condensed matter—we call the brain.

The cave in the center of the head is occultly defined as that place where land, air, and water meet, because this is the center in which etheric, mental, and astral substance is focused (in that order) for condensation into form."

I should like to insert here that air has been used in connection with the mental plane as a part of the veil of Truth. Actually that statement is an occult fact, since air is everywhere equally present, but it is also incomplete.

When this is considered in the light of the preceding instruction, it begins to convey real meaning.

The Soul has created a devic form out of the four elements of the Buddhic sphere. Let us say, for our purposes here, that that form has to do with the Soul's expression in the three worlds, via the medium of an illumined persona. The consciousness, which the Soul would express and which has been imprisoned within the newly-created form, has to incarnate into the physical brain, i.e., it must be focused there within its new form before it can manifest in the three worlds.

The Soul, still on his own plane, looks down, via the channel created from the causal sheath, through the head center to the cave and readies himself to drive the created devic form downward into a focus in the cave.

In the cave the substantial forces of his bodies meet, and in this center they will claim or clothe the new deva.

He is now concerned with these forces and their effect upon his created form. He has, then, to look through the center where etheric, mental, and astral devas meet, into the bodies themselves, to ascertain their readiness to cooperate with this effort.

Lesson 31

The condition of the bodies is reflected back into the cave. For just as the forces concentrated there have created them, so do they impact upon their center causing reaction therein.

More will be given anent this stage of the creative process in the next lesson.

As an assignment, please explain in your own words your understanding of the four elements.

The Nature of The Soul

LESSON 32

Ceremonial Magic,
or the Manipulation of
the Devas of the Lower Four:

The Devas of Mental, Astral, Etheric,
and Physical-Dense Substance
(or Energy, Force, Substance, and Appearance);
The Evolution of the Devic Lives;
The Use of Will when Impacting the Devas;
The Parallel Evolution of Consciousness
(as Being) and Matter (as Intelligence);
The Soul's Assessment of
the Condition of the Lower Four

LESSON 32

The term "ceremonial magic" is one which has been used deliberately, both as a veil and as an occult indication of Truth. It refers to that conscious manipulation of energy, force, and substance which produces phenomenal appearance in the world of affairs.

In the last few lessons we have concerned ourselves almost completely with the creative process as it is initiated from the level of the Buddhic plane by the Soul-centered disciple. While this is pure creativity, and while we have referred to it as magic, it is not actually ceremonial magic, for ceremonial magic deals with the manipulation of the lower four.

Here we come to a further unscrambling of Truth in order to understand a subject which has been clothed in so many veils as to render it seeming fancy.

We have described the lower quaternary as the four frequencies of prime matter, or earth, air, fire, and water. These refer to prime matter in the planetary sense, which is found in the Buddhic sphere, and which is used by the creator as he initiates from the level of Soul that which is to take form in the three lower worlds. In other words, we have described the process of creating a Soular deva (causal form), which may or may not take on an appearance in mental, astral, and etheric substance.

The devas of the lower four refer to:

1. the devas of the mental plane

2. the devas of the astral plane
3. the devas of the etheric plane
4. the particular devas of appearance

or:

1. energy
2. force
3. substance
4. appearance

In other words, the work on Buddhic levels is pure creativity, while the work below that level is ceremonial magic, i.e., the manipulation of four orders of devic life.

The kingdom of devas is a parallel evolution of substance or intelligence which relates to consciousness in such a way as to give substantial form and appearance to it. Thus does Logoic Purpose work out into manifestation via the consciousness aspect in its relationship to the devic evolution. Via this relationship, a man is enabled to think, to feel, and to act, for it is the deva who gives body to that which he would express on any level.

To the man in the brain, or the consciousness imprisoned within the confines of the three lower worlds, the Soular deva, whose creation we have considered in the last few lessons, is the archetypal form. To the devas of the lower four, the Soular deva is not only the archetypal form, but the higher directing life toward which they aspire, and whom they seek to obey.

Just as the imprisoned consciousness aspires toward, and seeks union with, its higher correspondent, so do the devas of the lower four evolve similarly. Just as the consciousness finally reaches such union via devic life, so does the deva reach his union via consciousness.

Thus, both kingdoms are interdependent and can reach the fulfillment of their respective purposes and goals only through a cooperative effort with one another.

Every form that is perceivable to the five physical senses is constructed of the devas of the lower four, and indwelt by consciousness. The bodies themselves are constituted of devic lives, so that the two evolutions of deva and consciousness are closer than are Logos and Soul, even though the latter two are One.

The very mind with which you think is a deva. The feeling nature through which you perceive, sense, and touch, is another deva. The substantial body behind your appearance, and the appearance itself, each is an intelligent life within this devic evolution. These lives have to be deliberately contacted by the consciousness, and cooperated with in the working out of God's Plan on earth, before either can realize its Purpose and goal.

The devic evolution is the Third Aspect, the negative pole of manifestation. At its highest level, it is the third Logos, but in its highest grade available to man, it is the Holy Ghost, and in its lowest grade, it is the physical element.

Consider for just a moment these two parallel evolutions in their unconscious relationship to one another.

A man in his mind (mental deva) is enabled to think only because the deva obligingly arranges itself according to the dictates of the man's will, which is the positive pole.

A man in his feeling nature (astral deva) is enabled to perceive via the senses, to sense and touch only because the deva obligingly relates him within a sphere of activity or vibration. It puts him in touch with other forms and states of consciousness or isolated egos, according to the dictates of his Will.

The Nature of The Soul

A man in his inner substantial Soul (etheric deva) is enabled to act only because the deva gives substance to what he would do.

A man in his physical body or appearance (a combination or interaction of etheric deva and elemental) is in appearance only because the elemental gives him appearance (reflects what he is) according to the dictates of his will.

In this way, the human evolution lives within, and unknowingly manipulates, devic lives in order to manifest at all. The deva always cooperates with the will aspect as it is wielded by a man's consciousness. Thus does it serve his evolutionary purpose.

The man consciously cooperates with the evolutionary purpose of the deva only when he transfers or impresses upon it with clarity the Divine Will, rather than a separated will. Thus is the deva enabled to contact, and finally merge with, its higher life, namely Spirit.

Consciousness is the evolution of Being, of Identity.

Matter is the evolution of intelligence or substance.

The attention of these two evolutions will not be directed to the evolution of the First Aspect in this particular Solar incarnation, though some few revelations anent it will come in toward the end of its day. The third or final incarnation of our Solar system in the cosmic physical plane will reveal the evolution of Spirit, and hence complete the final equation of Spirit, matter, and consciousness on its own level, or in a Solar sense.

For our purposes, then, the devic evolution is the polar opposite of the Will aspect, and via its manipulation the Divine Will, will finally reveal itself. These devas are the builders of the universe, who, in obedience to a directing will, arrange themselves in activity to produce form.

Lesson 32

In our last lesson, we had arrived at that critical place in the creative process where the Soul, on its own level, must ascertain the readiness of the lower devas to cooperate with his effort.

"The Soul, still on his own plane, looks down, via the channel created from the causal sheath, through the head center to the cave, and readies himself to drive the created devic form downward into a focus in the cave."

Three factors here concern the Soul. They are: The state of the incarnate consciousness as it is reflected by:

1. The etheric deva, who shall give first action to the newly created form, i.e., life in the three worlds. In other words, out of its own substance, the etheric deva shall build the etheric network, the inner substantial body, or constitutional framework, of that which is to take birth in the three lower worlds.

This deva must then reflect a ready consciousness via its upward movement of poise. It is held steady and receptive to higher impact. Its breath is quiet, i.e., in the higher interlude of reception.

2. The mental deva who shall give Purpose and direction, or Potency, to the form. This deva reflects the readiness of consciousness via its alerted attention to higher impact. The lucidity of its substance is noted. Is it such that the higher purpose of the precipitated form can be impressed upon it? Will that purpose reflect as meaning in the mind nature of the new form?

This deva must clothe the new form with that body of mind which ensures the precipitation of its creator's intent. That intent is reflected, via meaning, as the life plan of the form from its end to its beginning.

I should like to clarify somewhat this occult statement of "from its end to its beginning." That which is reflected downward from the mental body to the astral is an inversion of the created image, so the last (beginning) comes first in the sequence of manifestation. Thus, the mental deva receives and builds from the end to the beginning.

This deva has to be coordinated with the etheric deva in the higher interlude of reception.

3. The astral deva who, out of his own substance, shall create a field of activity and relate the newly created form within its own sphere, to that field of activity which is to be its world of affairs.

This deva must evidence the readiness of the incarnating consciousness via its utter quiet, i.e., peace. Only out of peace is that chaos of activity born which results in a new precipitation of purpose and Plan.

This deva is coordinated with the other two in the lower interlude of reception.

We have herein considered the requisites to magical function insofar as the devas of the lower three are concerned. They indicate the three requisite conditions of the incarnating consciousness as being:

1. that it has been brought into a point of focus (abstraction from the world of horizontal impacts);

2. that it is aligned and receptive via mind to the higher purpose and Plan;

3. that it is capable of entering that silence known as Peace, i.e., its focus is one of poise.

LESSON 33

Using the Higher and Lower Interludes
of the Creative Process to Manifest the Form

The Relationship of the Ashramic
Meditation to the Moon Cycles;
Coordination of the Soul's Lower
Interlude of Meditation with the
Higher Interlude of the Persona;
The Higher Interlude's Connection
with the Full Moon and Illumination;
The Lower Interlude's Connection
with the New Moon and Precipitation;
The Minor Cycles of the Twenty-four Hour Day

LESSON 33

"Throughout the entire incarnation
the Spiritual Soul is in meditation deep."

Let us now consider a hypothetical case of a group Soul (an ashramic group life) who has created a new life in the form of a Soular deva. That deva contains the Divine Purpose of the incarnating group, its service plan in the three worlds, and whatsoever of The Wisdom is necessary to the manifestation of its service.

It is suggested that those students of this text who consider themselves to be integrated into a potential service group give the above concept their deepest consideration.

The soul on his own plane has ascertained the readiness of the incarnating consciousness, and its instrumentality, to cooperate with the Divine Purpose and Plan. He has now to drive the newly created Soular deva downward into a focus in the cave, where the devas of the lower four will give it a form and an activity that is comprehensible to the human consciousness.

In order to do this, the overshadowing Soul must coordinate the lower interlude of his meditation with the higher interlude of the meditating persona.

This concept gives added light to the pure reason of meditation itself. When the incarnating consciousness makes himself available to the overshadowing Soul on the high mount of meditation, that Soul precipitates its Purpose, Wisdom, and Plan into the mind, brain, and affairs of its persona.

The first time this act really occurs, the third initiation is underway. The Overshadowing Spiritual Soul is incarnating into its prepared vehicle of manifestation via the process of illumination and transfiguration.

The meditation interludes are as follows:

A. The higher interlude is reached when the consciousness enters its highest point of receptivity, otherwise known as the occult silence. This is the moment of greatest aspiration to that which is transcendent.

While a higher interlude is reached cyclically in each meditation, the highest peak of all is normally reached once during each moon cycle, on or about the time of the full moon.

B. The lower interlude is reached when the consciousness, after having taken unto himself the overshadowing illumination, precipitates that illumination into a lower frequency of appearance. It is, then, the moment wherein magic is done.

As with the higher interlude, each meditation should provide for the cyclic moment of precipitation. None the less, the lowest interlude of all (the moment of greatest magical opportunity) is normally reached once during each moon cycle, just after the dark of the moon.

This means that the Overshadowing Spiritual Soul makes its major cyclic approach to its persona during the full—moon period covering from 12 hours to 3 days, depending upon its point of evolutionary development. This is its lower interlude, the moment apropos to its precipitation of illumination into the meditating consciousness of the persona.

The Overshadowing Spiritual Soul makes its minor cyclic approach to the meditating persona once each twenty-four hours during the morning period covering from sunrise to high noon, depending upon its point of evolutionary development.

The indwelling consciousness establishes its cyclic interludes via the meditation practice of approach. The minor cycle of the higher interlude is approached each morning via a carefully practiced alignment, focus, and silent aspiration. The major cycle of the higher interlude is approached via the utilization of the daily high point for a specific Purpose during the period from new moon to full moon.

In other words, the daily meditation during this period is considered as a cyclic approach to the greatest moment of opportunity for illumination upon a specific seed-thought. No one realization reached during this major cycle of approach is considered, or accepted, as the goal of the meditation until that moment.

The meditation, from new moon to full moon, is one meditation approach carried out cyclically.

The process then reverses with the minor cycle of the lower interlude being utilized each day via the practice of a lower alignment, contemplation, or reflection, and the act of precipitation.

The major cycle of the lower interlude, which is actually an approach via gradual descent, utilizes each daily meditation for a specific Purpose during the period from full moon to the dark of the moon.

During this period, the higher interlude is used as a time of contemplation or thought-form building of that illumination already received. A new seed-thought is not taken during this cycle, nor are new realizations sought. The purpose of the period is the embodiment of that received during the higher interlude.

When the major cyclic moment is reached, the real work of magic is entered, and the full cycle of meditation concluded.

The meditation from full moon to the dark of the moon, is one meditation descent from a higher interlude into a lower one, carried out cyclically.

This means that the daily meditations, from one new moon to the next, are but the cyclic activities of one full meditation, utilizing a continuity of one seed-thought or goal.

I should like to bring out one other point of major importance at this time. When the disciple can enter into meditation upon arising, and maintain or hold the meditative state of mind throughout the day, his minor cycle of precipitation is reached during the period from sunset to midnight.

If the meditation cycles are not properly utilized, the whole meditation is thrown out of balance and cannot be expected to bring the best result. After the probationer has become somewhat reoriented to the life of the Soul and seeks to serve the Divine Plan, he must then learn to make right use of these cycles.

If the approach to the higher interlude is not carried out, with an inner dedication to Purpose, conscious Soul contact cannot be expected to ensue. If the approach via descent to the lower interlude is not maintained for the specific purpose of embodiment, how, then, can the probationer expect to master the form nature? If the continuity of the full meditation is interrupted, the next cycle is thrown out of balance, and confusion is the natural result.

During your study of this series of instruction, your practice of meditation has followed a much shorter cycle; however, you are now ready to initiate the continuity of meditation as practiced by the Hierarchy and its disciples.

Proceed then, keeping in mind the following ideas as you do so:

1. That the Overshadowing Soul is a group Soul attempting to appropriate, via its lower interlude, the incarnating consciousness of its instrumentality.

2. That that instrumentality consists of:

   a. the world group of disciples,
   b. the ashramic group life of which you are a related part,
   c. the group unit with which you are in incarnate contact.

As you proceed with your alignment, include a horizontal one with these three aspects of the instrumentality of the Soul.

Consider, for a moment, the tremendous power potential of a group of disciples who could, and would, establish and maintain the continuity of meditation together as one.

The higher interlude would find each focus in the cave, or a higher center, in one state of silent receptivity where the separated consciousness has merged into a one life. The illumination could then be precipitated into the consciousness of the entire group, and each one would cognize the same Purpose, Wisdom, and Plan.

The lower interlude would find each focus in the cave synthesized into the white magician, where the act of group precipitation could take place via the total instrumentality.

The Nature of The Soul

Thus does the disciple become a conscious part of the One Life, and thus does the One Life become a conscious part of him. In this way, the Purpose, Wisdom, and Plan of the ashramic group life is cognized and precipitated into a world service activity.

> 3. That that which carries the illumination from the over-shadowing Soul to the incarnate consciousness is a Soular Deva, created specifically for that purpose.

This deva will be driven downward by the Overshadowing Soul when the higher interlude of the persona is coordinated with the lower interlude of the Soul.

At this point, an annual meditation cycle which utilizes both the major and minor cyclic interludes, is offered to those of you who are intuitively guided to make right use of it.

This meditation can best be initiated during the first new moon of the new year, or during that new moon which follows the Wesak festival.

The purpose of the full year of meditation will be the precipitation of the Wisdom into the consciousness of humanity as it relates to the following twelve seed-thoughts. Each seed-thought will cover one full cycle of meditation from each new moon to the next in the order given.

> 1. "The Power of Truth is God."
>
> 2. "The Love of Truth is Wisdom."
>
> 3. "The Light of Truth is 'Every Man a Christ'."
>
> 4. "The Truth Shall Make you Free."

342

Lesson 33

5. "The Will to Synthesis is the Spirit of Peace."

6. "The Will to Love is the Cause of Peace."

7. "The Will to Good is the Action of Peace."

8. "The Divine Motivation of Force is the Life of God."

9. "The Wisdom of Force is the Love of God."

10. "The Right Use of Force is the Love of Humanity, Individually and Collectively."

11. "Love Transcends Conflict."

12. "The Divine Plan for Humanity Manifests Through the Divinity of Every Individual Unit."

The Nature of The Soul

LESSON 34

Problems of the Young Disciple as
Ceremonial Magic is First Attempted:

The "No-Man's Land" Between
Identity as Soul and Persona;
The Problem of Dissatisfaction
with the World of the Persona;
The Dilemma of "Impotence"
and the Glamours of Futility,
Depression, and Self-Pity;
Wielding Divine Laws
as Methods of Coping;
The Law of Economy and
the Nature of Obsessing
Thought-Forms;
Right Relationship
with Finance

LESSON 34

The young disciple who is entering the realm of initiate magic for the first time finds himself beset with obstacles and conflicts, which, in their total impact, give the appearance of utter confusion or chaos. He moves within that no-man's land between two worlds, each with a distinct set of laws, finding that he can enter into neither.

The old world of the persona, within which he has lived, and moved, and had his being for untold centuries of experience, is no longer open to him. He long since took a path which led directly out of it, and with little recognition, he has finally moved through the gate which bars him from reentry into it.

Ahead he sees—but dimly yet—a new world of the Soul, wherein new laws of life must be learned before he can begin to function. As he practices meditation, he is learning the rudiments of mobility, communication, and cognition. He stumbles, as does the baby when it is learning to walk; he stutters, as with the child who is learning to talk; and he makes mistakes similar to those of the youngster with his three R's.

His horizons have extended far beyond the circumference of his physical vision. A new and different light than that of his sun shines upon all that is, making it grow according to an inner half-seen pattern. Life is no longer a space of time between birth and death, but has become an everlasting growth of consciousness and changing forms.

Yet, this newly born one (newly born to the Spirit) still

occupies a persona, still finds himself in this world, if no longer of it.

What, specifically, are his problems? Those of you who have come thus far will recognize such problems when they are stated, even though you yourselves might be unable to define them.

First, of course, is the sense of "so little real knowledge," which every young disciple feels with such an acute awareness. The vast expansion of consciousness which he has experienced—and it is vast when compared to that of but a short time ago—is as nothing in sight of that which he has yet to attain. His vision of the world of reality, with all of his new knowledge, is but a place of shadows. The laws that he must manipulate are but definitions which sound and feel right to him, but which, as yet, hold little practical meaning. That Soul which he is (his very identity) is as yet little more than theory.

Secondly, and at the same time, the young disciple experiences an increasing dissatisfaction with the world of the persona, which grows out of all proportion to his new knowledge. Here he cannot find joy or peace of mind. He grows tired of his very life work. He finds every contribution he would make to society utterly inadequate. The gift is given, but without the spirit of the giver.

This is a dangerous period, a test of the very process of initiation, which claims the failure of many a beginner.

In addition to these two problems, the young disciple very often experiences such things as financial and social failure, influential failure, and the futility of impotency in all of the activities which count with him. Magic no longer works, not even the simple magic of the mind, which he learned long ago.

What are the answers to this complex maze of chaos?

What is the path that leads out of it into the new world which stands as a dim beacon before him? There are answers; there is a way, and this lesson shall devote itself to both.

Learn, first, what it is you experience with the feeling nature. What is that weight of sorrow you have suddenly taken on your shoulders and cannot put down nor bear to hold? What is this burden imprisoning you from natural joy?

It is the weight of the world sorrow pressing in upon you. It is the eternal cry of the imprisoned Soul for release, the Soul of humanity, which suffers the indignities of the evil nature of ignorance.

My brothers, you have scarcely touched it; you have but tasted of the pain of human suffering (and I speak now not of the persona, but of Soul suffering) that every initiate and adept knows so well. What moves God to wait upon humanity? What moves the great consciousness and Light of the Christ to sacrifice His heaven to overshadow and intervene in human affairs? What moves the Hierarchy to stay within the dark star, when the Cosmos waits without? What is it that calls forth compassion from every Life that is free of it? What is the need for compassion?

You have felt that burden, have experienced its likeness, as you have opened your heart to the Soul of humanity, and in most cases, you have considered it your own. You have claimed it, have interpreted it via self-pity, depression, futility. This you think is your own? Ah, my brothers, such ego, for no one unit could have reason or access to such sorrow.

Here is the first step toward freedom. Realize, once and for all, that you have or can experience nothing of yourself alone, for you are not alone. The depressions and sorrows experienced by every mystic or occultist are the sorrows of the World Soul in its total imprisonment. As you become conscious of the One Life, you open the door of awareness to this condition within a part of it. As you merge more and more closely within the One Life, you will know and experience this condition to its very depths. This is a part of the Consciousness of the Soul. Would you escape it? This is your share of Planetary karma.

Yet it need not be the cause of your failure as a disciple. Even in the midst of its awareness, joy can also be known, both the natural joy of life itself, and the joy of knowing that you can serve to alleviate some little bit of that great suffering.

Thus is this pair of opposites balanced, and the initiate born to serve humanity.

Learn to stand with that Divine Strength which does not permit an astral subjugation to it.

The second step to freedom follows closely upon the first. It has to do with Law. Those Laws which manipulate Spirit and matter, or Plan and form, have to be ascertained and wielded with a fearlessness characteristic of The Christ.

First, we look at the old set of laws that have brought us this far, moving into an awareness of the new ones through cognition of higher correspondence.

What is the medium of exchange in the world of affairs—the medium that governs and controls the movement of all energies, forces, and substance in the physical plane of appearances?

It is the financial system via which commerce and exchange of all kinds is possible. This system carries the life blood of human affairs, and is the part of the economy which makes such life possible. It has built the present civilization and sustains it.

In the present world, this medium of exchange is the reflection of the inner etheric network of the body of humanity, that network which holds together and makes possible, via exchange, the interrelationships of all parts to one another and to the whole.

The word of power, which manipulates the energies through the financial system, is "money"—crystallized Third Ray energy. Money, then, is not the medium of exchange, as is supposed by many, for that medium *is* the system. Money is that form into which power has been directed or designated.

In the world of affairs, money is a reflection of the sacred word of the Soul, which moves the life of humanity through its etheric medium of exchange. Its power lies in its mantric form, for both the OM and money are essentially mantrams, i.e., words of magical power.

The forms in the physical world are manipulated through their exchange, within an elaborate system of exchange, via the sounding of that word which has the power to move them. These forms we shall define as the 'devas of appearance.'

In a similar manner, the devas of the etheric, astral, and mental planes are manipulated through their exchange via the sounding of that word which has the power to move them.

Consider now the disciple who brings a gift (something which he wishes to exchange) which has no monetary value (no real place yet) within the financial medium of exchange. His problem is very real, for if he would exchange that which he has, for life within the world of affairs, he must make a place for it *within* the economic system of the world.

The Nature of The Soul

Yet, a gift of the Spirit has no monetary value, nor can it truly be given such, for to do so would limit it to the world of form.

Thus, the young disciple moves in a no-man's land between the world of concrete facts and the world of so-called miracles.

He has first to realize that his gift of the Spirit can only be exchanged behind the scenes of ordinary affairs via the manipulation of the devas of the etheric, astral, and mental planes. That gift will be carried from one consciousness to another by those devas, when the word of Power is sounded.

But that which is subjective does take on an appearance, and a new deva of appearance must be created that can be exchanged for life and influence in the world of affairs.

The disciple knows the form he exchanges is not his gift; it is not his contribution to humanity, even though it may appear as such.

He detaches the sense of importance from the form or appearance of his service, knowing wherein his real service lies.

Then, calmly, without emotion, he aligns the devas of appearance with the devas of the Plan, aligns the lower word of power with the higher one, and sounds that mantram which gives him control of the form nature.

The mantram that he sounds is more than a word. It is a synthesis of Light, sound, color, and vibration into a new ceremony, the ceremony of life itself.

With this ceremony, we shall deal at some length in the following lessons. In preparation for such illumination, it is suggested that you consider the particular devas of appearance with which you are most familiar.

First, what is a deva of appearance? It is the obsessing thought-form just behind, or controlling, the appearance of the outer picture, an interaction between the etheric deva and the elemental.

Consider the obsessing thought-form behind the monetary value of any article of goods, of any act of public service, of any act of work, etc.

Consider the obsessing thought-form behind the color of a man's skin, his racial characteristics, his social class and consciousness, his likes and dislikes, etc.

Consider the obsessing thought-form behind nationalism, Catholicism, Protestantism, Buddhism, Capitalism, Communism, etc.

Consider the obsessing thought-form behind peace and war, good and evil, life and death, love and hate.

Anything that is makes its appearance in the three worlds via a thought-form which obsesses consciousness. This we call the deva of appearance, which finds its place between, and yet within, the etheric deva and the elemental form.

If the disciple is to control the form nature, he must deal with these devas, choosing those with which he will be obsessed, and with which he, in turn, will obsess. If this comes as a shock, realize that you are only considering the facts of life.

The Nature of The Soul

LESSON 35

Aligning Devas via the Ceremony of Life:

Participation in the Ritual
(Formal and Informal) of Aligning Devas;
The Light Body of The Christ, See-la-Aum;
The Light Body of Humanity, Selah;
The Use of Sound, the Brain, and
the Center System in Formal Alignment

LESSON 35

A disciple's medium of expression, and therefore of exchange, is the etheric Light body of the Planetary Logos. We view it first as a One Life, a great Light deva, whose substance enters into, permeates, and holds in right relationship, all parts of the One Life in an integrated totality.

Insofar as our planet is concerned, the Buddhic sphere is the point of origin, or more correctly, the door of entry of this light body into the seven vibratory spheres of planetary activity. Thus, via this medium of expression, the Life of our Logos flows into, and through, all of its parts from the Buddhic sphere, the natural habitat of the Soul, which is the heart of the Logoic Life.

Pause for a moment and consider the Buddhic sphere as the heart which distributes the life of the Logos throughout the Planet via a great Light deva, which emanates spherically from its center to its periphery. Thus does that Life reach into, and direct, the affairs of the seven planes or spheres of vibrating matter that make up the Logoic physical body.

Via this emanating Life which is Love, the conscious Soul, according to its awareness, has access to, and expression within, all seven spheres of planetary activity, for this deva not only carries the life aspect, but is also the vehicle of consciousness.

When viewed from the perspective that sees it in its totality as a One Life, it is the Soular deva; the etheric Light body of the Logos Himself. This is the Third Aspect of manifestation constructed of light, sound, color, and vibration, or the elements of earth, air, fire, and water.

The Nature of The Soul

Insofar as the disciple in the three worlds is concerned, this great Life, in its highest aspect, is the Lord of the Devic evolution, the energy and substance of The Christ.

It is via this deva that The Christ makes His Presence known to the meditating disciple, and via this deva that His plans and Purpose are revealed.

Christ is the redeeming principle within the planetary Life. The great Light deva is the instrument of that redemption, giving causal body to each focal point of Logoic fire within the Buddhic sphere.

Thus, a man's Soul Body is but a part of the great Deva of Light, the body of Christ, in process of redemption.

Upon completion of that redemption, the periphery of the Soular deva is shattered, permitting the Life and consciousness to merge with that life of which it is a part.

We speak of the Divine Plan for humanity as being held in focus by the Mind of The Christ. That focus within which the Plan is held is the great Deva of Light whose name, as close as can be translated into formulated sound is See-la-Aum. The meaning of this name is the Plan, and it can only be cognized through meditation and expressed through loving service.

The sounding of this name in the proper combination of notes, and accompanied with the cognition of Divine Intent, invokes Divine Intervention into the life and affairs of humanity. The release of this information is in preparation for that time during the latter part of the twentieth century when the world group of disciples shall, in coordinated effort, invoke the reappearance of The Christ in a mass initiation.

Lesson 35

This, however, must be preceded by many changes, both in the consciousness, and in the affairs of humanity. The integration of all disciples into a world group effort toward rehabilitation and reorientation of the mass must proceed almost at once if the cycle of opportunity is to be taken advantage of. This effort will go forward via the practice, by such disciples, of the true Ceremony of Life, as that ceremony is revealed by the incoming Seventh Ray.

The consciousness of the One Life is identified as The Christ. The body of the One Life is identified as See-la-Aum. The Christ pronounces that body into existence; and the disciple of The Christ becomes its custodian, its transmitter, and its focal point of precipitation into manifest appearance.

Let us look now at the lower correspondence of this great deva, the etheric network of the body of humanity. All human beings live, move, and have their being within a great network of etheric substance, which is an emanation of this Light deva. It holds them in relationship to one another, and is the medium through which the life energies of the human kingdom circulate throughout its many parts. This network, while an emanation, and, therefore, a part of yet a greater life, is also a life in itself: another great deva who is the vehicle of human consciousness, i.e., consciousness which is persona-identified. It responds to the mass mind, which is both astral and mental in nature, reflecting the conditions of that mind into the world of affairs via the devas of appearance. Its name is Selah, and its response is to that which reaches it via a brain.

When the disciple deliberately, and with consciously formulated intent, sounds the name Selah upon the right note (such note being in the key of F), this deva gives him its attention and carries out his intent via the making of a deva of appearance.

The Nature of The Soul

We have already defined a deva of appearance as the obsessing thought-form behind, and controlling the details of the outer picture. We have said it is the interaction between the etheric deva and the elemental form. What is it that turns a thought in the minds of a few men into a public opinion, or into a custom? What gives it life in the affairs of humanity? It is Selah, the etheric network and body of humanity, who takes that thought unto himself and gives it life force, such life force flowing into an elemental group life waiting for it.

The deva of appearance, then, is the life force of the thought as it flows from the etheric network into a particular form. That life force can only be given it by Selah as Selah responds to the directing will within a brain.

When a thought, both mental and astral in nature, is given life force by the etheric network of humanity, it becomes an obsession, because its power is now the power of the form nature which does obsess the consciousness of humanity.

Consider the effects, within the life and affairs of humanity, which could be engendered by a group of trained thinkers. This is the work of the world group of disciples as they take on the service responsibility of preparation for the Reappearance of The Christ.

The Ceremony of Life has to do with the bringing together of See-la-Aum and Selah, so the Plan can take appearance in the world of men. Remember, Selah only responds to the directing will as it is focused through a man's brain, thus the Plan can only be precipitated through a group of trained thinkers within the body of humanity.

The sound which brings these two great devas together, after each has been contacted by the disciple, is the OM.

This sound, when chanted on the right note (such note being in the key of A), creates a channel, between See-la-Aum and Selah, through the disciple's own etheric light body. When it is chanted on the right note (such note being in the key of G), the circuit is completed between the created deva of appearance within Selah, and its higher correspondent within See-la-Aum, without the instrumentality of the disciple. This saves the disciple from his own work.

This is most important, for if the disciple unknowingly creates a deva of appearance, and does not complete the alignment with the Plan, it invites the attention of those who would misuse it. In such instances, it might also move back upon its creator, obsessing his mind out of proportion to its purpose, thereby distorting his understanding and often causing insanity. When one considers that its life force is the force of kundalini, one understands why such precautions are necessary.

The disciple, who is the intermediary between the two great devas for the sake of human consciousness, brings every aspect of his life and affairs into a divine ceremony, which becomes his service activity.

Ceremonial magic is a concept which can, if not correctly approached, result in a very great glamour. Glamour, remember, is the interpretation given a truth by the astral consciousness. The glamour of ceremony makes of it an outer act without inner meaning. Such is the case with so many of the so-called ceremonies in use today.

True ceremony is an inner state of being, which is channeled into every outer act.

We begin with that consciousness who knows himself to be Divine, i.e., a part of the One Life. As he opens his eye to the morning, it is with full realization of this fact;

and because of it, it is with a deep appreciation of life that he greets a new day.

Consciously realizing and appreciating Life for what it is, he consecrates himself, consciousness and instrumentality, and all that he has, to that Life. This he does in Love in the interior part of his being. This is ceremony. Everything that impinges upon his vision, his thought or feeling, receives his Love and appreciation because it is part of the One Life. He is cognizing and communing with God via the only language permissible between God and man—the exchange of Love.

Whatever the early morning routine, it is a part of the ceremony, since it is being carried out by the disciple with a deep realization of the inner meaning of life.

The older and wiser the disciple, the greater is his cognition of this meaning, and the more powerful, therefore, is his ceremony.

The probationer who is attempting to become the accepted disciple may initiate such ceremonial with a quiet contemplation of the One Life as he goes about the daily business of arising from sleep and preparing for the day. Just having learned that all forms are composed of intelligent substance, and that all intelligent substance constitutes devic lives, which, in their sum total, are the matter aspect of the Holy Trinity, he channels into such devas his awareness of love, as he contacts them via form. Every form with which he comes into contact, and every act in which he is engaged, receives his conscious love and appreciation as a part of the One Life. Thus, he initiates his day with a ceremony which continues throughout its twenty-four hours.

The accepted disciple and initiate adds to this the simple ceremony of aligning the manifesting devas of appearance, within his immediate environment and his sphere of influence, with their higher correspondent, the Plan. He does this via a channel created between See-la-Aum, through his own etheric light body, and Selah— and back again from Selah to See-la-Aum—via the etheric light body of the Planetary Logos as it emanates through the three worlds of human endeavor and into the body of humanity.

The channel descends from its apex at the level of The Christ to its midway point in the cave in the head, from there to the manifesting devas of appearance within the etheric network of humanity via the ajna center, and ascends, at an angle, back up through the three worlds of human endeavor outside of the disciple's instrumentality to its high point of origin.

On the descent, the OM is chanted in the key of A seven times, each time in a lower octave than the one before, the sound becoming audible only at the midway point in the cave, and continuing audibly until the descent has been completed. The consciousness must be cognizant of what he is doing, and why, for this to be effective.

On the ascent, the OM is chanted in the key of G seven times, each time in a higher octave than in the one before, the sound becoming inaudible on the fourth note, and continuing so until the high point of origin has been reached.

During the ascent, if the disciple will realize that human kundalini (not his own but that of humanity) is being aligned with God's will as it is focused by The Christ, the ceremony will be more effective.

A few more words. I should like to emphasize at this time the note of Selah is in the key of F.

The note of See-la-Aum cannot be disclosed at this time.

The Nature of The Soul

The note which aligns See-la-Aum with Selah, in readiness for invocation, is in the key of A.

The note which aligns Selah with, and evokes kundalini upwards toward See-la-Aum, is in the key of G.

Each note is seven-fold in nature, affecting the substance of each of the seven spheres of vibrating matter within the logoic-cosmic physical body.

A few words of warning before I bring this lesson to a close. Do not permit the import of this release to overwhelm your consciousness. You have entered into the great cycle of revelation as the Seventh Ray comes into active incarnation in world affairs. Accept the atmosphere of it with ease and move forward into real Light.

LESSON 36

The Soul's Assessment of Its Instrument:

The Paradox of Causality;
The Overshadowing and
Indwelling State of Consciousness;
The Alignment of Devas,
and the Ceremony of Life,
Used to Manifest the
Divine Plan in Physical-Dense;
The Call to a Deeper Capacity
to Love and Wisdom as Applied Truth

366

LESSON 36

If we have learned anything thus far, we have learned that the primary concern of the Conscious Soul Incarnate is with his direction of energies and forces through the etheric network of his three-fold environment, and the effects they create within the indwelling consciousness of that environment.

Let us approach this subject somewhat differently than before, looking more closely into that which constitutes cause and effect.

We have said previously that a man's state of consciousness is the true cause of all that happens to him, since experience is but an outpicturing in substance of the inner state of consciousness. This is a truth which, if not rightly comprehended, can result in an interpretation of contradictions which bring the probationer to a state of impasse.

A man *is* his own cause, yet there are other causes which supersede and relate to the inner state of consciousness as cause to effect, and it is with these that we are here concerned. Paradox is polarity. It is not contradiction. This must always be taken into consideration if a student is to grasp and to appreciate Truth.

Let us look very closely at this paradox:

1. The indwelling consciousness is causal to the outer experience via its reflection in substance.

2. The conscious Soul, whether incarnate or overshadowing, is causal to the indwelling persona-

identified consciousness via:

a. His reflection into the substance of the three worlds as a persona, and

b. His direction of force throughout the etheric network of the environment within which he is related as a persona.

For as long as the consciously-identified Soul is overshadowing, he is directly causal only to his own persona-identified consciousness. In other words, his alignment with, and entry into, the body of humanity as a causal factor is only via the persona for which he is a focus of light.

While such a persona may appear as a causal factor within his environment, meting out pain or pleasure to others, it can only be in response to their attraction of such experience via their own inner state of being. Thus do fully-identified personae work out together a group karma through natural attraction of one to another in an association of karmic factors.

Example: A dominating and possessive woman will be attracted to, and attract unto herself, those whose karma (the conditional state of the incarnating consciousness) demands the experience such an association will engender.

The moment the Overshadowing Soul begins to infuse its persona with an awareness of itself as Soul, a change takes place in its causal power potential.

Such a one becomes causal to the conditional state of consciousness of those around him, becoming, in point of fact, much more than an instrument of personality karma.

Lesson 36

As that infusion continues, and the incarnating consciousness becomes more and more Soul-aware and Soul-identified, he becomes the instrumentality of The Christ and of the Plan for humanity. He cannot then be the instrument through which ordinary personality karma is worked out.

Example: He could not be the dominating and possessive woman. If he were placed within a group whose demands were for such a persona, his obligation to them would be to instigate that growth which would lift them above such needs. Thus, he becomes causative to the incarnating consciousness within his environment, effecting its growth into a new conditional state of cause.

This is service to humanity. Such service is rendered via the direction of force into and through the etheric network within which humanity lives.

All force, whether of mental, astral, or etheric nature, reaches the consciousness of an individual, or a group, via the etheric lines of force which connect him or it with its originating source. The impact upon the indwelling consciousness results in an outer experience which, in turn, produces growth.

Observe the Conscious Soul Incarnate within his environment. Consciously identified with the One Life, and cognizant of its etheric body of manifestation, he relates to those within his environment as interrelated parts of the totality. He then relates the Plan to the consciousness aspect of the environment. What new growth is indicated in the tonal quality of the relationship between Plan and indwelling consciousness?

Example: He knows the Plan for humanity in general to be Christhood. He relates that planned goal to the incarnating consciousness, and compares the tonal quality of such consciousness to that of the Plan.

His understanding will, of course, depend upon his comprehension of the meaning of Christhood. What does such a goal mean to him?

As he relates that meaning to the condition of the incarnating consciousness, he works out the details of the Plan in time and space.

Example: To the probationer disciple, Christhood means brotherly love, peace, goodwill, security, harmony, etc. His understanding even of these is highly abstract.

As he observes the incarnating consciousness of humanity today, he sees separativeness, greed, resentment, hate, war, etc.

Thus, he compares tonal qualities, and if he is not very careful at this point, his consciousness can become so overwhelmed by the vast difference in the two tones he hears as to become lost in the glamour of futility.

He must work to relate more carefully the Overshadowing Plan to that which is in manifestation.

As he looks into the conditional state of the indwelling consciousness, he comprehends that the negativities there are only the result of spiritual ignorance and the hold of the form over the consciousness. Man is not basically evil. He is by nature divine, though perhaps as a child, ignorant of that divinity.

While there is some aspiration, it is not rightly directed to invoke that Truth which man so desperately needs. In addition to this, he will discover and begin to comprehend the appalling lack of human sensitivity to an overshadowing, obvious truth.

Realizing that, as yet, humanity en masse can only be reached with divine ideas and forces via a constructed form, he turns his attention to the world of form.

Here he sees a world whose economy both serves the Plan, and the opposition of the separated self to that Plan. The mass of humanity lives within a wartime economy, basing this exchange of life force, and experience in the world of affairs upon a highly organized war effort. They call this a peace plan, devote their time and effort to it as to a great cause, for there is a motivation and a deep desire within humanity for peace. Yet they fail to realize that a wartime economy must result in war, unless quickly altered. The pressure of such psychology, and the constant production of destructive weapons, must find an outlet, for these constitute force turned toward a specific end.

At the same time, the economy serves the Plan, in that it has brought about a closer relationship between peoples and nations. No one today can live in complete isolation, no matter how he tries, for humanity has become interdependent. Each needs the other, and whatsoever the other has to offer, in order to live within this civilization.

The probationer disciple, observing the conflicting note sounding in time and space as a result of such contradictions, comprehends and takes upon himself his share of the responsibility of working out the details of the Plan in the world of affairs.

Such details are obvious: a true peacetime economy in this instance, with the force of brotherhood manifesting free trade among nations; co-existence and a distribution of the world's goods into those areas where they are needed; food for the hungry; fuel and clothing for the cold and the ragged; medical wisdom and supplies for the sick, etc., wheresoever such needs are in evidence.

Here are some of the details of the Plan, and they are

easy to draw. Observe any manifesting condition, relate its tonal quality with that of Christ, and the answer is obvious.

The greatest need of the world today is for Wisdom. This civilization has been created by the West with its Christian religion. Jesus brought to the West the concept of love. His teaching is simple and direct. Yet the Western brother who claims Jesus as the savior of humanity prays for peace and goodwill, on the one hand, and advocates war and disaster upon the other, via his action.

To love one's neighbor, to love one's enemy, to love those whose treatment is cruel and unfair, to turn one's cheek, these are the teachings the Western brother seeks to bring into the world. Yet with an appalling, blind rationalization, he violates them consistently in the world of affairs.

Probationer disciples who seek to serve the Divine Plan may comprehend the details of that Plan easily and simply by comparing that which is in manifestation to these aspects of the Divine Plan as held in focus by the mind of the Christ. That mind is ever with humanity.

Is there one in your environment who would harm you? Do you feel the sting of resentment or jealousy as it is loosed upon you by another? What are the dictates of the Plan in such an instance? How do you become causal to the conditional state of such a consciousness, effecting its growth into an awareness of love?

Through love. By demonstrating real love via a constructed form which will convey it. No enemy can remain an enemy in the face of such an act.

Jesus beat the money changers out of the temple, and Jesus was finally crucified. There is more than one lesson in this. Did a beating teach such men the value of love, or did it teach them the right use of money? No, my brother, it brought a response of bitterness and growing hatred, which was finally demonstrated in the ignoble death of a savior.

Yet, the lesson, if it can be finally faced by a humanity that seeks Truth, can free the world of pain. It can free the indwelling Christ from a continued crucifixion upon the cross of the form nature.

The seeker can learn all he will of Truth, but this will not give him Wisdom until he applies it. Love is Truth. Its forms are obvious. The Will to Love is a force which, when directed into and through the etheric network of humanity, will manifest each detail of the Plan in Divine Law and Order.

The Nature of The Soul

LESSON 37

The Science of Right Human Relations,
as Related to Esoteric Mathematics

God Unmanifest and Manifest;
The Process of Involution
and Evolution of the Logos;
The Numerical Equations
and Symbols of this Process
and its Relation to the
Unfoldment of Kundalini

LESSON 37

Discipleship in the new age will deal largely with *right human relations* as these are discovered and made manifest via a research into, and practice of, a new science of mathematics. Until that new science becomes known to the leadership of the world, right human relations cannot be brought into outer manifestation, for those equations which reveal them have not been found.

Ceremonial magic and alchemy in the new age also will be based upon the new science, and on an understanding of planetary kundalini. Two courses of instruction entitled "The New Science of Mathematics" and "The Science of Relationship" will be made available to humanity as a part of The New Thought-Form Presentation of The Wisdom.

In the interim, students preparing for Discipleship, via a study of this course of instruction, will find in these last few lessons some of the basic concepts from which the new science will proceed. It is suggested that they be taken into meditation and reflection, both in an effort to awaken the intuitive faculty in this direction, and to provide a magnetic field of receptivity in the three lower worlds for the inflow of the new science.

Numerical measurement in our present system of mathematics is based upon a scale of numbers from zero to nine. Since the zero, out of which one comes, is intended to convey nothing or naught, the system of counting is based upon a false premise, which throws the entire sequence of logic into a series of false conclusions.

The symbol used to convey the idea of nothing is a universal symbol that really means the totality of everything that is. This is God transcendent, or God overshadowing and unmanifest. While in one sense it is a no-thing, yet it is in essence everything that is, was, or will be, i.e., pure Spirit.

This everything, and yet no-thing, we have symbolized as a circle, yet in reality it has no beginning or end, no center or periphery. In actuality it is a sphere which cannot be circumscribed, though we take the liberty of drawing it so in order to establish a symbol of first cause. Yet, we must realize when we do this what is the essential meaning of that circle. We cannot give it position in time and space, for these are contained within it.

We have next the problem of manifest life coming out of the zero, and to understand how this can be, we must proceed in the natural order of universal symbology. This is somewhat difficult, for the tendency of the human mind is to count from one to three, and this is in opposition to the creative process. One does not come out of the zero.

The first manifestation of God is a Trinity; a one life, yes, but in structural reality, a three.

It is symbolized by the circle with the dot, which has been interpreted in the past as a one. It is a One Life but it is held in three interrelated dimensions which are inseparable; therefore, its so-called Oneness is entirely subjective.

Lesson 37

The first dimension is the Overshadowing Totality that has been focused into a positive polarity identified by the dot. The dot symbolizes the first dimension, yet present-day science gives that dot position but no dimension.

The third dimension is the Overshadowing Totality that has been focused into a negative polarity, identified as the periphery of the circle.

The second dimension is the space, or magnetic field between, which gives the Overshadowing Totality, Soul or awareness.

It must be understood that these three cannot manifest in sequence as a one-two-three, for they come into objectivity together. When a center is visualized, it must have a periphery and a space between, or when a space is visualized, it must be the magnetic field between two poles.

The new scale proceeds, then, from zero to three, and is symbolized by the uncircumscribed sphere, which we call zero, and the circle with the dot.

From out of the three (polarity, and space or magnetic field) is born identity, a one which, oddly enough, is symbolized by an elongated triangle. If the A used in AUM were made to look and sound like this, the symbology would be mathematically correct. This also is the correct drawing of the numeral one.

Any one identity we refer to as Logos, meaning the central directing life of any organized system of life. Life is a term which describes the interrelated activity of the first three dimensions, as that activity is precipitated, via the word (Logos or focal point of consciousness), into four lesser dimensions.

The first Logos is the Indwelling self-conscious God of the manifest Cosmos, Who reproduces Himself into the many via the process of creation. This is the One Central Life of that highly and divinely organized system of life we call the Cosmos; the One about Whom all lesser lives revolve, and in Whom they live, move, and have their being.

This is a focal point of consciousness born into expression from the first three interrelated and impersonal dimensions, and is the fourth dimension sought by present day science.

Man lives in the fifth, sixth, and seventh dimensions, which he calls the first, second and third, and is, in his own consciousness, the fourth dimension he seeks.

The reproduction of the One into the many is symbolized by the squared circle with the dot at the center, which looks like this:

This is The Christ crucified upon the cross of matter

into the many focal points of consciousness, which we call incarnating Souls. We use the term "incarnating," in this instance, as it relates to the planet and Buddhic sphere, rather than as it relates to the three worlds of human endeavor.

This is a four, and the above symbol is the correct drawing of that number. This signifies the many who are in actuality a One. Realization of the One Life or Christ is attained as the identity enters into the fourth dimension and experiences that One-ness in consciousness. Such a one we call a Conscious Soul Incarnate. He is a four because the positive and negative polarity of the dot and the periphery have been reflected into the consciousness so it, too, is dual.

This duality in consciousness results in the fifth, sixth, and seventh dimensions, called the three worlds of human endeavor, within which the incarnating Soul is imprisoned.

A focal point of consciousness, besides being aware, which is its own characteristic, inherits from that positive and negative polarity that gave it existence, the characteristics of will and intelligence. Thus, because of its own inherent creativity, it produces those outgoing frequencies which create the three lower worlds.

The fifth, sixth, and seventh dimensions are reflections of the first three dimensions, which have been focused into and through the focal point of consciousness, as through a lens. Here again we see this fourth dimension of consciousness as a door, the midway point between the higher triad and the lower.

The fifth dimension, which is the mental plane, is a reflection of the Will aspect, or the dot in the center of the circle. This is the positive polarity of the lower four.

The Nature of The Soul

The seventh dimension, which is the etheric plane, is a reflection of the intelligence aspect, or the periphery of the circle. This is the negative polarity of the lower four.

The sixth dimension, which is the astral plane, is a reflection of the dual consciousness and is, then, the plane where the pairs of opposites are reflected as a condition in consciousness.

The physical plane is the outer appearance of these three interrelated dimensions. It is time and space and will continue only for so long as consciousness remains dual in nature.

This duality of consciousness is the result of its inability to identify as itself. It identifies with its positive and negative polarities (of which the sexes are but an out-picturing), imprisoning itself thereby in the form nature of its own creation.

The symbol of the three lower worlds is the swastika. It is numerically a seven, for here, in three interrelated dimensions, is the reflected activity of the first three and the focal point of consciousness, which is a four.

Thus, we see the created soul incarnating within a lesser trinity, creating its own world of appearance.

The Evolution of the created soul into The One Life of Christ produces a change in the polarities of the mental and etheric planes. The life force imprisoned within the etheric is gradually attracted upward into the mental, so that the lower triad becomes negative to the higher triad.

Lesson 37

Thus, a tremendous shift takes place, the substance of the three lower dimensions becoming negative to the energies of the three higher dimensions, and consciousness taking its rightful place as the mediator between the two. The seven are synthesized into a causal triad which functions then on the Cosmic physical plane rather than in the subfrequencies of the Cosmic physical.

The life force which has to be lifted is Planetary kundalini. It is symbolized by the serpent and is numerically a 22.

Here is the real matter aspect, the serpent fire of creation, which gives life to the forms dictated by the Will.

Planetary kundalini, which should reside in the mind nature, has fallen into the etheric body of manifestation, giving the form in the world of appearance dominance over the incarnating soul.

The serpent kingdom, which is not a true kingdom in Nature, is an outpicturing of this mis-creation or misdirection of force.

As the kundalini fire is lifted into its rightful place, the outer picture of the serpent will disappear from the earth. Here is the constant reminder, to the human family of this planet, of its failure to orient within the Cosmic scheme.

The new science of mathematics will proceed, then, from the following numerical scale of measurement:

Involution		Evolution
03147	22	74130

The equation as it relates to the human family today reads $03147 = 22$. Here is the serpent coiled.

The Nature of The Soul

The equations, as they will relate to the human family when it takes its rightful place in the scheme of things will read: 03147 + 22 = 74130. This is the serpent standing upon its tail.

The equation, as it will relate to the Planetary Logos upon completion of His initiation will read 03147 + 22 + 74130 = 22. This is the serpent with the tail in its mouth and reveals the place of our Logos within the Solar Scheme. He is the custodian of Solar Kundalini.

Within this latter equation is hidden the divine name and nature of our Logos.

LESSON 38

The Awakening of Kundalini and
the Redemption of Matter:

The Division of the 22 into
2 via the Fall of Humanity;
The Unfoldment of Kundalini
Through the Center System;
The Redemption of Matter by
"Sealing the Door Where Evil Dwells"

LESSON 38

We have entered into an area of occult science that is most difficult for the human mind to comprehend. If the student will realize that he is not expected to understand the text at present, and if he will not make an attempt to either accept or reject it, but rather to become receptive, allowing the consciousness to respond in its own time, the way will be made easier. This text is not written for the human mind. It is written for the Soul consciousness, therefore, the method of comprehension is via the higher intuitive faculty rather than the intellect.

It is the division of the twenty-two, within and by humanity, into a two, which is "the door where evil dwells" insofar as this planetary system is concerned. Twenty-two is the number of the true negative pole of manifestation in the Cosmic physical body of our Logos. This has been called kundalini, symbolized by the serpent, and likened unto Fire.

How has it been so misinterpreted as to have become divided into two parts, and to have manifested as the source of planetary evil? To understand this, the student must become cognizant of the nature of kundalini.

In itself, kundalini is the latent fire of matter residing in the very heart of the atom of substance. It appears as the central directing life of the atom, and in one sense, it is that in manifestation. But it is the true negative pole. In other words, it is pure spirit vibrating at its lowest possible frequency. This means that the only universal life property which could be discovered and studied by the human mind is the lowest manifestation (and such terminology carries the wrong connotation) of that which we call Spirit or God.

Kundalini, then, in its essence is manas, the principle of Intelligence, which has fallen from its place in the Buddhic sphere into its own reflection, or its own magnetic field. It has moved into that color (a reflection of its own fire) which livens the form aspect. Thus, the consciousness is carried into, and imprisoned within, the form.

This is symbolized in the story of the Fall of Man from out of the Garden of Eden. Eve (the creative aspect of the Soul, now defined as the persona) was tempted by the serpent (fallen kundalini) to taste of the apple (sensory experience of substance) from the tree of knowledge (form aspect). After eating, Eve then tempted (attracted) Adam (the Overshadowing Spiritual Soul) to eat of the apple, and the process of reincarnation in the three lower worlds began. They were driven out of the Garden of Eden (Buddhic sphere) by the Father, for the purpose of redeeming the fallen kundalini.

Kundalini in its present manifest condition has been divided into two poles, one aspect residing in the lowest center of the etheric center system, and the other residing in the highest center of the etheric center system. Consciousness has been imprisoned between the division and has, therefore, lost its kingdom.

This means that the positive pole toward which man is aspiring is the true negative pole of manifestation, while that which is the negative pole from which he arises is an illusion of his own making. The life between these two poles can only be of the form, and this is why the average man cannot even conceive of an identity apart from the form.

Lesson 38

The bodies, then, are given the perceptive faculties, and a man's perception is based upon the sensation of the form as it responds to the fire of creation.

This fire of creation, which we call kundalini and symbolize by the serpent of knowledge (which in his risen state is the golden dragon of Wisdom), is the creative force itself. This is that intelligent life which is moved by a man's, or a God's, will to give life and reason to a form.

We see polarity manifesting the pairs of opposites within the Planetary life and affairs because the negative polarity of this planet has been split in two. This is why Christ can only be reached via the Presence by the meditating disciple in the three worlds.

The Holy Ghost aspect is achieved when the kundalini fire residing in the lowest frequency of the Cosmic physical is lifted up into the fourth ether, where the consciousness can be animated by the Divine Intelligence of the Higher Triad.

Consider the effect of the creative force within the body of humanity today. The kundalini fire resides in the center at the base of the spine. The motivating principle of Intelligence resides in the head center. This motivating principle is the heart of manas, the true negative pole which receives the direct impress of the will. The kundalini fire, which should burn around that heart, lies below it in frequency so that the motivating principle must lower its own frequency before it can activate the latent fire. That fire, once it is activated, burns upward, reaching toward its own desired center of polarity. In so doing, it enters into and stimulates into vibratory activity, those lower centers which lie between it and its attracting pole.

Please understand that this creative fire gives life to that into which it enters. The form, which houses or is enlivened by kundalini, becomes the vibrant center or focal point of life force so that it generates its own life and affairs, or series of experiences.

The kundalini attracted upward by the impulse of the motivating principle enters into the sacral center and, for a time, remains there, making this the stage of activity.

The sacral center itself is that frequency in substance which has to do with the lower kingdoms in nature, and their appearance via procreation.

Insofar as humanity as a whole is concerned, the kundalini has uncoiled one-and-a-half times. In other words, the fire burns in the center at the base of the spine and the sacral, and reaching upward, stimulates into a great, related activity the solar plexus center.

Thus, the power factor of manifestation (the astral body) and man's desire nature (the lowered motivating principle) are linked with, and directly related to, the center of procreation.

If we look at the Planetary Life and affairs, forgetting humanity for a moment, we observe in manifestation the lower kingdoms in nature. We do not see evidence of a higher intelligence, or higher way of life, than that which is evidenced by those kingdoms. These kingdoms are the life and affairs generated by the Planetary sacral center, which is now the home of the serpent.

When we place humanity in the picture, we still see the life and affairs of the sacral, but with a difference. Humanity brings the kundalini up into the solar plexus, where intelligence in the form of a desire nature can work to lift that creative fire still higher. Humanity, then, is that great life (Christ) in incarnation, whose sacrifice makes possible the redemption of substance, and the form, and the imprisoned consciousness of the Logos, via the redemption of the kundalini. Humanity itself is the great avatar in incarnation.

We see, then, that the form aspect has been given the creative impetus, and the strange phenomenon of creation without an intelligently planned cooperation by the consciousness takes place.

The etheric body has become the negative pole of manifestation, the custodian of the senses, so that a man's perception and his comprehension, even his desire nature, are based upon the sensory nature of substance rather than the intuitive faculty of consciousness. The form nature rules, and man follows the dictates of the sensation-loving form.

Thus, a Soul is imprisoned within the confines of substance. His incarnation into the world of appearance can only take place via the process of procreation. It is the result of the activity of the form, is dependent upon that activity, and is imprisoned within and by it.

As the kundalini continues to uncoil, it activates the heart and throat centers, causing a shift in the life and affairs from the instinctual level into the aspirational and intellectual level. Man begins to think in terms of self-improvement, and he aspires toward an ideal.

As the kundalini reaches the throat center, it is attracted up, out of the sacral, by the positive polarity of the mind nature. The creative fire leaves the former stage of activity, and man becomes creative in a new way. He is creative in his mind, rather than in just his lower form nature. Thus, he builds beauty into his surroundings, entering upon the creative way for the sheer joy of it.

The kundalini burning in the solar plexus and the heart

centers causes a purification process to begin in the astral-desire nature. Man relates to his brothers in love and sympathy and begins to think in terms of their good rather than just his own.

As the kundalini reaches into the ajna center (the result of conscious effort to meditate), the abstract nature of mind is stimulated into great activity. Man is coming closer to home. Eventually, that kundalini burns so brightly in the ajna as to pull it up, out of the solar plexus. It is then burning from the heart, through the throat, and into the ajna.

The stage of activity shifts so completely that the man begins to live entirely in his mind, where he can begin to cognize his identity as consciousness. No longer are his comprehension and his desire nature limited to the sensory experience of the form. He sees through the eye of his mind, hears with the sensitive attunement of his light body, and understands with his consciousness— which has become his heart. He is a Conscious Soul Incarnate.

Eventually, and finally, the serpent brings his tail up out of the heart and throat centers, and burns around the motivating principle of Intelligence. The three major centers have merged into one (the kundalini redeemed), and the man's consciousness is released to merge in awareness with that avatar which he is. There is, then, only Spirit, matter, and Consciousness as Christ.

Discipleship in the new age, and particularly during the next fifty years as a preparation for the Coming, will work to lift Planetary kundalini from the sacral center up to the throat center, via the medium of humanity. The effort to establish right human relations in the world of affairs is necessarily linked to this, for only via the lifting of the kundalini up, out of the sacral center, will such be possible.

Lesson 38

How can such an effect be created? Disciples have to become the positive polarity via group activity, which will attract the kundalini force within humanity upward.

They must, as a group, embody the ideal so as to exert that strong and steady magnetic influence that will attract the response of the creative fire within all human beings. The "twenty-two" has to become a reality in the world of affairs before the "two" (lowered kundalini and the door where evil dwells) can be swallowed up by the dragon.

The Nature of The Soul

LESSON 39

Group Consciousness:

Initiation as a Group Process;
Group Consciousness as Evidence
of a Conscious Soul Incarnate;
The Problem of Disillusionment
and Passivity in Humanity;
The Need for Humanity
to Cultivate Right Action;
The Problem of Subjective
Integration of the Group Life;
The Problem of Objective
Embodiment of the Group Idea;
The Problem of Taking Positive Action

LESSON 39

Those of you who have received and given serious attention to this course of instruction have responded to the Hierarchial note which is now being sounded within the body of humanity. That note affords the probationer disciple an opportunity unparalleled in human history. It presents him with the opportunity to participate in a group initiation which, if successful, during the remaining years of this century, will ensure the mass initiation of humanity into the fifth kingdom of Conscious Souls.

It is realized that as yet there can be but very little grasp of the meaning of such an event. Yet, I urge each one of you to think deeply upon it, to attempt via the intuition to cognize that meaning, and to let it inspire you into a new and powerful effort to serve this goal for humanity.

Group initiation is a concept about which there is little known, for it is a new Hierarchial effort that until now has met with little real success. This does not mean that all such efforts have failed, but that progress is seemingly slow, and to date has been at great seeming cost to the personalities involved.

The group with which the Hierarchy is concerned is not a group of personalities defined as aspirants, probationers, or disciples. It is a group consciousness within the body of humanity, which is most receptive to, and capable of expansion into, the world of overshadowing ideas and concepts now impacting upon humanity as the new way of life.

The great difficulty encountered by the Hierarchy in

this effort has been the lack of response, within those contacted and worked with, to the real group idea. The moment the word "group" is used, the human mind thinks in terms of personalities and thus misinterprets the concept, losing the higher reality of it. Those persons who are involved forego the reality for the glamour of it, and in an illusion of self-importance as personae are rendered ineffective insofar as the group idea is concerned.

From the perspective of the Hierarchy, the group is a state of consciousness within the body of humanity, which is shared by many persons. That state of consciousness, though it indwells a goodly part of the many, is One. It is then worked with as such, while the personae that make up its instrumentality are seen as its hands and feet, etc. It is the state of consciousness that is deliberately overshadowed with the planned activity, that is evoked into a response, and that is watched and guided into the initiatory effort.

The Hierarchy is concerned, then, with the response of that state of consciousness as a *one life* or a *group*, rather than with the response of any separated persona, or group of personae. Not until the total group consciousness responds and embodies the new concept will the Hierarchy consider such a group in *manifestation*.

When looking at this state of consciousness which is attracting the attention of the Hierarchy, we find it has two characteristics and qualities which indicate its place upon the path.

1. It is disillusioned with the world of affairs, almost satiated with the experience of an astral nature, yet it tends toward an unexpressed idealism. The greatest concept entertained by it is the idea of "if." If the world were not the way it is—if Christianity could learn to practice the Law of

398

Lesson 39

Love—if we were not under the constant threat of war—etc.

This state of consciousness, which indwells so many, is of a negative influence in the world rather than a positive one because of its use of the concept "if." As a group, it radiates this "if" into the life and affairs of humanity as a condition of defeatism, so we find humanity responding to the positive solutions of its problems only with an apathetic "if."

2. At the same time, this state of consciousness is responsive in its mind nature to the overshadowing. It is aligned with, and receptive to, the ideal in such a way as to give that ideal a thought–form. Its service potential, then, is great, for once that mind nature begins to control the disillusioned astral body with its defeatist attitude, it can influence humanity into right action.

Furthermore, the consciousness itself is seeking via its mind for universal principles. It intuits its own need for growth and stands at the very door of discovery. The Hierarchy seeks to plant that discovery in its thought-life. "Self-initiated growth and development into the ideal of Christ, as the application of a Universal principle," will become its sounding note in the three worlds of human endeavor. This discovery will open the door of initiation.

The instrumentality of the group is composed of many personalities in all walks of life who are, for the most part, ineffective in the world of affairs. There are few in this particular level who are in positions of power or importance. They constitute the upper regions of the mass consciousness, yet are not really of that mass, since they do not agree with its thought and desire life, though they do share it in manifest condition and experience.

The Nature of The Soul

A part of the consciousness has responded to the Hierarchial effort and can be seen entering into greater activity, but that activity must become much more effective for good in the world, and more widespread, before any real success of a group nature can be achieved.

The probationer disciple who is a part of the instrumentality of the group consciousness must understand that he cannot, and will not, take initiation of and by himself, but as the group does. Therefore, he does not aspire to a personal or individual initiation into the One Life, but rather works steadily for the illumination of the group.

This is a somewhat difficult concept for it is a new one, and the initiatory process involved is necessarily new and different than that of the immediate past. The effort now being made is toward a synthesis of several initiations into one major illumination and transfiguration. It involves the tests and trials in a greater concentration of several degrees, so that when complete, something altogether new, insofar as this planet is concerned, will have been achieved. The third–degree initiate will evidence a broader consciousness, greater wisdom, and, therefore, more control of the form side of nature, than the third–degree initiate of the immediate past. Thus, his effect upon humanity will be of far greater consequence than that of the brothers who have gone before him.

The movement of a large group into such an expansion holds the hope of the Hierarchy for the restoration of humanity. It is upon this movement that Hierarchial hopes, prayers, and effort have been directed.

Several problems confront the effort in this particular time, which should be given deep consideration by all of those involved.

    1. The problem of subjective integration.

Lesson 39

When the subjective thought and desire life of the group have been integrated into a One Life, with a powerful influence for good in the world, the first major effort will then have been completed.

At this moment we observe that mass of thought and desire acting as barriers which hold each unit of consciousness in the three worlds separate and apart from each other, both in reception of an idea and in radiatory influence. Yet, each unit of consciousness is essentially so alike, both in evolutionary development and in general karmic complication, that it is seen from the perspective of the Hierarchy as a group.

As each one aspires to the Soul, he is helping to supersede the barriers of separation. As each one meditates, he comes closer to a conscious realization of the group life. The subjective integration can be brought about more quickly if those of you who are receiving this instruction, or one similar to it, will carry out the following suggestion.

    a. Think outwardly with love toward your group brothers, and realize that wherever the group membership may be in the world of affairs, all are consciously serving the *same* Purpose, "The Divine Plan for Humanity."

    b. Then realize that regardless of the varied activities of the group membership, each is consciously working toward the same goal, "the embodiment of peace, goodwill, and brotherhood by humanity in our time."

    c. Realizing this same purpose and goal which is shared by the entire group, dedicate the power of your thought and desire life to that group, and, in turn, dedicate the group, through your instrumentality, to The Christ.

d. Try to carry this realization with you through-out the day, offering whatsoever re-alizations you might receive, the truths you are attempting to embody, the strengths and talents you may have acquired, to the total group consciousness. Make these available via your *related touch* with and within the group.

2. The problem of objective embodiment of the group idea.

The Hierarchy stands ready to precipitate into the total group consciousness many concepts and ideas, plus practical techniques for their embodiment and use in service, *when* the group stands receptive as a group.

The effort is hampered now by the tendency of the group membership to misinterpret such an effort as one of individual contact and guidance. An individual becomes conscious of the attention the group is receiving, takes that attention unto himself, and fails to record the im-pression correctly because he is so englamoured with the thought and desire of personal contact with the Hierarchy.

This serves as a greater obstacle than you can realize at present. The projected concept is directed into the group consciousness to impact upon the minds and brains of those involved via their own Soul alignments. When many group members receive that impact, and immedi-ately misinterpret it as coming direct from a member of the Hierarchy to themselves as individuals, a great cloud arises in the astral-mental environment of the group, which distorts both their receptive and interpre-tive abilities. Thus, it becomes necessary for the Hierar-chy to withhold its guidance, and the entire effort is hampered.

Lesson 39

If you become cognizant of a projected concept, and the energies accompanying that concept, realize that it does not come to you alone as an individual, but that it has been made available to the group. Then, as a part of that group, receive it, interpret it, and attempt to embody it. You can receive nothing specifically of, by, and for yourself as an individual unit of consciousness, from the Hierarchy. A disciple in the Hierarchy does not confine his thought or attention to an individual. He has mastered the form nature and works with consciousness at that level where all consciousness is one.

Let your receptivity when in meditation be as, and with, the group. In this way you will add to the receptive power of the total group.

3. The problem of taking positive action.

This is a problem which always appears to be an individual one, but which is, in every sense, a group problem. The solution, then, is of a group nature and until this is realized, the disciple is constantly frustrated in his attempt to take a positive action toward, or in, service.

This particular problem includes finance, discipline, environmental control, etc., and will be considered more fully in the next lesson.

In the meantime, endeavor to cognize, more fully than heretofore, the meaning of group consciousness. As an assignment, intuit and bring to the next class a seed-thought which contains the depth and breadth of that meaning.

Those who wish to receive a grade for this series of instruction are advised to give their teacher the total meditation report written thus far, and the notebook regarding the difference between Soul and persona, suggested earlier.

The Nature of The Soul

404

LESSON 40

Moving From the Hall of Learning
to the Hall of Wisdom:

The Distinction Between
Knowledge and Wisdom;
Wisdom as "Love in Action";
The Need for Courage,
At-one-ment, and Cooperation
with Fellow Disciples;
The Problem of a Weak and
Impotent Will, and an
Unrefined Etheric Instrument

LESSON 40

We have said that initiation is a new beginning, a new birth in awareness. The test of any initiation, whether of an individual in the past, or of a group in the present, or of the mass in the future, is the ability of the consciousness involved to use that awareness to the betterment of those within the entire sphere of influence.

You are in the process of initiation. Your consciousness has been initiated into a new field of awareness that concerns the whole of humanity. You have been taught to think in terms of the One Life, to consider the Good, the True, and the Beautiful as it applies to that One Life. While you have been totally concerned in this study with The Wisdom, you are still within the Hall of Learning. Yet, the passageway which connects the Hall of Learning with the Hall of Wisdom lies straight before you with its doors wide, its light clearly showing the marked path, and many brothers awaiting your entry.

Wisdom is more than knowledge. It is more than the contemplation of Truth. Wisdom is "Love in Action," the application of all that is known for the love of humanity.

In the Hall of Wisdom, the student becomes the accepted disciple. His school now becomes the school of service, the new school for humanity, and his teacher is The Christ. His heart is filled to overflowing with the love Christ knows for humankind; and as it spills out into the world, it brings healing, life and restoration to an ailing humanity. Such a one becomes the custodian of the Law of Grace, wielding that law with an exactitude which surpasses even the exacting nature of karma. He is a giver of peace in the midst of conflict; he is food for the hungry, pure water for the thirsty, and ease for every pain.

He is all of these because he has become them himself. He no longer hungers, or thirsts, or cries out in the bitterness of pain. His gift is of himself, therefore it is one of Peace.

All of this is Wisdom.

The step from one Hall into the other appears great, as if over a chasm, yet when the passageway is seen, it is clearly one of light, which bridges that dark space between two worlds in the space between two moments. In the twinkling of an eye is a man reborn and transfigured into the appearance of Christ.

The Soul spends eons developing within the womb of matter, and is born forth into the world of Spirit after the pain of labour has subsided. Love gives birth after pain has done its work, and Love is born.

The Soul who stands ready upon the brink of the chasm, fearful for himself, trembling before the awe he senses, but cannot yet see, receives this encouragement:

"Dare to drop your conflict. Dare to become filled with Love. Dare to stop all thought and receive the Spirit of God. Dare to take the step with the eye lifted away from the chasm, fastened upon the Light."

If I speak to you in symbols, it is because they convey the simple truth. The way is always hazardous right up until the last moment—and that moment is in the heart, not in time. The path of initiation appears to increase the conflict, to sharpen the pain, to increase the burden, yet the Final Glory blazes forth in that moment when the life is filled with peace.

Lesson 40

The applicant has within himself the Power to bring an instant cessation to pain and conflict. His choice it is, and this is the final choice, yet the one always before him.

It makes little difference what his circumstances in the body, that body will become filled with peace when the consciousness enters the final act and wields the power of decision.

While all of the above describes the final act of initiation, and the state of consciousness of him who is initiate, and while this act awaits only that moment of fearlessness in the heart of the applicant, still it has to be approached. The student disciple who has yet to build in his strength of decision does so via a clearly marked path of approach that is characterized by positive action in service.

Throughout the world there are those probationer disciples, numbering about one-sixteenth of the world's population, who are in their totality the group now receiving Hierarchial attention. Theirs is the karmic right of opportunity, during this crisis in human affairs, to consciously restore God's plan on earth. They form a vast state of consciousness of potential power sufficient to turn the tide of human affairs in whatsoever direction they choose, almost overnight.

When this group consciousness and its instrumentality can be integrated into a focal point or center, its invocative and evocative strength will be sufficient to bring in the Reappearance of The Christ. Consider such a group in meditation upon one seed-thought having to do with some specific aspect of the Plan in the world of affairs. Such a meditation would result in the rapid manifestation of those events necessary to bring the specific aspect of the Plan under consideration into appearance in the light of day. Here is the answer to the solution of the world's problems.

The Nature of The Soul

The probationer disciple in Great Britain or India, or any other part of the world, is so similar to you in consciousness that you could be of the same family. The outer conditions within which he lives may differ, yet he struggles with the same inner conflicts, aspires toward, and works for, the same ideals as do you. Your problems are his problems, your frustrations are his frustrations, and your success is his success. You realized one morning, in some degree, that you are a Soul. So did your brother, wherever he was. You were momentarily overcome during the December '56 lunar cycle with a sense of futility and helplessness. So were your brothers throughout the world. You thrill to the joy of a newly received Truth, or you despair to find yourself reacting to the form nature. So do your brothers. It is a One Life.

When this is realized, even in some little degree, disciples will have found the way toward positive action. When you have a problem, regardless of the nature of that problem, realize that it is not your own. This is a group problem, which has to be dealt with by the group. You are but a focal point through which it is making itself known to the consciousness of the group.

Achieve as great a realization of this as is possible via meditation and reflection, and then realize further that if you, or a group unit, can arrive at the solution, the way is made easier for the entire group of probationers throughout the world.

Then, working from within the realization of this one group life, invoke the power of the group Soul to manifest the solution, whatever it might be, throughout its total consciousness and instrumentality.

If you find yourself faced with some particular reactive pattern, which acts as an obstacle to the embodiment of Truth, accept that pattern only as a condition to be corrected within and by the entire group. In this way

Lesson 40

you de-personalize the apparent difficulty and clear the channels for a positive action from the level of the group Soul.

This also turns the attention away from the separated self, permitting the group life to pour through the instrumentality.

When this attitude has become habitual, the probationer disciple may then take another positive step toward inner and outer integration.

The group as a whole is now overshadowed with the higher Third Aspect. This means that the Angel of The Presence stands ready to pour the Christ Life into the group the moment that group is developed sufficiently in invocative strength to bring it down.

Two related conditions arise within the group life to block the descent of the Holy Spirit into the group instrumentality.

1. The will is weak and impotent.

2. The etheric instrument is not raised to a high enough frequency to conduct the higher frequencies of the Spirit through, into outer manifestation.

In order to grasp the significance of the overshadowing and the importance of its descent, please consider for a moment the group life (both consciousness and instrumentality) as a potential antahkarana anchored within the body of humanity as a passageway between The Christ and the world of affairs. When the Holy Spirit (higher Third Aspect) fills the group life, it will have become that antahkarana. Any disciple, then, may use it to invoke the Power of The Christ into manifestation in the midst of any circumstance or situation. Thus, the saving or redeeming Power of Christ is brought into activity in the life and affairs of the disciple. It is available to him. This is the Power which renders the work of magic potent and instantaneously effective.

It must be understood that when a disciple works from this level of perception and available power, he does so in the Name of Christ. That is, he works as a part of The Christ Life. He cannot then be divided within himself.

The two conditions which block the descent are so interrelated that they can only be considered together, as two sides of one problem.

The impotence of the will is very marked in today's probationer disciple, as evidenced by the tremendous difficulties he encounters within himself whenever he attempts to discipline his own form nature, or to initiate a planned service activity.

Many opportunities of service are being missed by the probationer because of his own inability to establish a control of the devic life within his own environment. The deva responds to the consciousness as that consciousness wields the will energy. Lack of adequate material supply, of right conditions and opportunities, of inspired cooperation from others, or even of inspiration within oneself are symptoms of a weak and impotent will. When the will is functioning, all of the necessities to the manifestation of a planned service activity are assembled together via those devas whose response has been attracted and initiated. The Power to build the structure of the planned service activity is then transferred into them via the invocation of the Power of The Christ. The higher Third Aspect (Angel of The Presence) is invoked into command, and the builders obey his command.

Lesson 40

When the will is weak and impotent, the etheric body will be sluggish and unresponsive to higher impact. It cannot then conduct the Light on into outer manifestation.

The development of the Will, and the lifting of the etheric body in frequency, are two interrelated activities which are initiated together.

First observe the tone of your life. What are the habits of the etheric body itself? It causes the physical to sleep, to eat, to drink, to move, to speak, to follow specific patterns of reactions in given circumstances. What are those reactions? What has that etheric body been trained to like, to dislike, to want, to do?

Wherever you find you are a slave to an unnecessary habit, that is, unnecessary to the good of the Life itself, achieve freedom from that habit. Do this not for moral reasons, but for the sake of developing the will and bringing your etheric deva under complete control.

At the same time, consider the necessity to lift the frequency of the etheric into one which is compatible with that of The Angel of The Presence. Visualize the body as one of a vibrant blue-white light, harmless in its radiation, and potent as an instrumentality of the Plan.

Meditate upon *purification, consecration, and transfiguration* in connection with the etheric, and as you intuit the necessary disciplines, use your will to impose them upon the life of the instrumentality.

Let your will become the will to serve, and for the sake of that service, use it.

Before the probationer disciple can control the devas of his environment, he must control his own devas of appearance. Before he can take action in the Name of Christ, he must become filled with His Life.

One other point, if the personal will is not adequate to the task, *invoke the Divine Will of The Christ, via the group, to appropriate the personal will.*

And now we come to the end of this series of instruction. Its value to a needy humanity will be determined by your response to, and application of, those basic concepts of truth contained within it. If your life is enriched in spiritual growth by one of its concepts, it is serving its Purpose. If someone else's life is enriched by you, because of that growth, you are serving the same Purpose. Let its Truth pour forth through you into all walks of life, into all departments of human living, into the consciousness of humanity.

How To Study
The Nature of The Soul

The Method of Study

The Nature of The Soul has a threefold approach to study:

- the text
- the meditation work
- the discussion

Together they balance the overshadowing wisdom of the course, the inner experience of that wisdom, and its expression in the world of affairs.

Many students are now studying the course on their own or in study groups, and there is a growing need for information about these methods. The following suggestions and examples focus on:

- *Individual Study,*
- *Study Groups,* and
- *The Meditations.*

Individual Study

The Nature of The Soul is a course in self-initiated spiritual growth and development. It is designed to facilitate step-by-step unfoldment from individuality to group awareness and conscious service to the One Life. Each lesson in this course is a step in a transformative process. This process includes:

Studying the Material

The information included in the course is presented in a rhythmic sequence. Each lesson builds a foundation for understanding and prepares the way for the next lesson. This progression from one lesson to the next creates a harmonic rhythm which aids the transformation process.

In order to establish and maintain this rhythm, we suggest that all students of the course do the following:

♦ Begin with the Introductory Lesson and study each lesson in turn. Skipping around or starting in the middle will break the rhythm and cause confusion.

♦ Spend at least one week (seven days) studying each lesson. Begin every new lesson on the same day of the week. You may devote more than one week to each lesson, but if you do, consider spending the same number of weeks with every lesson.

♦ While studying the course, concentrate your attention on the course. Avoid practicing internal exercises from other disciplines, as they may not combine well with the exercises in *The Nature of The Soul*.

We do not mean to imply that this course is in any way superior to any other course or discipline, yet, in order to maintain the internal rhythm of this course, you must stay in the course. Once you have completed N.S. *(The Nature of The Soul),* we encourage you to include other schools and disciplines in your study and practice.

♦ Complete the assignments. The structure of the course is similar to that of a textbook and includes frequent assignments. These assignments can be divided into three types:

● Subjective: These include internal activities such as the meditations.

● Objective: These include external activities such as writing a paper.

● Subjective and Objective: These combine internal and external activities in a single assignment (such as keeping a meditation log).

In each case, the assignment is there for the specific purpose of assisting you to expand your awareness or embody a new concept. Completing the assignments is part of the rhythm of the course.

♦ **Practicing the Meditation Techniques:** The internal disciplines included in *The Nature of The Soul* are presented in a natural progression from basic to advanced. The meditations are the heart of the course; the information in the lessons is designed to aid your practice and comprehension of the meditations.

1. Practice each of the meditation techniques exactly as described.

2. Keep a meditation log. A daily written record helps you move the abstract realizations gained in meditation into your outer life and affairs. Each entry should include the day and date, the meditation technique, and any noticeable results.

Include all realizations and internal experiences which occur during the meditation, and any related insights and experiences which occur during the day or in your dreams.

3. Learn the meditation forms. Be patient with the process. Over time the results will become apparent. We encourage you to practice these techniques as an on-going process for your inner growth.

◆ **Embodying What You Learn:** *The Nature of The Soul* course is designed to help you find your place, and take up your work, in the One Life. It does this through:

1. The Course of Instruction: This instruction consists of 41 lessons and lasts at least ten months. During this period concentrate on learning the ideas, practicing the techniques, and making The Wisdom part of your daily life and affairs. Studying the lessons and practicing the techniques begin the process of self-transformation.

2. The Embodiment Cycle: The months of instruction are followed by a matching period of application. *The Nature of The Soul* course is completed by moving what you learn from the instruction into and beyond your immediate environment. This application or embodiment of The Wisdom includes:

   • Subjective activity: Most of your service will be subjective, and may include many of the techniques you learned in *The Nature of The Soul* and its sister courses. As you continue to practice The Wisdom after completing the instruction, you will create an opportunity to help transform your environment.

   • Objective service: Your subjective practice

may result in opportunities for providing objective service to family, friends, co-workers or the environment.

Approaching the Material

Because students often approach a new course with preconceptions based on previous experiences, keeping an open mind and an open heart will allow your intuition to integrate those experiences with the new material presented in the course.

There are a variety of methods of studying *The Nature of The Soul*. A positive approach is one which helps the student initiate his or her own growth and development. A method which is very supportive of self-initiation is Individual Self-directed Study.

Initiating your own spiritual growth and development means choosing a path of study, practice, and application which is right for you.

The primary value of individual, self-directed study lies in:

♦ **A stronger focus of will:** Every time you decide to study a lesson, practice a technique, or do an assignment, you are exercising your will. As with any other kind of exercise, in order to receive the benefit you must do the work. No one can do it for you. That process is described in this recommendation from *The Path of Initiation, by Lucille Cedercrans, Vol. II, lesson 4:*

> "Many students reading this lesson will wonder how to do this work of lifting the polarization without direct contact with a teacher. I shall answer that question in several ways. Firstly, let us understand that all aspiring to the Soul are in direct contact with a teacher, namely their own

Soul; and by continued aspiration, they will soon come to recognize the contact.

Secondly, aspirants are enabled, through their right aspiration, to contact higher levels of awareness, and from these levels draw down those concepts of Truth which provide a sure foundation for their later understanding.

Thirdly, aspirants learn to recognize experience as a great teacher, and through their efforts to live the Truth which they have grasped, they develop in the school of experience a consciousness rich in understanding. They do this deliberately, in full awareness of the activity, and their everyday life becomes a thing of beauty, regardless of appearances."

♦ **Self-initiated service:** As you respond to the inner needs of your environment your awareness of your place and function in the One Life expands. This in turn leads to conscious service to that Life as you take your place in It.

Teaching the Material

If you are considering teaching *The Nature of The Soul*, we earnestly suggest that you first experience the course. Experiencing the course will help you become aware of the difficulties attached to teaching. These include:

♦ **The sage on a stage:** The idea of being a spiritual teacher can be so attractive that seekers attempt to create the outer form without first achieving the inner content. This difficulty can be avoided by:

- Studying the course materials: You cannot teach what you do not know. First experience it for yourself, then facilitate the course.

- Practicing what you learn: You cannot teach what you cannot perform. Practice and perform the meditation techniques yourself, then teach others.

♦ **Being a "successful" teacher:** The teacher's attention must be on the Wisdom. A teacher does not need a lot of students, nor does teaching have to occur in a conventional classroom.

Study Groups

We encourage each study group to consider the following suggestions. Some suggestions may seem appropriate for your group, while others may not. As your group gains experience and develops its intuition, it will refine its group process. Adapt these suggestions to your own circumstances as your alignment indicates.

The Length and Frequency of Each Meeting

Most groups meet once a week, while some meet more often and some less. The average length of a group meeting varies from group to group. Some meet for as little as 1½ hours (and take several meetings to cover a single lesson). Others meet for over 3 hours (and may try to cover each lesson in a single meeting). The length of the meetings, and how many meetings it takes to cover each lesson, are entirely up to each group.

Suggestion: Find a point of balance between hurrying through the lessons and lingering over them.

- Choose a time frame that enables you to take full advantage of the lesson material.

- Adapt the suggestions to your time frame.
- Meet at a regular time and place.

Before Each Meeting

Suggestion: Some have found it helpful to preview/review material prior to each group meeting.

During each meeting

♦ **Meeting Facilitators:** The role of the meeting facilitators vary from group to group. Basically, the individuals are responsible for keeping the group focused. This responsibility could rotate from one meeting to the next so everyone has the opportunity to take a turn or to pass.

♦ **Opening Exercise** Suggestion: Begin each meeting with a group meditation. Use the form of meditation which the class is presently studying. During the first few lessons, when you have not yet been given a meditation form, you could use the short meditation form found in *The Nature of The Soul*, on p. 66.

1. "Turn the attention to the physical body and realize that you are not your body.

2. "Turn the attention to the emotional nature and realize that you are not your emotions.

3. "Turn the attention to the mind and realize that you are not your thoughts.

4. "Focus the attention in the ajna and meditate for three minutes on the following seed-thought:

   " *'Having pervaded this body, emotions and mind with a fragment of myself, I remain.'* "

Further Suggestions:

- The meeting facilitator could lead the meditation.

- The meditation could conclude with The Great Invocation found in the front of the book.

- Late comers enter quietly or wait outside if the meditation is in progress. A noisy entry can disturb a group already practicing the meditation.

The Readings

♦ **The First Reading** Suggestion: Begin each lesson by reading the entire lesson aloud, from beginning to end, without stopping for questions or comments. During this first reading, be receptive to the meaning behind the entire lesson. Options for this first reading include:

Example 1: The meeting facilitator could read the lesson aloud.

Example 2: The group members could take turns, with each person reading one paragraph aloud, continuing around the group until the lesson is complete.

Example 3: The entire group could read the entire lesson aloud, with everyone speaking the same words simultaneously.[1]

This first reading is done at the beginning, and only at the beginning, of every lesson. As the group gains practice with the process of alignment, it can consciously align with and stand receptive (as a group) to the thought-form of the Wisdom which overshadows the course. This alignment will enhance the learning process.

---

[1] This method can work well with small groups, but may be awkward for larger groups.

◆ **The Second Reading** Suggestion: Following the first reading, do not stop to discuss the lesson that you just read![2] Instead, pause for a few moments of contemplative silence before beginning a second reading which will focus on one paragraph at a time. After re-reading a paragraph, use your intuition to discuss it and relate it to your life and affairs. Repeat the process with each paragraph. There are several ways to organize this second reading, including:

Example 1: The meeting facilitator could read each paragraph aloud.

Example 2: The group members could take turns, with each reading a paragraph aloud as the group progresses through the lesson.

Example 3: The entire group could read each separate paragraph aloud, with everyone speaking the same words simultaneously.[3]

Contemplating The Concepts

Suggestion: After reading a paragraph the second time, pause for a few moments and contemplate the abstract concepts.[4] Then discuss, explain or question those concepts.

Example 1: After allowing the group to gather its

---

[2] It is vitally important to move directly into the second reading without any talking or discussion! Any premature discussion will dissipate the descending energy, causing ideas to be stillborn, and dropping the remaining energy (and the resulting discussion) to a lower frequency).

[3] This method works well with small groups, but may be awkward for larger groups.

[4] Don't be afraid of the silence! A few moments of silence are appropriate at this point.

thoughts, the facilitator could ask if anyone has comments or questions.

Example 2: The group could take turns commenting or asking questions about the paragraph, with each person being given the opportunity to speak or to "pass."

Example 3: The person who read the paragraph aloud could break the silence by offering or inviting comments and questions.

Relating The Concepts To The Everyday World

Suggestion: After discussing the concepts, pause for a few moments to contemplate how the concepts relate to the everyday world. Then attempt to feel and describe that relationship.

Example 1: The facilitator could ask if anyone has a story or comment that relates the abstract concept to everyday life or the world.

Example 2: The group could take turns offering comments.

Example 3: The person who read the paragraph could initiate offering examples, comments, and/or questions.

Repeat the above steps with each paragraph in turn until you complete the lesson. Give yourself as much time (and as many meetings) as you need to complete each lesson.

Closing Exercise

Suggestion: Close each meeting with a group meditation led by the facilitator or other member. This meditation could take the form of a new technique encountered in the current lesson or (if there is no new technique) one the group has been practicing.

After Each Meeting

♦ **Practice the techniques:** The meditation exercises are an *essential* part of the course. You cannot get the full benefit of the course unless you practice the techniques! We therefore *strongly recommend* that you practice the exercises when and as indicated.

The Meditations

"Meditation is a technical process whereby Soul contact is realized and Soul infusion achieved." p.38

Meditation trains the persona to align with the Soul, discover its purpose, and apply that purpose in inner and outer activity. The Soul becomes causative to the persona, and the persona becomes receptive to the Soul.

Foundational Techniques

The meditation techniques used in the course can be divided into two types, invocation and evocation.

♦ **Invocation** brings a divine energy down into manifestation, giving it shape and form in time and space. These techniques help bring an overshadowing potential into its first appearance (as when a person is born).

♦ **Evocation** brings an indwelling divine energy out into full appearance. These techniques help move the first appearance into full expression (as when an infant grows to maturity).

The Motion of Consciousness

Meditation is also the downward and outward motion which produces inward and upward growth. The techniques produce this motion through a three-step process, including an ascent, meditation proper, and a descent.

♦ During the first part of the meditation exercises, the consciousness:

  • Ascends through the persona instrument, relaxing the body, calming the emotions, and focusing the mind. This prepares the persona to act as an instrument of contact with Divinity.

  • Aligns with and becomes receptive to an aspect of Divinity, such as the Spiritual Soul. This prepares the persona to act as an instrument of transmission of Divine quality, characteristic or energy.

♦ During the second part of the exercises, the consciousness contacts an aspect of Divinity, and either:

  • Invokes a Divine quality downward into appearance, and/or

  • Evokes a Divine quality outward into full expression.

♦ During the third or descent portion of the exercises, the Divine quality, characteristic or ray is radiated forth into appearance. The radiatory process includes the entire persona instrument (mind, emotions, and body), each part of which receives some portion of the Divine energy.

- Invocative radiation impresses a Divine quality (on either the substance or consciousness).

- Evocative radiation draws a Divine potential out (of either substance or consciousness) into full expression.

The descent grounds both the Divine energy (giving it shape and form) and the meditator.

All of these alignments, connections, and radiations are created by the directed focus of the consciousness. This directed focus is developed through the regular practice of the techniques in Lesson 3 (on p 39 - 40) and Lesson 13 (on pp. 141 - 145). These two techniques are the foundation for all the meditation work in The Nature of The Soul. They are the heart of the sequential process which develops the persona skills, and the alignment between the Soul, mind and brain, which make the Soul work possible.

Placement of the Consciousness

The meditation exercises work on the principle that "Energy follows consciousness." The self or identity is placed between, and relates, Divine potential to manifest condition. This relationship causes the overshadowing solution and the manifest condition to become one. The stronger the relationship, the quicker the transformation.

In the exercises, the consciousness places itself in a point midway between a manifest condition and an overshadowing potential, then extends its awareness up to the potential solution and down to the condition. This creates a relationship, in consciousness, between the solution and the problem, a relationship which the Divine energy of the solution must follow.

The point of placement is usually one of several centers (organs of energy) located in or near the head. At first, the point of placement is closer (in frequency) to the persona instrument than to the Overshadowing Spiritual Soul. Later, as the student gains more experience, the center used is midway between the overshadowing Soul and the persona.

This progression from place to place is an essential feature of the meditation exercises. The earlier, more persona-oriented techniques prepare the instrument for the later work. They build the alignment between persona and Soul and from Soul to persona, which allows the downward and outward motion of Divine energy to take place. Thus, practicing the earlier techniques (especially the Transmutation Technique on *p. 92*) *is* an *essential* part of the course. One cannot truly practice the later techniques unless the necessary alignments have been built.

The Science of Impression

The early techniques are relatively simple, and focus on impressing a Divine energy on one's own personality. Later techniques assume the earlier work was done and the alignment built, and focus on impressing a Divine energy on the environment.

In either case, whether one is impressing one's personality or environment, one is still transmitting a potential. The meditator is a midwife to a potential solution. One helps the overshadowing potential to manifest, but does not choose, create, or dictate the form it may take.

The problem solving mechanism included in the techniques is process oriented. It helps the consciousness find whatever it needs, rather than presenting a ready-made solution. The techniques provide a process for translating the potential solutions of the Soul into practical activity in the world of affairs. This translation process must be learned, but it eventually becomes automatic and (like walking) requires little or no attention.

Personal Work

The problem solving process can be applied to our personality, surroundings, community, nation, and planet. We usually begin learning the process by applying it to our personality and immediate surroundings. At this point, the consciousness is focused on the individual and the dominant motive is individual growth and development. This is natural. As the consciousness expands, there are corresponding shifts in the motive behind the inner and outer work.

The efforts to improve the personality are also, in the end, a service to the One Life. The physical body learns to be relaxed, receptive, and responsive. The emotional body learns to be calm, aspirational, and forceful. The mind becomes focused, creating and organizing. The characteristics of the Soul are built into the persona, transforming it into a fit dwelling for the Spiritual Soul and instrument of service to the One Life.

Adjustment and Transmutation

The course uses a variety of adjustment and transmutation techniques to improve the personality. The adjustment exercises offer a new frequency, so that change *may* take place. In an adjustment one can align with a ray energy, invoke or evoke the ray, and radiate the ray. Thus, each of the ray seed-thoughts may be viewed as a persona adjustment, a method of developing a subjective feel for the ray energy, and a means of gaining experience in wielding the ray.

The transmutation techniques impress a new frequency, so that change *will* take place.

The most important of the personality exercises is the Transmutation Technique in Lesson 8 on p. 92. This exercise trains students to identify as Soul and to be causative to the persona equipment. Regular, persistent practice of this technique eventually leads to the redemption of the individual persona. As practitioners evolve, this technique evolves with them, enabling them to move their transmutation work beyond their individual personas to their surrounding environment. This type of transmutation is the most important work individuals can do for themselves.

Service Work

Eventually, the motive of the practitioner moves from improving the personality to serving the One Life. The adjustment and transformation techniques are still used, but the way they are used changes. The purpose resides over, the point of focus moves above, and the outer activity moves beyond, the individual persona. At this point, opportunities to serve through the meditation work appear.

The mind, emotions, and body are still used. However, through the character-building adjustments and transmutations, and the alignment with the Soul, the personality has become an instrument through which the practitioner serves. In the end, it is through moving the identity out of the persona and into the Soul, and transforming the persona into an instrument of service, that the persona is understood and "perfected."

As the focus moves from the persona to the One Life, the techniques which had been used to adjust or transmute the persona become tools of service. Thus, all the techniques in the course can be used for service.

The course's invocative adjustment techniques include the:

Second Ray technique on p. 80
Fourth Ray techniques on pp. 154 & 155
Seventh Ray technique on p. 225

The evocative adjustment techniques include the:

First Ray technique on p. 49

Many of the techniques in the second half of the course are specifically designed for service. The most important of these service exercises are the *Ceremony of Life,* and the *See-La-Aum* exercise on pp. 363 - 364.

The service techniques are always done as Soul for Soul, not to or for the persona. The soul for whom an adjustment is done is given the opportunity to create its own solution, rather than a pre-determined solution favored by the meditator. Helping a soul to find its own way is, in the end, part of the service to the One Life.

Summary

As you practice the techniques, you will learn both how to perform them and how your equipment responds to the energies. This requires patience, tolerance, and perseverance, but the results are well worth the effort.

INDEX TO THE NATURE OF THE SOUL

own, 110
Anguish and pain, 212
Animal Kingdom, animal Soul, 20
Animal man—
consciousness—
integrated with mineral
consciousness, 242
integrated with vegetable
consciousness, 242
lowest level of individualization,
242
Animal Soul—
definition, 19
definition and focus, 140
relates man to animal Kingdom,
20
Antakarana—
being reconstructed, 304
broken, 303
reconstruction, 305
Appearance—
of all forms, 219
underlying cause of, 15
Apple, taste of, 388
Archetypal form—
appearance of, 109
enabled to view, 307
Soular deva, 330
Armageddon, nature of, 210
Art and science of form building—
prerequisites to learning, list of,
96
Art and Science of Magic, 229
Artist, 139
Ashram—
aura of, 231
definition, 160
enters during meditations, 322
exists in consciousness only, 160
exists within consciousness, 161
magnetic radiatory field of, 232
periphery of, 231
protection of, 223
visualized, 161
your life in, 243
Ashramic—
group, aware of, 234
group life, 341—

exists in consciousness, 231
position within, 231
Soular deva created by, 337
office, 231—
assuming responsibility of,
234
Auric Influence, 232
Peripheral Manifestation,
232
Ashrams—
disciple working within, 46
seven major, 240
subject of, 159
Aspirant—
as takes his place, 37
attitude of, 118
defined, 118
Disciplines of embodiment of a
Spiritual ideal, 38
focal point of attention, 71
harmonizing agent, 61
recipient of greater Light, 118
Aspirants, 6—
to become disciples, 48
Aspiration—
activity of, 117
daily silent, 339
defined, 118
definition, 117
degree of rightly motivated, 244
desire lower correspondence, 115
directed to a knowable Source,
105
directed to The Christ, 283
directed to the Soul, 119
evolves, 118
meditation and application, 115
moment of greatest, 338
newly awakened conflict with, 87
persistent, 121
puts student in tune with the
Soul, 120
right, 6
selfless, 135
summation, 119
to be of service, 232
to embody Soul quality, 61
to serve, 135

Index

to use the mind for the
betterment of humanity, 97
Aspire, to The Christ, 283
Assignment—
disciplinary measures, 132
effects of meditations on Love, 81
explain four elements, 325
fifth ray, 175
four-week, 185
intuit group consciousness seed-
thought, 403
noting effects of Will energy, 62
personal and service karma, 268
sleep meditation, 248
special notebook, 252
summary of fourth ray, 155
understanding of sixth ray, 195
understanding of the seventh
ray, 213
your understanding of the
Ideal, 111
Associates, right relationship with,
267
Astral—
aura, 129
body, 136—
control the, 97
higher, 138
center, 139
consciousness, 129
desire body of the Soul, 68
energy, motion, 129
experience, satiated with, 398
forces—
control of, 184
power factor of
manifestation, 88
form—
cyclic, 129
definition, 291
forms, life of their own, 130
individual focused in, 88
instrument of healing, Plane—
instrumental contact, 171
contains, 129
Sphere—
desire characterizes, 117
establish a condition

within, 50
transmutation, and Power, 68
Astral force, power of, 129
Astral plane—
defined, 321
definition, 128
devas of, 330
Astral-emotional body, less turmoil
within, 117
Astral-emotional nature—
great transmitter of force, 68
vehicle for feeling aspect of
consciousness, 68
Atlantean—
civilization, cataclysm, 304
Consciousness, first law violated,
305
episode, 302
period—
human beings conscious
magicians, 303
veiling since, 301
Atom, of substance, 387
At-one-ment, goal of speech, 100
Attachment, to the form, 193
Attack—
glamour, 222
source of own, 222
Attacks, so-called, 222
Attention, Soul maintains via third
eye, 297
Attitude—
different, 47
toward others, 70
Attributes, four, derived, 149
Auric, influence, 165
Authority, behind the written word, 4
Avatar, consciousness released to
merge with, 392
Avatars, Great, source, 106
Awareness—
dark areas, 222
specific change in, 282

B

Bad, transmuted into good, 155
Balance—

Index

Breaths, taking seven deep, 40
Brother, relationships within the
    One Life, 267
Brotherhood—
    a fact in nature, 8, 46
    lack of, 117
    manifestation of, 70
Brothers—
    service to, 9
    wrong relationship between, 48
Buddha—
    energy of, 200
    Teachings of, 107
Buddhic—
    levels, work on is pure creativity,
      330
    plane, substantial body of, 321
    sphere—
      creator's aura, 321
      distributes life of Logos,
        357
      door of entry, 357
      expression within, 240
      four elements of, 324
      natural habitat of the Soul,
        357
      of the Soul, construction in,
        308
      prime matter found in, 329

C

Causal, triangle of manifestation,
    311
Causal form, soular deva, 329
Causal triangle, of the manifest
    planet, 306
Causal truth, 155
Causative triangle, energies, 149
Cause, glimpse, 9
Cave—
    active, 143
    center, brain cavity, 141
    constructed of, 293
    definition, occult, 292
    from polarization in, 297
    heart of a man's being, 293
    Identify within, 283

    location, 141
    magnetic field of light in,
      creating, 253
    move back into, 143
    Soul polarization in, 294
    Soular deva focused in, 337
Center—
    Between the brows
      focused in, 90
    predominate, 139
    System, imbalance, 219
Centers—
    defined, 137
    location and shape, 137
Cerebro-nervous system, purpose,
    130
Ceremonial magic—
    definition, 329
    glamour of, 361
    mathematics, 377
    seventh ray, 209
    three-fold activity, 221
    work below Buddhic is, 330
Ceremony—
    an inner state of being, 361
    definition, 362
    sacrificial, 235
    throughout 24 hours, 362
Ceremony of Life—
    bringing together of See-la-Aum
      and Selah, 360
    revealed by seventh ray, 359
Chaos—
    first manifestation of intelligent
      activity, 88
    period of, 50
    restore order out of, 45
Character building—
    as a science, 37
    as the path of return, 35
    importance, 36
    three types of energy, 115
Child, unloved, 80
Childhood, resentment, 90
Christ—
    adult Son, 16
    appearance of, invoke or reject,
      212

Index

Index

forms, manifestation of, 210
gratification through fulfillment,
117
lower correspondence of
aspiration, 115
phenomenon of emotional
nature, 115
summed up, 117
to escape, 201
versus aspiration, 61
Desire nature, purifying, via fixed
ideal, 8
Detach, from form, 193
Detachment—
from karmic form of
relationships, 267
It may or may not be true, 31
Deva—
and consciousness, 331
definition, 330
deliberately contacted, 331
feeling nature, 331
mind a, 331
of appearance, 360—
defined, 360
if disciple unknowingly
creates, 361
making, 359
misuse of, 361
union via consciousness, 330
Deva of appearance, definition, 353
Devachanic experience, length of,
262
Devas—
builders of the universe, 332
in obedience to a directing will, 332
manipulation, etheric, astral,
and mental plan, 352
of appearance, 330
of the astral plane, 330
of the etheric plane, 330
of the mental plane, 329
Development, point of, determined,
151
Devic—
evolution, 330, 331
form—
construct, 307

physical-etheric, 308
stuff, 307
Devic evolution—
polar opposite of Will aspect, 332
the third aspect, 331
Devil—
born along with Christ, 314
who is, 211
Devote, yourself to the Divine Plan,
204
Devoted—
mistake of, 204
to personality, 202
Devotee, sixth ray, 209
Devotion, object of, 202
Dharma, of probationer, meeting, 98
Disciple, power released, 230
Disciple—
Accepted, 46—
harm-less-ness, 21
meditation, 120
of The Christ, 9
attracts love outward, 80
auric influence, 125
auric influence characteristic of,
159
breathes truth, 194
brings gift which has no
monetary value, 351
conscious part of the One Life, 342
creative will, 219
custodian of body of One Life, 359
defined, 125
develops invocative strength, 233
dissatisfaction with world of
persona, 348
Divine Will of his Soul, released,
233
entering realm of initiate magic,
347
Equipment, Divine Love-
Wisdom, 75
finance, 403
financial and social failure, 348
has sensed the Divine Plan, 50
hypothetical ray makeup, 151
impotency in all activities, 348
instrumentality through which

441

Index

Index

445

Index

point of, establishing, 40
Food, Soul's attitude toward, 296
Force—
  blocks, 219
  defined, 218
  direction throughout etheric
    network, 368
  erroneous flow, 219
  precipitating, 219
  steady flow of, 218
Forces—
  of creation, made available, 211
  impact of, 173
Forehead, point of focus within, 40
Form—
  appearance on any plane, 301
  as prison, 201
  aspect, not yet perfect, 203
  Building, art and science of, 95
  Definition, 291
  directed via speech, 221
  disintegrated, 193
  driven downward into
    manifestation, 323
  empowered via feelings, 221
  enlivened by kundalini, 390
  free of the limitation of, 252
  freed himself from, 294
  impress purpose on, 185
  instrument of service, 253
  Intelligent Activity made
    manifest, 100
  mourn the lost, 193
  nature—
    attempts to discipline, 220
    control over, 141
    creative will, 222
    mastery of, 174
    nature, refining, 296
    nature of to respond via
      sensation, 296
  no longer a prison, 253
  old and outworn, 193
  Solid, slowest rate of frequency of
    energies, 58
  substantial intelligence in
    controlled motion, 99
  the appearance of reality, 291

Forms—
  disintegration process, 119
  will power to, 220
  within his consciousness, 97
Formulated intent, projecting, 145
Four—
  correct drawing of, 381
  driven into manifestation, 308
  frequencies of matter, 311
Four elements—
  1. light, 307
  2. sound, 307
  3. color, 307
  4. vibration, 307
  earth, air, fire and water, 307
Four rays, of attribute, part of Soul,
    153
Four spiritual principles, 311
Fourth dimension, 380
Fourth ether, 389
Fourth principle, of vibration, 320
Fourth Ray—
  definition, 153, 159
  esoteric sound, 163
  invocation of, 164
  invoked, 163
  of Harmony through Conflict, 149
  peculiar motion, 155
  quality of the in the mind, 164
  the balance of Power, 230
  tunes frequencies, 164
Frequency, the major, 189
Frequency range, higher, 7
Frequency ranges, activity in, 100
from its end to its beginning, 334
Fulfillment—
  in service, 21
  inability to find, 21
Full Moon—
  higher interlude reached, 338
  period, 338
  precipitation of illumination into
    persona, 338

G

Garden of Eden, 388
Get thee behind me Satan, 211

447

Index

idea, objective embodiment of, 402
illumination of, 400
in manifestation, 398
instrumentality of, 399
life—
a potential antahkarana, 411
conscious realization of, 401
meditation, 409
personalities, friction, 11
relationship, to the Plan, 229
service potential, 233
subjective thought and desire of, 401
Group initiation, a new Hierarchial effort, 397
Group Soul, individualizing, 245
Groups—
come into incarnation, 10
warning regarding, 11
Growth—
experiences necessary to, 242
from hate to love, 212
intelligent activity speeds up, 86
rapid, 99
self-initiated, 8

H

Habits, freedom from, 413
Hall of Learning, 407
Hall of Wisdom, 407
Harmless, in thought, word, and deed, 38, 70
Harmlessness, 125—
aspirant endeavors to practice, 69
Harmonic, movement into manifestation, 311
Harmony—
an attribute of the Soul, 159
and Word of God, 154
dynamic, 154
everywhere equally present, 159
expression of Love-Wisdom, 155
Fourth ray, 159
invocation of, 159

known through conflict, 315
prerequisite to right relationship, 155
produces that understanding, 155
through Conflict, 149
Hate, polar opposite of Love, 79
Head—
polarization, from a, 179
residence in, 71, 184
take up residence, 78
Head center—
active, 143
definition, location, function, 137
Head, cave, and ajna centers, aligned and active, 144
Healing, energy of, 194
Healings, miraculous, 88
Health, made manifest, 48
Heart—
physical, 138
region of, 117
Heart and the head approach, merging, 116
Heart center—
activation of, 391
definition, location, function, 138
Heart of God—
alignment with, 78
Alignment with, Not a valid bookmark in entry on page 76
Heaven, fifth Kingdom, 19
Hierarchial—
Ashrams, disciple working within, 46
effort, thwarting, 275
intent, disciple is enabled to focus, 121
Light, periphery of, 160
note, sounded within humanity, 397
Hierarchical, effort, a group movement, 266
Hierarchy—
alignment with, 234
Divine ideas from, 121
glamour, 159
its hope for humanity, 50

449

Index

Index

balancing another aspect, 262
building of new, 285
group, through natural
    attraction, 368
inner meaning, 285
Law of, 7
manifest as experience patterns,
    284
manipulating to serve the Plan,
    323
new concept of, 285
observed and accounted for, 322
personal—
    precipitating for
        adjustment, 276
    resolving, 276
precipitated and adjusted, 51
service, 285
Karmic—
    cause, as he overcomes, 286
    causes, adjust, 286
    limitations of physical
        environment, 261
    necessity, 152—
        choice, 285
        equipment reveals, 284
    of a personality, 256
    obligation, personal, 263
    patterns, eliminated, 165
    relationship, removed from
        consciousness, 261
    right of opportunity, 409
Key of A, 361
Key of F, 359
Key of G, 361
Kindliness, application of, 130
Kingdom—
    Fifth, 19
    human, evolution through, 241
Kingdom in nature, one Soul, 17
Kingdom of devas, definition, 330
Kingdom of God—
    enter, 191
    Inner, way entered, 120
Kingdom of heaven—
    enter into, 140
Kingdoms—
    in nature, consciousness of, 241

lower, evolution, 241
mineral, vegetable, animal
    consciousness, 241
Kundalini—
    activation of heart and throat
        centers, 391
    defined, 387
    divided into two poles, 388
    evoked upwards, 364
    fire, resides in, 389
    in the ajna, 392
    life force of deva, 361
    manifested as the source of
        planetary evil, 387
    mystery, 139
    planetary, understanding, 377
    redeemed, 392
    redemption of, 391
    symbolized by the serpent, 387
    uncoiled, 390
Kundalini center—
    definition, location, function, 139

L

Law—
    appearance of form in
        cooperation with, 301
    ignorance of, 220
    of attraction, 32
    of cause and effect, considered, 50
    of Grace, 286
    of Love, 286
    the Atlantean consciousness
        violated, 305
Law of Grace—
    analogous to, 87
    custodian of, 407
Law of Harmony, work with, 151
Law of Love, application of, 130
Law of Paradox, 155—
    applied, 164
Laws, probationer learning to
    manipulate, 291
Leader, imperfection of, 203
Liberation, from pain, 181
Life—
    after death, 171

453

Index

born of Will and Intelligence, 16
created all knowledge, 67
doctrine of, 199, 200
evolution of, 16
Expression, negated by
    environment, 80
expression inwardly, 153
flooding emotional nature with, 61
good an expression of, 80
idea of, 199
in the mind, think in terms of, 78
intelligent application of, 5
interpreted as an emotion, 77
life problem involved with energy
    of, 79
manifesting it in the emotional
    nature, 79
of Humanity, 9
polar opposite, 199
polar opposite of, 79
produces—
    comprehension, 75
    intelligent, productive
        thought, 75
radiating, 145
the consciousness of, wields
    Spirit and Matter, 95
tonal quality of, 204
wielding from a mental level, 97
-Wisdom, highest aspect Pure
Reason, 76
Loving understanding, 285
Lower quaternary, 311
Lower quaternary, of
    manifestation, 312
Lower response mechanism, 142

M

Magic—
    age of, 210
    an act of, 282
    Art and Science of, 229—
        defined, 291
    era of, 193
    potent and effective, 412
    process which we call, 301
    real work of, 340

under law, 301
white or black, 210
Magical—
    application of esoteric sound, 165
    effect of harmony, 155
    operation, invocation, 164
Magician—
    concerned first with equation of,
        312
    four elements, 307
    must sound the Word, 312
    way of becoming, defined, 294
Magicians—
    all human beings were, 303
    premature, 293
Magnetic—
    field, 16, 27—
        consciousness, 15, 16
        consciousness aspect as, 65
        definition, 65
Magnetically receptive to the
    teaching, 272
Man, 16—
    1. a Positive Pole, which is the
        Spirit, 86
    2. a Negative Pole which is
        Matter, 86
    3. a consciousness, 86
    a developing, growing,
        consciousness, 67
    adrift from Logoic Purpose, 304
    an aggregate of energies, 150
    and his body became one, 242
    and his feeling nature became
        one, 242
    approaching the second
        initiation, 9
    awakening of, 3
    awareness of himself as a Soul,
        282
    becomes a living Soul, 101
    by nature divine, 370
    characteristic of identification, 29
    common goal of, 70
    completing the first initiation, 9
    conscious creator, 139
    conscious of Being, 29
    created in the Image of God, 17

Index

Index

Non-violence, message of, 203
Note, intuited by the Soul, 297
Notebook, Soul and persona, 403
Nothing, idea of, 377
Numeral one, correct drawing of, 380

O

Observation, seek out and know
    Divine Plan via, 61
Observe, truths, 194
Observer—
    emotions reveal themselves to, 90
    permitting Soul to reveal, 90
Obstacle, to the embodiment of
    Truth, 410
Occult—
    knowledge, foundational, 58
    light, 292
    path, beginner on, 31
    schools, teacher may serve in, 255
    secrets revealed, 293
    study, 150—
        basic formula, 17
Occultist—
    problem of, 66
    who is also the mystic, 120
Occultology, science called, 172
OM—
    chanted in the key of A, 363
    magic word of the Soul, 297
    softly sounds, 143
    sound which brings Selah and
        See-la-Aum together, 360
    sounding of, 145
One—
    about Whom all lesser lives
        revolve, 380
    does not come out of zero, 378
    focused into the many, 169
    many who are in actually a, 381
One Humanity, living totality of, 273
One Life—
    builds many forms, 18
    contribution to, 183
    evolution of the, 18
    individual tone and color, 231
    initiating a contribution to, 234

    integration of Group thought and
        desire into, 401
    one-ment with the, 306
    out of which all lessor lives
        stream, 106
    perfect action within, 282
    sacrifice of ambition and desire
        to, 9
    sacrificial action within, 282
    substantial body of, 171
    technique, 199
    union with, 183
    violation, 303
One Soul, an atom in the body of, 18
One, The, function as, 315
Oneness, concept of, 18
One-pointed, toward spiritual
    enlightenment, 200
Opportunity—
    new cycle of, 301
    refuse to accept, 207
Opposites, balance of, 154
Opposition—
    dormant in prime mattter, 315
    to consciousness, born, 314
    violent, 220
Organic functions, imbalance, 219
Organization, 230
Organs, reproductive, 139
Outer experience, cause, 369
Outer space, contact with, 171
Over-Soul—
    evolution of itself, 281
    Soul individualized expression of,
        18
Overshadowing Self, attentive to, 144
Overshadowing Soul—
    a group Soul, 341
    and persona, differentiation, 251
    aspires to the Monad, 282
    direct alignment with, 143
    long trained by, 256
    subray of, 255
Overshadowing Spiritual Soul—
    alignment with, 185
    extension of, 144
    identity, 252

The Nature of The Soul

P

Pairs of opposites—
embodied, 60
harmony renders them whole, 154
manifest by the Second Ray, 79
observing, 154
recognize, 154
reflected, 382
result of Sixth Ray, 199
transmuting, 60
within the mind, 60
Paradox—
all truth is, 264
is polarity, 367
Parapsychology, 230
Parapsychology, field of, 272
Past age, guiding energy, 191
Past life—
detaches from, 261
review, extracts wisdom, 262
Path—
cause of difficulty on, 89
involutionary and evolutionary,
245
liberation from pain, 182
more available and difficult, 160
of decision, forked, into the open,
210
of Discipleship, series of
incarnations, 162
of experience, 46, 69
of initiation—
after consciously enters, 76
appears to increase the
conflict, 408
aspiration evolves, 118
as a probationer, 180
definition, 263
is the path of discipleship, 46
man tempered to endure, 61
meaning, 263
obstacles, 21
of least resistance, 218—
energy becomes force, 218
inability to complete, 219
of non-action, misinterpretation,
154

of Return, 208—
new, 160
Path, The—
beginner on, 46, 47
place on, 135
Paths, of least resistance, two, 151
Peace—
desire for, 371
lasting, 3
made manifest, 48
Peacemaker, 194
Peacetime economy, 371
Perception, based upon the
sensation of the form, 389
Perfect Love, produces perfect
understanding, 76
Perfect understanding, 68
Perfected instrument, definition, 96
Perfection—
in form, result of, 209
manifest in form, 32
Periphery, manifest aspect of the
Plan, 233
Perseverance, a needed asset, 50
Persona—
abstraction of from physical
body, 261
and Soul, separated by time and
space, 252
ascent and integration, 143
aspires via discipline, 282
at transition, 261
consciousness, 252
created prior birth, 321
definition, 169
freed from form, 253
inclusion in ashramic life, 162
integrated ray of, 152
integrating ray, 254
manifesting Divine Ideas, 141
mask of the Soul, 282
merges with Overshadowing
Soul, 282
neither attracted nor repelled by,
71
part of the Soul, 252
personal will of, 210
ray, 151—

460

Index

Index

final secrets of, 294
of thought and sound, 142
Protect, others from mistakes, 223
Protection, from outside impact, 223
Psychiatrist, 89
Psychiatry, 230
Pure Reason, 5, 29
Pure Reason, all knowing, 76
Purpose, 16—
    incarnating cycle, 244
    of evolution, at-one-ment, 18
    persona of itself is without, 69
    to his life, 69
Purpose and goal, common, 266
Purpose and goals of the
    meditation, 135
Purpose, Evolution, and Activity, 17
Purpose, Power, and Will,
    potentials, 229

R

Race, majority of the, 126
Ray—
    energies, seven, expressions of
        God, 55
    group, place within, 230
    makeup, 229—
        hypothetical case, 255
        ascertaining, 153
    predominant, 189
    Soul functioning, 229
Rays—
    all available, 154
    planetary, three major, which
        the probationer is perfecting,
        115
    seven Lords of, 240
Reaction, defined, 130
Reality, foundation in, 155
Reasoning, hampered, 80
Rebirth, Law of, 7
Redemption, of consciousness and
    substance, 304
Reformer, average, 47
Reidentification, 169
Reincarnation, 30—
    Law of, 7

prematurely, 262
process began, 388
psychological findings, 171
Relationship—
    first realization of, 131
    problems in, 153
    tonal quality of, 369
Relationships—
    quality of, 68, 131
Relaxation, of instrument, 39
Release, from desire and ambition, 9
Religion, right relationship with
    every, 274
Religious, affiliation, present, 274
    form, will not break up, 200
Religious and philosophical,
    systems, re-evaluation of, 171
Reorientation, period of, 261
Results, Immediate, work without
    noting, 50
Rhythm, within astral body, 117
Right activity, within the physical
    body, 145
Right aspiration, in consciousness
    of beginner, 69
Right hand path, way of disciple, 212
Right Human Relations, 271
Right relationship—
    Divine Law and Order reasserts
        itself, 98
    harmony prerequisite to, 155
    on plane of personality, 71
    with associates, 267
Ring-pass-not—
    conflict within, 180
    of human kingdom, 18
    of Logos, 217
    raging within, 179

S

Sacral center—
    definition, location, function, 139
    kundalini enters, 390
Sacred planet, why ours not, 315
Sacrifice—
    of conscious reservation, 235
    of personal ambition, 266

464

Index

of the separative self, 277
School, of experience, 7
School of service, 407
Science—
 and Religion, conflict between, 193
 new era of, 194
Second dimension, the space or magnetic, 379
Second initiation—
 approach, 181
 union, 183
Second Logos, 65, 191—
 conscious unit in, 30
Second ray—
 differentiated expression of, 192
 Education, 230
 negative, 79
 relationship to the reasoning process, 75
Secret Place of the Most High, way entered and known, 120
Seed-thought—
 Alone I stand upon the scales, 98
 definition, 40
 dropped, 41
 for Soul who seeks to serve, 316
 Having pervaded this body, 66
 I am That I am, 284
 I am the Soul, 111
 identity, 144
 I sound forth in time and space, 132
 Not my will, O Soul, but thine, 118
Seed-thoughts—
 twelve, 342
Seek within, 191
Seekers, vast group of, 6
See-la-Aum—
 aligned with Selah, 364
 and Selah, channel between, 361
 body of the One Life identified as, 359
 Deva of Light, 358
Selah—
 function, 360
 gaining attention of, 359
 human network of etheric

substance, 359
 note of, 363
 only responds to will focused through a man's brain, 360
 responds will within a brain, 360
Self—
 illusion called, 170
 separated, 115
Self-denial, rigid, 201
Self-disgust, 50
Self-glorification, attainment, 20
Self-initiated, disciplinary training, 8
Self-initiated growth—
 and development, 399
 a possibility, 179
 concept, impact, 182
 concept of, 181
Selfish—
 in these lessons, 115
 will of man, 115
Self-less love, within the emotional nature, 145
Sensory system, impact of astral force, 129
Separated focus, 306
Separated self—
 escape pain, 181
 glorification of, 20
Separative, dangerously, 59
Serpent—
 coiled, 383
 fallen kundalini, 388
 home of the, 390
 of knowledge, 389
 standing upon its tail, 384
 symbol of Planetary kundalini, 383
 with the tail in its, 384
Serpent fire of creation, real matter aspect, 383
Serpent kingdom, not a true kingdom, 383
Service—
 activity—
  defeat the Purpose of, 274
  fear initiating, 265
  initiating, 62
  planned, 109, 204—
   avocation or vocation, 271

465

Index

Index

Index

Index

473

Index

Made in the USA
Lexington, KY
18 October 2013